The Mystery Solved:

OR,

IRELAND'S MISERIES;

THE GRAND CAUSE, AND CURE.

BY THE

REV. EDWARD MARCUS DILL, A.M., M.D.,

MISSIONARY AGENT TO THE IRISH PRESBYTERIAN CHURCH.

NEW YORK:

ROBERT CARTER & BROTHERS,

No. 285 BROADWAY.

1852.

T. B. SMITH, STEREOTYPER,
216 William Street, New York.

R. CRAIGHEAD, PRINTER,
53 Vesey Street.

CONTENTS.

PART I.—IRELAND'S MISERIES.

CHAPTER I.

GENERAL WRETCHEDNESS.

PAGE

Country's present appearance—Commerce—Manufacture—Agriculture—Depopulation—Evictions, &c., . 9

CHAPTER II.

THE FAMINE.

Frightful mortality—Scenes of horror—Affecting incident, &c., ... 14

CHAPTER III.

EMIGRATION.

Extent—Progress—Miseries—Evils: moral, political, and social, &c., ... 16

CHAPTER IV.

INCREASING PROSTRATION.

State of gentry — Farmers — Peasantry— Growth of pauperism—Decrease of births and marriages, &c., . 22

CHAPTER V.

SINGULAR EXCEPTION.

PAGE

Superiority of Ulster—In manufacture, commerce, agriculture, &c.—Object of this volume, ... 32

PART II.—ALLEGED CAUSES.

CHAPTER I.

THE PHYSICAL.

THE COUNTRY—Soil—Climate—Resources, &c. THE RACE —Celt and Saxon—Wales—Highlands—Irish mind, and heart, &c., ... 39

CHAPTER II.

THE POLITICAL.

THE AGITATOR—Natural history of agitation—O'Connell —Ulster, &c. THE LEGISLATURE—The constitution— Laws—Repeal—"Misrule," &c., ... 53

CHAPTER III.

THE SOCIAL.

HABITS—Feudalism—Style—Extravagance, &c. PURSUITS — Trade— Agriculture — Rack-rents — Tenant-right, &c., ... 64

CHAPTER IV.

THE MORAL.

KNOWLEDGE—General and religious ignorance—Superstitions, &c. &c. VIRTUE—Military, police, and criminal statistics—Consequent disorganization, &c. &c. CONTRAST IN ULSTER—Light—Morality, &c. &c., . 77

CHAPTER V.

THE RELIGIOUS.

PAGE

THE COINCIDENCE—Superiority of Protestantism in England, Scotland, Ireland's provinces, counties, parishes, towns, people. THE INFERENCE—the key of history in Ireland, Europe, &c. &c., ... 93

PART III.—THE GRAND CAUSE.

Basis of demonstration, ... 109

CHAPTER I.

ROME ECLIPSES THE MIND.

The Bible in Ireland—Altar harangues—Maynooth training—Priestly *instructions*—Impostures—Miracles—Rome the enemy of all light—Congregation of the *Index*—Parent of barbarism—Fruits in Ireland, &c. &c., 112

CHAPTER II.

ROME CORRUPTS THE CONSCIENCE.

PRINCIPLES—Absolution—Confession, &c. &c. IRISH PRIESTHOOD—Profane swearing—Drunkenness—Sabbath-breaking—Adultery, &c. &c. IRISH PEOPLE—Frequency of crime—Its atrocity, &c. &c., . . . 132

CHAPTER III.

ROME DESTROYS THE HEART.

Her hatred of the Bible—Payments—Tortures—Lough Derg—Purgatory—Priestly foragings—Robberies—Butcheries—In Ireland and all countries—Truculent spirit unchanged, &c. &c., ... 151

CHAPTER IV.

ROME DEBASES THE WHOLE NATURE.

PAGE

Makes mental imbeciles, social cripples, moral slaves—Dreadful engines of subjugation—Women—Convents—Confessional—Degradation—Filth—Improvidence—Idleness—Beggars, in Ireland and all Popish lands, &c. &c., ... 170

CHAPTER V.

ROME BLASTS MAN'S TEMPORAL STATE.

FINANCIAL CURSE of Ireland—Destroys prosperity—Robs community, &c. &c. PHYSICAL CURSE—Effect on soil, climate, race, &c. SOCIAL CURSE—Paralyzes energies, perpetuates feudalism, aggravates landlord tyranny, &c. POLITICAL CURSE—Curses our civil blessings—Trial by jury—Elective franchise, &c.—Creates agitation, despotism, &c. &c., ... 189

CHAPTER VI.

ROME CLOUDS MAN'S ETERNAL PROSPECTS.

Protestant pseudo-Liberals—Paganism of Popery—Popish mummeries—A scene of *devotion*—Sacerdotal *piety*—The *heaven* of Rome—Her *saints* and *sinners*, &c. &c., ... 212

PART IV.—THE CURE.

Recapitulation—"The Mystery Solved," . . . 227

CHAPTER I.

THE MEDICINE—THE POPULAR REMEDIES.

THE CIVIL—The Land question—Ireland unfit for liberty—The mockery of freedom, &c. THE EDUCATIONAL

PAGE

—National Board—Sectarian zealots—Godless philosophers—Insufficiency of mere education, &c. THE INDUSTRIAL— Industrial. Schemes—Advantages—Defects, &c.—THE SCRIPTURAL—Touching incident—The two atmospheres—Power of the Bible—Its amazing triumphs—Glory of Britain, &c., ... 230

CHAPTER II.

THE MEDICINE—THE GRAND SPECIFIC.

PHILOSOPHY of the Gospel—Indispensable to virtue, happiness, and general improvement of mankind—Atonement— Regeneration—True Catholicon — Monstrous folly of endowing Maynooth—FRUITS of the Gospel—Awakens the mind—Purifies the conscience—Gives a heart—Elevates the whole nature—Blesses for time, and eternity—A word to our statesmen, . . . 257

CHAPTER III.

THE TREATMENT—INFORMATION.

Protestant ignorance—The *practical* of Rome—Its Satanic philosophy—The eclectic system of evil—Rome's tactics in these lands—*Blustering, cunning*—Hatred of, and designs on England, &c., ... 282

CHAPTER IV.

THE TREATMENT—LEGISLATION.

Rome a *temporal* power—THE CONVENTS—Their decoys —Their horrors—Our duty. MAYNOOTH COLLEGE—Its history—Course of Instruction—Moral influence—Endowment—Infatuation of our rulers—Duty of the people, &c. &c., ... 293

CHAPTER V.

THE TREATMENT—EVANGELIZATION.

PAGE

Ireland's grand hope—Past neglect—Missionary statistics—The Irish Society—Dingle—Achill—Birr—"Irish Schools"—"Scriptural and Industrial Schools"—Awakening in Connaught, &c.—The grand requisite—*Revival in the Churches*—Prayer—Faith—Wisdom—Union, &c., ... 315

CONCLUDING APPEAL.

Alarming progress of Popery—Increase of Irish in England—Scotland—Australia—America, &c.—Hope for Ireland—Evangelization—Emigration—Immigration, &c. &c., ... 335

THE MYSTERY SOLVED, &c.

PART I.

THE MISERIES.

APPEARANCE OF THE COUNTRY—COMMERCE—MANUFACTURES.

THE present condition of Ireland is perhaps without a parallel amongst the nations of the earth.

Misery has long been this country's peculiar portion. Her history has been written with tears and blood. Her children are familiar with sackcloth and ashes. But in God's awful providence she seems at length to have reached the climax of woe; and is now passing through such a complication of miseries, as has excited the astonishment and pity of the world.

CHAPTER I.

GENERAL WRETCHEDNESS.

THE first thing that strikes the traveller, is the air of desolation which begins to pervade whole districts—especially in Munster and Connaught. As he wanders through these provinces, he sees half-decayed towns, which once were so flourishing as to send members to the Irish parliament. He finds whole villages in ruins so complete, that nothing remains but a few tottering wall-steads, to tell that the hum of life was ever there. In some cases, even these monuments of desolation have disappeared, and the coachman points to a bare deserted spot, as the site of a former hamlet. And as to the destruction of farmsteads and cabins, he can scarce move in any direction but the scene appears as if some invading army had passed by.

He finds, on inquiry, that this decadence had commenced long prior to the famine, and was only hastened by that fearful visitation. On the eve of that calamity, and while yet the tide of events flowed in its usual channels, Ireland contained one third the population, with one fourth the surface of the United Kingdom; and yet her national revenue was not one eleventh, being £4,500,000 sterling out of £52,000,000. The registered tonnage of her shipping was not one twelfth, being 250,000 tons to near 3,250,000. And the proportion of persons employed in her factories was one twenty-third, being, in round numbers, 23,000 to 540,000;* while her agricultural condition could scarce be compared to Britain's—

* See Thom's Irish Statistics for 1849, pp. 54, 55, 177, 178, 182; Oliver and Boyd's Edinburgh Almanac for 1848, pp. 141, 142.

there being then in Ireland near 1,000,000 of holdings on 13,500,000 of acres of arable surface. And of these holdings, one seventh did not exceed 1 acre each; one third consisted of from 1 to 5 acres; not one twentieth were above 50 acres each; and two thirds, at least, were wretchedly cultivated.*

If we look to the circumstances of the population of that period, our results are not less remarkable. While the English upper classes have long been the wealthiest in the world, few of the Irish were even out of debt, and numbers were hopelessly embarrassed. While the English middle classes have long been surrounded with comforts, Ireland can scarce be said to have ever had a middle class. And of the few that even then existed, the means were so slender, that often the Irish merchant was poorer than the English clerk; and the Irish farmer would have been thankful for the food which English servants threw away; while the entire agricultural class, representing seven tenths of Ireland's substance, were fast sinking into poverty. How, then, shall we compare the lower classes of both countries—the starved Irish peasant in his wretched hut, with the happy English hind in his cheerful cottage? More than three fourths of all the dwellings in Ireland were at that period built of mud. Near one half of all the families in Ireland lived in dwellings of but one apartment each.† Two thirds

* See Thom's Statistics, 1849, pp. 168, 169.

† Census for 1841.

of the entire population lived by manual labor, and subsisted on potatoes. Near one third were out of work, and in distress thirty weeks in the year;* while not less than one eighth were paupers, or on the very verge of pauperism.

We think no one can read these statistics without being able to account for all the horrors of the famine of 1847. No prosperous country could be utterly prostrated by the failure of one crop—least of all, the potato—for no prosperous country depends upon it. It is the staple food of poverty or sloth. That nation must have been foundering, which such a calamity could so completely engulf. The above statistics demonstrate that Ireland *was* foundering—that the people were already so impoverished, as to be unable to bear any additional privations; and many of them, indeed, so sunk in the gulf of wretchedness, that the least rise of its waters was sure to overwhelm them.

The census of 1851 has accordingly shown the disastrous effects of the famine upon Ireland. Ten years before, the population was 8,175,124. At the same rate of increase which had marked all previous decennial periods, it should at least have been 9,000,000 in 1851; and many believed it had reached that number in 1846. Yet it was found to be only 6,515,794—thus revealing the astounding fact, that in five years, the population of Ireland had virtually decreased *two millions and a half*, or near one

* Third Report, Poor Inquiry Commission.

third! This number is within about 370,000 of being equal to the entire population of Scotland. We have only, therefore, to imagine the almost total extinction of the Scottish nation, in order to form some estimate of our loss. Moreover, in the year 1841, there were 1,384,360 dwellings in Ireland. According to the census of 1851, the number was then reduced to 1,115,007,—showing, that in the mean time, no less than 269,353 of all the habitations of the country had been levelled to the ground! We find, from the same source of information, that this dreadful clearance has chiefly taken place among the small farmers—that humble class so graphically described by the poet, whose little plot

"Just gave what life required, but gave no more."

In 1845 there were, as already stated, near 1,000,000 of holdings in Ireland; and of this number, those which contained from 1 to 5 acres each, amounted to 310,436, and supported 1,862,250 individuals—more than one fifth of the population. The census of 1851 has revealed the awful fact, that near three fourths of this entire class have been swept away—there being then but 91,618 holdings, supporting 549,708 individuals! We find, moreover, that of all the holdings which were under 15 acres each, one half have disappeared, involving the clearance of 1,500,000 souls. All this in a few short years! yet even now, the depopulation goes on as rapidly as ever. Who that has a heart can read these details without emotion? NEAR TWO HUNDRED AND SEVENTY THOUSAND DWELLINGS swept away! And in these the pulse of affection once beat warmly; for nature has endowed the peasant with feelings as well as the prince. To these, the poor man proudly brought his bride. In these, they no doubt spent years of humble contentment, cheered amidst their sorrows by each other's love. There the mother has smiled over her infant's cradle, and perhaps wept over its coffin too; and the hardy father has had his toils beguiled by the innocent prattle of his little ones. And there, too, have they often knelt around their dying embers, and in their own humble way and simple strains presented their evening prayer to heaven!

CHAPTER II.

THE FAMINE.

SUCH are the general statistics of our depopulation—the brevity of this sketch forbids minuter details. It is enough to say, that of the above 2,500,000, the famine destroyed about 1,000,000, and emigration has removed the remainder; and let any one imagine, if he can, the scenes of woe embraced in these fearful figures! During the horrors of 1847, our country was transformed into a grave-yard and a lazar-house. It was quite common to see the people staggering like drunken men along the roads from the utter exhaustion of nature, their faces and legs being swollen with hunger ; and pages might be filled with the bare record of cases the most affecting, of starvation, pestilence, and death. Let us just present the reader with an instance or two. At Killalla, the famished creatures used to crowd round the house of the Rev. Mr. Rogers, wolfish with hunger ; and men once athletic and muscular would stand before his windows, take the skin which once covered a brawny arm, but now hung loose and wrinkled, and double it round the bone in order to prove the extent of their emaciation ! One woman was found stretched on the bed by the side of her dead husband, and after having just given birth to a poor wasted infant. It was not uncommon to find whole families dead in their cabins together. Nor were cases rare in which the famished creatures became deranged before expiring ; and in one such instance, the most awful of all the occurrences predicted against the Jews, was found to have taken place—the delirious mother had fed on her dead infant ! Our missionaries were doomed to witness daily the most heart-rending scenes. The Rev. Mr. Brannigan one day observed a man and his wife digging in a stubble field. He approached and inquired what they were doing. They told him they had five children, whom they had for a fortnight supported on cabbage and mill-dust, but that they were now actually starving ; that for the last two days they had kept them in bed to try to sleep off the hunger; and that they had that day been out from the early morning in quest of some wild roots, of which they exhibited a handful as the fruits of their protracted labors. Mr. Brannigan was moved, and, uttering some kind words, he handed them two shillings. This relief coming so unexpectedly on the poor man weakened as he was by sorrow and hunger, completely unmanned him, and he sobbed and wept in the minister's face; while his wife, still less able to control her feelings, clasped her husband in her arms, exclaiming—"My dear! our children won't die yet." And yet these are mere samples. How many scenes more tragic still were enacted during that dreadful calamity, which no chronicle has ever recorded, of whose existence the world never heard, and over which no tears of sympathy were shed, except perhaps by some fellow-sufferers! Nor must we forget that, in consequence of the partial failure of the potato ever since 1847, many districts have been suffering an annual famine, and have now, therefore, almost equalled Egypt's seven years of dearth without its previous seven of plenty.

CHAPTER III.

EMIGRATION.

For many years a large portion of Ireland's shipping trade has been mere emigration. And its aggregate amount can be best seen from the fact that, according to a late estimate, there are in America 3,000,000 of native Irish, and 4,500,000 more of Irish descent. In other words, America now contains of inhabitants of Irish blood, 1,000,000 more than does Ireland itself! Even previous to the famine of 1847, the annual number of emigrants had in six years steadily risen from 40,000 to 95,000; and since that time it has increased so prodigiously, that the Colonial Land and Emigration Commissioners give the number emigrating in 1851 at 279,000. The daily arrivals of emigrants at the port of New York alone, range from 700 to 1000, and of these the great mass are Irish. Thus, after flowing westward for half a century, the stream of emigration, so far from diminishing, has swollen into a mighty flood, and the world now gazes on a phenomenon which can only be likened to the migrations of the Gauls or the Huns, or other wandering tribes of yore. Multitudes are flying from their once loved homesteads, as though Ireland were the scene of some physical as well as social convulsion, to a land which comprises all they can henceforth call a country; deeming even its wild forests an asylum from their woes. They daily hear of the untimely end of thousands of their fellow-emigrants by shipwreck on the passage, or hardships on their arrival; but so far is every other feeling overborne by the one desire to escape, that the most timid brave the deep, and the most infirm encounter the

2

hardships. Of the crowds that thus hurry along in this general "exodus," scarce one returns, save the few who come back from ill health or indolence, *nulla vestigia retrorsum;* so that a large portion of the country's business arises from emigration. From it our railways are reaping a transient and ruinous harvest—the numbers continually pouring along the Great Southern and Western alone are surprising. And seacoast villages, which vessels were never known to touch before, ships now regularly visit for their human cargoes. Churches and chapels are fast being emptied. The country begins to feel the fearful drain, and faints from excessive depletion; yet on goes the increasing tide, and on it promises to go. In many cases the wail of the emigrants who crowd our ports is not so heart-rending as that of their friends whom poverty compels to remain behind; and had the people but the means of getting away, whole districts would rise and take their departure. Even the warmest advocates of the clearance-system begin to feel alarmed. Instead of a competition for land, as formerly, there has at length commenced a competition for tenants; and some are seriously speaking of the necessity for parliamentary interference with the emigrant, to save the country from complete depopulation—it being a matter truly of easy enough calculation, that at the same increasing rate of emigration, a very few years indeed would leave Ireland a lonesome solitude.

Here is a state of things as mournful as it is unparalleled. We refer not so much to the previous dreadful hardships which such a general flight implies; when, by a people proverbially attached to *home*, a Canadian log-hut is now deemed a blessing; when the spell of *country* is so completely broken, that America, once their last resource, is now the goal of their hopes; and what used to be dreaded as a land of exile, is now sighed for as a place of refuge. Nor do we refer so much to the anguish endured by our warm-hearted countrymen when thus torn from their humble, but yet beloved homesteads! What this must be, the heart-rending cries of the emigrants who throng our quays but too painfully show; or their still more bitter wail, when taking their last farewell of those homely abodes which were endeared to them by a thousand recollections! Not surely that these woes are to be overlooked or underrated; on the contrary, they must command the deepest sympathy of our nature. He cannot be a man who could witness such scenes without emotion, or feeling all that our native poet has so touchingly expressed—

> "Good Heaven! what sorrows gloomed that parting day
> That called them from their native walks away;
> When the poor exiles, every pleasure past,
> Hung round the bowers, and fondly looked their last;
> And shuddering still to face the distant deep,
> Returned and wept, and still returned to weep."

Most affecting of all is it to see amongst those

mournful groups, not the young and active merely, but many a poor old man who had hoped to lay his bones in his fathers' sepulchre :—to see trembling old age thus turned out on the world when almost leaving it; doomed to recommence life's pilgrimage at its close ; and forced to encounter hardships fit only for elastic youth, and beneath which gray hairs are all but sure to sink. But we refer not now to these calamities.

We allude rather to the moral and social evils of this unnatural state of things. For many years it has been the very flower of the people who have been leaving—our enterprising upright yeomanry—who were not content to live on dry potatoes. It is the bones and sinews of the country we have been losing, who, besides contributing their labor and skill to America's national wealth, have been carrying with them each from £10 to £1000. By the departure of this class it is reckoned that since 1845 the country has lost in cash alone about half a million sterling. Thus Ireland has for years been little else than a nursery ground for America, whence the hardiest plants are being annually removed, while the least thriving and healthy are left behind. The cream of the nation has thus for years been flowing off: like some liquid of which the purer portion at the top has been repeatedly drawn away, till the very sediment itself begins at length to run off. Such has been the draining process of Irish emigration, on which Britain has looked with indifference, till now the best of the people are gone to rear cities beneath a foreign banner, and all that remains for England's proud flag to wave over, is the pauperized and prostrated remnant.

Nor are the political bearings of the case to be wholly disregarded. It were idle to deny that America now holds that place in the hearts of most of our countrymen which England ought to possess. Hearken to their conversation, and America is the theme of their eulogies; while England is spoken of in terms of invidious contrast, and in a spirit of moody discontent. Never was this fact more clearly proved than during the American ambassador's late visit to Ireland. While at a recent festival in Limerick, the health of our beloved Queen was received with hisses by some of the party, the people everywhere gave Mr. Abbot Lawrence a royal reception, and flocked around him as though he had been a visitant from some better world. In truth, the hearts of the people are now in America. Enter almost any dwelling, and the great aim of the very servants is to save what will "take them out of this country" to that land of promise. Converse with our struggling farmers, and the last hope of many is that their sons, who have gone before, may be spared to send for themselves and their families, and enable them to exchange the condition of British subjects for that of American citizens. Follow that youth to those distant shores, and you find him sustained amid their summer droughts and winter snows by the hope of soon rescuing his revered parent from hunger and "oppression," and welcoming him to that "land of liberty" and wealth.

CHAPTER IV.

INCREASING PROSTRATION.

SUCH is the history of the millions we have lost—let us now glance at the state of the millions who remain. It would be some consolation for the loss of the former, if, as many hoped, it would have conduced to the good of the latter. According to our *over-population* theorists, Ireland was like some over-crowded ship; and what was chiefly necessary to save her from sinking, was simply to lighten her of her human cargo. Well, this has been done, and to their hearts' content—has it enabled her to weather the tempest?

Look to our *upper classes*, and how many of those who were embarrassed in 1846 are absolute bankrupts now! Their property has so fast been passing through the Encumbered Estates' Court, that 2000 petitions have already been presented, of which 1600 have been fiated; and yet it is the opinion of many that the labors of that court are only commencing. You now pass by numbers of decaying mansions which were once the homes of splendid hospitality; you see their magnificent demesnes neglected, and their various monuments of elegance fast going to ruin. And you find the only tenant of their lonely halls to be, perhaps some Chancery *keeper*, or else some old caretaker of the family, who entertains you with stories of its ancient "grandeur." Some of these dwellings have been turned into poor-houses—sad emblem of our country's state!—and those who were once their lords are now penniless exiles in distant lands, or earning a pittance in some department of the public service. The sons of several of our gentry have been glad to enter the constabulary as common policemen, and a few at least are now private soldiers. A baronet is this moment a common turnkey in a prison, and at least one gentleman of high family has been discovered in a poorhouse! There is something peculiarly affecting in these facts. By a merciful arrangement of Providence, those who have been cradled in hardships are for that very reason best fitted to endure them; but it is pitiful to think of hundreds in actual want who were reared as tenderly as any of our readers, and whose infant locks the rude winds of heaven were scarce ever permitted to toss. We have had applications from the daughters of gentlemen, couched in terms enough to make the heart bleed, begging to be made teachers of our industrial schools on £20 a-year. One of our missionaries was some time since sent for to visit a reduced lady who was reported to be dying. He found her in a wretched dwelling, and sinking mainly from sheer privation; and the only relics of former years he could see, were a riding habit and a silver-mounted whip, which belonged to a beloved daughter! And the most affecting feature of the case is, the shifts to which these persons frequently resort in order to conceal their distress. In one case, the author accidentally discovered the starving condition of a gentleman with a large family, who had held a high situation in the Customs; and having at length so far gained his confidence as to induce him to make known his wants, he learned amongst other things that the only covering which the gentleman and his wife had over them at night was an old green baize cloth to which he pointed on the table before him!

Look now for an instant to our *middle class* —or rather to that class which in Ireland comes nearest to what is meant by this term, and embraces not only our merchants, shopkeepers, and higher agriculturists, but our traders, farmers, and private householders, of respectable character, but limited means. There is scarcely any better index of the condition of this class, as well indeed as of all who stand between it and our humblest peasantry, than the state of our savings' banks. Now, in 1845 the number of depositors in the savings' banks of Ireland was 96,422; and the amount deposited, £2,921,581; whereas in the year 1850 the number of depositors had fallen to 47,987, and the amount deposited to £1,291,798!

Another most important indication of a country's prosperity or decline, is the amount of its imports and exports. Now, in 1845, when we had a population of 8,500,000, our exports in grain alone were worth £4,500,000 sterling; yet, in 1850, with only 6,500,000 of a population to feed, the value of our corn exports was but £1,500,000 sterling;—in other words, this principal source of our wealth had, in the above brief period, fallen away *two thirds!* Nor has this decline been confined to our grain trade. Our exports in cows and pigs amounted in 1846, to above £4,500,000 sterling; while, in 1850, they had fallen away to £2,200,000, or less than one half. And when it is recollected that seven tenths of Ireland's wealth is agricultural, these figures but too plainly demonstrate the rapidity of her decline.

If next we look to the private circumstances of the farmers, we know that their live stock is one of the most important items, and *sources*, too, of their wealth. Every one knows that much of the value of their farms depends on their ability to stock them well. Now, in 1841, the average of live stock on each holding under fifteen acres, was £9, and the total value on all the farms of this extent in Ireland, was, in round numbers, £10,500,000 sterling; while, in 1851, the average value of live stock on each had fallen to £6 10*s.*, showing that more than one third of this source of our national wealth has also disappeared. And it has been truly affecting to mark, in so many farmers' dwellings, those sure and steady strides of poverty which the foregoing statistics indicate; to see, first of all, how the farmer's little savings were gradually drawn from the savings' bank till all was gone—then how his cattle were sold, one by one, till frequently the last cow disappeared—then how his household furniture itself went, piece by piece, and the very apparel of the family began to be sold or pawned; and how the long-maintained, but fruitless struggle, was finally closed by the poor man giving up his farm on which his fathers had dwelt for generations, and mournfully bending his steps to the poorhouse or the sea-port. The last five years have hence been unexampled for the number of auctions and other sales; and when so many were selling, and so few able to buy, the sacrifices often made at these were, of course, enormous. Nor have the pawnbrokers been less busily employed than the auctioneers. We have known even their yards and outhouses to be filled with articles from their surrounding neighborhoods. And in some cases they have suffered from the very excess of their stores, so many have been pawning and so few purchasing!

Of course, there are many exceptions to this general decline, both in our middle and upper classes. We speak of the majority, though we fear it is the large majority; for if so many signs of distress appear in those ranks of Irish society whose fondness for keeping up an appearance is so proverbial, and whose dread of being thought poor is so great, that they would almost rather starve than let their wants be known, we cannot but conclude that, were we admitted behind the scenes, we would discover an amount of privation which would more than justify the picture we have drawn.

If, then, such is the condition even of our gentry and yeomanry, what can we expect amongst those *lower grades* from which our vast armies of paupers are chiefly recruited? Perhaps our poor-law statistics will form the best answer to this question. Let the reader just look at the subjoined table,* which marks the progress of our pauperism, with all its ruinous expenditure, for 11 short years. From it he will find that, whereas in 1841, the numbers relieved were 31,000, and the cost of relief was £110,000; in 1849, the numbers relieved were no less than 932,000, and the cost of relief near £2,-200,000;—that is to say, for eight years the scale continues to ascend till the number of paupers has increased thirtyfold, and the cost of relieving them

*

Year.	Expenditure.	Paupers.
1841	£110,278	31,108
1842	281,233	87,604
1843	244,374	87,898
1844	271,334	105,358
1845	316,025	114,205
1846	435,001	243,933
1847	803,686	417,139
1848	1,835,634	610,463
1849	2,177,651	932,284
1850	1,430,108	805,702
1851	1,110,892	768,570

THOM'S *Statistics*, 1852, p. 203.

twentyfold! Indeed, in 1848, the number receiving relief, including out-door paupers, exceeded 2,000,-000, or a fourth of the population; and if the last two years exhibit a diminution, we fear this is to be ascribed to something else than returning prosperity. A depopulation of 2,500,000 should alone go far to explain the phenomenon; while the country is so fast sinking beneath a load of poor-rates, that in several poorhouses it is found impossible to accommodate the paupers of the district; and those who find admittance, in many cases perish in such numbers from their miserable maintenance, that they begin to shun the poorhouse as a sepulchre. In two houses alone, those of Ennistymon and Kilrush, there died in the year ending March, 1851, 3,028 paupers, being at the rate of 4 deaths a day in the one house, and 4½ in the other! The state of our poorhouses, therefore, is no certain criterion of the state of our pauperism. Some of our Unions are insolvent, and many are in debt; while the poor-rate is so fast hastening the general decay, that a number of the rate-payers of one year are uniformly found among the paupers of the next. The poorhouses built only 12 years ago, with ample accommodation for the estimated wants of the time, have in many places been found so inadequate as to have added to them three and four *auxiliary workhouses.* A large portion of the town of Millstreet is at present thus occupied by paupers; yet our poorhouse accommodation is still so deficient, that we fear the foregoing table scarce indicates three fourths of the existing pauperism of the country.

This prodigious amount of pauperism, embracing near one sixth of the population, is yet but too easily accounted for by a glance at the state of the peasantry. While the average wages of the English laborer is about 1*s.* 6*d.* per day, that of the Irish laborer is about 6*d.*; it occasionally rises to 10*d.* and 1*s.*; it is often as low as 3*d.* and 4*d.*; and, in the slack seasons, numbers are content to work for their food. We have seen that, for weeks together, they are unemployed; and in the west particularly the labor market is so wretched, that you will see them bringing ass's loads of turf and of chickweed for several miles into town, and selling them for ½*d.* or 1*d.*, and a messenger will gladly travel 10 or 12 miles for 6*d.* Their food is of the poorest description. Before the famine, it consisted chiefly of potatoes, with sometimes milk, often herrings, rarely meat, and frequently nothing; but since the famine, it largely consists of Indian meal stirabout, and this frequently but twice a-day; and most thankful are some of them to get even this. We have known them to live for weeks on boiled turnips or cabbage; and by the seaside you will see women daily dispersed along the strand in quest of mussels or limpets, or whatever else they can find. You examine their dwellings, and as you gaze on those wretched hovels, with their straw roofs rotten and leaky, their floors soaked with damp, and the green glut from the thatch often streaking their walls, you wonder how human beings can possibly exist in them! In truth, their accumulated hardships have, since the famine, wrought a melancholy change on this once hardy race. The children are now generally wasted and sallow, the parents have a famished look, disease is much more frequent, and longevity is daily becoming rarer. There are very few cabins which have not, within the last five years, been scenes of sickness or death; and you have only to enter and inquire for some parent or child, to be pointed to a wasted patient on a sickbed, or to the neighboring graveyard. Hence the number of orphans is now quite remarkable. You will meet them by scores in the poorhouses and begging along the roads; and we fear it is this mournful fact which, in a great measure, accounts for another far more deplorable—that juvenile prostitution has of late been increasing.

Nor has the distress of our peasantry failed to show itself in other affecting forms. It is indeed the last symptom of an expiring country and a famished people, when not only is the voice of the bridegroom and of the bride ceasing to be heard therein, but even that of the new-born babe. Yet, since the year 1847, the annual number of marriages in Ireland is reckoned to have decreased one third, and the number of births to have proportionally declined; while in many cases the wasted appearance of both mother and offspring is truly affecting to behold, and the powers of nature have been so far exhausted, that abortions are of frequent occurrence. It is also asserted, that in some districts lunacy itself is increasing. In a word, life has become with many a desperate struggle to live. Even our enormous poor-rates, while beggaring the country, have not yet left our paupers the alternative of a poorhouse or a grave; for deaths from starvation are still of frequent occurrence. Nay, even reduced below the alternative of flying to a foreign land or dying in their own, it has been proved that several prisoners committed the crimes they stood charged with, in order to obtain the privilege of transportation.

We shall now only add the marvellous fact, that all this decay has been proceeding in an age which, for general advancement, has been termed the age of wonders, and that Ireland has been thus fearfully retrograde in the very swiftest hour of the world's onward march. During the same period in which Britain has been rising to the highest pinnacle of greatness, Ireland, by her side, and beneath the same sceptre, has been sinking to this deep degradation: until now, the one is the mistress and the other the mendicant of the world; the name of the one is a glory commanding the respect of the nations, and that of the other a byeword commanding at best their commiseration. In the same time in which America has been transformed from a wild forest of Indians into a land of unparalleled prosperity, our people have grown so utterly wretched as to fly to her backwoods as to an asylum, to accept of her menial employments as a boon, and after being in many cases masters at home, to be thankful for the post of hired servants there. And what crowns the case is, that not only has this national consumption bid defiance to every form of treatment, but it seems rather to have grown worse under each successive remedy, and now appears likely to be arrested by nothing but dissolution. Each new measure has only blasted our hopes—each fresh loan has but increased our burdens—each remedial experiment has miserably failed, and often proved a curse rather than a cure;—until now our social maladies have reached such a height, that unless in some way arrested by God's gracious providence, in a few more years our country's funeral dirge must inevitably be heard.

CHAPTER V.

SINGULAR EXCEPTION.

To this general scene of wretchedness we must notice a partial, yet remarkable exception. The province of Ulster has long presented so strange a contrast to the rest of Ireland, as to have elicited the surprise even of continental tourists. Though warmed by the same sun, and watered by the same skies, this one province has prospered while the rest have declined; and you have only to cross the boundary line which divides them, to find a comparative desert on the one side and garden on the other.

If you look to Ulster's condition prior to the famine, you find it has long been the home of comfort and industry, and the headquarters of our commerce and manufactures. Of the 22,591 persons employed in our factories in 1846, nearly four fifths belonged to our northern province; the proportions being—Ulster, 17,304; Leinster, 3,732; Munster, 1,155; and in Connaught not a single one. To give one example of the relative progress of our northern and southern towns. In 1786, Belfast was an unimportant place with a wretched harbor, and the revenue of its port was but £1,500,000 sterling. In 1838 it contained 50 factory steam-engines; in 1841, its mills for spinning linen yarn alone amounted to 25, one of the principal employing 800 hands; in 1846, the Tidal Harbor Commissioners pronounced it "the first town in Ireland for enterprise and commercial prosperity;" and in 1850, its port revenues had increased to £29,000,000. On the other hand, Kilkenny was an important city when Belfast was a village; it once had several factories, 11 water-wheels, and such a carpet manufactory that Kidderminster petitioned for repeal of the Union. In 1834, Mr. Inglis saw one man in the principal factory which once employed 200; and he adds, that of the 11 water-wheels one was going, not for the purpose of driving the machinery, but to prevent it from rotting!

If you next turn to the period of the famine, those scenes of horror which were so common in the south were scarcely known in the north of Ireland; and many of those who did perish there were natives of Connaught and Leinster who poured into Ulster in quest of food. Of £10,000,000 of relief sent to Ireland at that period by public and private charity, scarce £1,000,000 is supposed to have reached Ulster; while that province actually contributed large sums for the relief of the south and west, and has ever since paid the rate-in-aid tax for the same end. Finally, if you look to its condition since 1847, you find that those calamities which have prostrated Munster and Connaught have fallen upon it with but mitigated severity. While Ireland has lost one fifth of its inhabitants, Munster almost one fourth, and Connaught nearly one third, Ulster has not lost one-sixth. Its capital, Belfast, which in 1841 contained above 75,000 inhabitants, had risen in 1851 to near 100,000, showing an increase of upwards of 24,000! In fact, the population of Ulster is now relatively greater than it was before the famine—consisting in 1841 of above one fourth, and in 1851 near one third of Ireland's inhabitants. Of the government advances made during the famine, the entire of the country owes near £4,500,000: of this Ulster owes little more than £500,000, or one eighth of the debt to near one third of the population. Its pauperism is not half so great as that of the other provinces; its proportion of the entire poor-rates of the country being also about an eighth. In a word, you find that Ulster, though exposed to every ordinary influence felt by Munster and Connaught, has scarce known the miseries which have given them such fearful notoriety. So soon as you enter that province, the entire aspect of the country changes. All around assumes that air of social health which is so easily perceived yet so difficult fully to describe. You have left behind the region of filthy cabins and swarming beggars, ruined villages and deserted farms; and you enter a territory of comparatively rich cultivation, studded with comfortable dwellings and thrifty towns. And you cannot but feel that, from whatever cause, Ulster is at least fifty years ahead of its sister provinces in all the true elements of national progress; and in its general aspect, so much more resembles Britain than Ireland, that one could almost fancy some physical convulsion to have severed it from the one island and attached it to the other.

Such is Ireland's temporal condition. We now proceed to that question which has been so frequently asked and so variously answered—What is the cause of such fearful wretchedness, particularly of the marvellous contrast we have traced between one of our provinces and all the rest? What makes Ireland a desert and Ulster its only oasis? or how came the Newry mountains to form the boundary line between the abodes of comfort and the haunts of woe?

On this subject how much has been written, yet how little seems to be understood! Each successive writer has found out the "true cause" of our miseries, and of course the infallible specific: yet these have been endlessly various and often directly opposite. In truth, to Ireland's other misfortunes this also has been added, that she has long been the practice-ground of social and political theorists. Never was laboratory the scene of more experiments, nor patient the victim of blinder quackery. Until now the only parallel to her case seems that of the woman who spent all her living on physicians, "and was nothing the better, but rather grew worse." The result, of course, has been calamitous. Not only has a vast amount of talent and treasure been wasted on Ireland which, if wisely applied, might ere now, under God, have achieved her salvation, but not a little of what was meant as medicinal has proved absolutely poisonous; and, untaught by the experience of the past, many of our most intelligent philanthropists and statesmen are to this very hour hanging over our expiring country,—perplexed about the treatment, because ignorant of the grand disease.

How long and anxiously have we looked for some one to arise and dispel this ignorance forever!—some one who would trace out the cause of Ireland's miseries with such clearness and candor, as would leave ignorance nothing to mistake, and bigotry nothing to say. No such person having as yet appeared, and our country meanwhile sinking at a rate so fearful, a very humble individual has been urged to undertake a task which can no longer wait for an abler pen. Nothing but the emergency of the case could have secured his consent. But what would be presumption in one class of circumstances becomes imperative duty in another; and in a crisis like the present, diffidence should yield to higher feelings, and the most obscure emerge from the shade, if he can but render his country the least possible service.

We crave, then, the reader's candid perusal of the following pages, whatever political or religious creed he may hold. We would especially bespeak for them our countrymen's calm attention. They are penned by one who can yield to none in devotion to his country and distress for her sorrows; who has spent the best years of his life in seeking her good; whose heart has often bled for her woes and throbbed for her future enlargement. He entreats them to lay aside, at least for one brief hour, the spirit of party; and if not on the high ground of their common country, at least on that of their common calamities, make this small sacrifice at the shrine of reason. Common woes and dangers have united the deadliest foes. The most hostile brothers have embraced over a parent's dying bed. And, oh! shall *we* ever permit the historian to tell, that even the grave, which entombed so many of our countrymen, could not bury along with them our feuds and dissensions; that these alone were flourishing, when all else around us decayed; that amid the throes of our expiring country, we could not suspend our suicidal strife; and therefore that her death was at least hastened by her own children's hands?

*** We may observe once for all, that we have found it impossible, in so small a volume, to notice the numerous sources from which our facts and statistics are derived. But the reader may rely on their correctness.

PART II.

ALLEGED CAUSES.

The alleged causes of Ireland's miseries may all be classed under the six following heads. Some have ascribed them to something in her *physical* state; some, to her *political* condition; others, to her *social;* others still, to her *moral;* while a fifth class has attributed them to her *religious* character; and a sixth has ascribed them, in part, to *each* of these. Let us briefly inquire how far each theory is accordant with truth.

CHAPTER I.

THE PHYSICAL.

This branch of our subject divides itself into the *People, and the Land of their Birth.* Does the cause, then, rest with *Ireland* or the *Irish?* Is the ground cursed with sterility, or the air with pestilence? Is the climate bleak, or the coast inhospitable? Is the island a Sahara or a Campagna di

Roma? Or is the now fashionable theory the correct one, that the *race* is hopelessly degenerate and *spent*—that, with them, "misfortune is another name for misconduct"—and that the Irishman, wherever he goes, is pursued by the curse of Cain or Cainaan, and for similar reasons?

The Country.—Is the cause, or any part of it, found in the *country?* The question scarce deserves an answer. Ireland is as much celebrated for beauty as misfortune. Volumes have been written on its scenery and resources. Swarms of tourists are annually lured to its shores. Poetry, often extravagant, speaks but sober truth in styling it the "Emerald Isle." And it is the unanimous verdict of mankind, that in all the requisites of national greatness, the entire island, but especially its southern province, is perhaps unequalled beneath the sun.

In truth, here Nature has lavished her stores. If we turn to the *climate*, Heaven never blessed a land with more genial skies. Its temperature rarely falls below 30° or rises above 75°; and thus it is preserved alike from the rigors of northern and the burning heats of southern climes. Its atmosphere is peculiarly free from disease, and altogether so pure, that till reduced by late hardships, its people were proverbially healthy; and so mild are the winter months of the south particularly, that the invalid takes shelter in its coves from the less kindly airs of Scotland and Ulster. If you look to the *soil*, it is proverbially fertile. Its fields wave with the finest harvests. Its very mountains are verdure to their summits. Notwithstanding its vast tracts of waste land, and the wretched cultivation of much that is reclaimed, Ireland exports twice as much provisions as it retains for its own population. The mere trade in its agricultural produce employs a fleet of steamers most part of the year; and you can scarce sit down to a table in Great Britain on which you will not find the produce of its soil.

Nor is it less bountifully provided with other elements of wealth. It is intersected by the finest rivers. Its bowels teem with the richest minerals. Its coasts swarm with shoals of fish. It contains some of the best harbors in the world; and such are its engineering facilities, that there is scarcely a tunnel in all its railways. While, as to still higher commercial advantages, it stands out on the world's highway—the Atlantic—with the fleets of nations daily passing by; and between the old world and the new, as though designed to be their link of communication, and enjoy the blessings of both. In a word, on this wretched country the God of Nature has showered his bounties so profusely, that one can scarce help thinking it was designed to be a garden of plenty instead of a land of paupers. You would say, that if on earth there was a spot which He had graciously exempted from the full effects of the curse on "man's first disobedience," it was this; and that nothing but *some malignant* agency could possibly have hindered it from becoming the model and envy of the nations, instead of being their prostrate suppliant.

Therefore, the country's physical condition, so far from accounting in the slightest for her miseries, makes them, in truth, more unaccountable. And the contrast between Ulster and Munster, as well as between Britain and Ireland, instead of being thus explained, becomes more perplexing than ever. Plants which even in England require a hot-house, flourish in Ireland in the open air; whilst Scotland is largely indebted to her even for poultry and vegetables. And as to other advantages, Nature has given to the south of Ireland the finest river in the three kingdoms—the Shannon; and the most magnificent harbor—Queenstown. Who would compare to the former the Bann, or even the Clyde, or to the latter the slimy port of Belfast, or the sandy entrance to Liverpool? Whatever "English jealousy" may be thought to have denied us, it has ever conceded that Ireland is naturally the finest of the British isles; and we shall only add, that Munster is confessedly the richest portion of the island. The farther you travel south, both clime and soil become more kindly. The snow-storms which visit Ulster, are scarce ever seen in Munster; and the "trap" hills of Antrim can ill be compared to the "golden vales" of Tipperary; while the same universal award which has conferred on Ireland the title of the

"Green Isle," and on Munster that of "the sunny south," has pronounced Ulster the "black north," and Scotland the "barren rock."

THE RACE.—Is the cause found in the natural character of the people? Is the Irishman more sparingly furnished than the Englishman, or the southern than his northern brother, with those qualities of mind and heart which form the elements of a noble race? Such is the favorite theory of some. Because our poor countryman has yielded to influences sufficient to degrade the finest race, degradation has been all but pronounced his normal state. Because he has not been more than human, he has almost been considered less. His worst misfortune has been thus converted into a fault, and he has been exposed to general scorn for the very thing which composed his strongest claim to general sympathy. The reproach which should have been heaped on the authors of his shame has been lavished on their injured victim, until now his very name is a byeword; you will hear even the expression in Christian circles, "a blessed land but a cursed people;" and the words of one of our finest sacred melodies have been uncharitably applied to him—

"Where every prospect pleases,
And only man is vile."

The doctrine just amounts to this—that the blood of the Saxon is naturally purer than that of the

Celt; and its advocates consider it at once the most just and charitable explanation of Ireland's wretchedness, that the Irish, as such, have some hereditary blemish, which we may pity but can scarce hope to cure. The shortest refutation of this doctrine would be to trace the distribution of the two great families of which the Celt and the Saxon are themselves but branches—to appeal, for example, to Celtic France, the second nation in Europe; to show how much England herself owes to the arms and arts of the Celtic Normans; and to prove, besides, the utter impossibility of knowing, at this time of day, what blood is Saxon and what is Celtic, in a race so mixed as the British.

But we are content to meet our theorists on their own ground; and, assuming that the Irish are Celts, and the English Saxons, we shall demonstrate the falseness of their hypothesis. If they mean no more than that the Irish as a nation have long been exposed to influences which are found in the course of ages to degrade a people, this is not to explain the mystery of Ireland's woes, but only to remove it a little further off; in truth, it is virtually to give up their theory, for this position none will deny; and the true question then is—What are these degrading influences? But if they mean that there is in Irish blood a deeper natural taint than what we all inherit from our first progenitors, we pronounce the theory false and absurd. The blue-eyed Saxon and the black-eyed Celt are children of the same common parent; and the corruption which has flowed from that original fountain, has been shared alike by all its streams. The history of every race has proved that none is *naturally* worse than another, but that each in its turn has risen and sunk according to the influences to which it has been exposed; and to charge the evils of Ireland on the Celt as a race, proves not the guilt of the accused, but the ignorance of the accuser. In the middle ages, when Saxon lands were shrouded in darkness, Ireland, then most purely Celtic, was the seat of learning for Europe; it is now when the least Celtic that she has grown most wretched; and this shifting on the social scale would itself demonstrate, that her children's degradation springs not from anything *within* them, but something *from without*. Again, the midland counties of Munster and Connaught contain a mixed race of Saxon, Norman, and Danish blood: while the pure aboriginal Celt is chiefly found in their western regions,—yet the fact is notorious, that it is these midland counties which are the chief scenes of blood, and those western regions which have the best excuse for poverty. Morever, on the Highlands of Scotland and the mountains of Wales, we find two other branches of the Celtic family; and who hears of their hills being drenched with the blood of murder? Where can you find over all their wide moors assassin-clubs nightly plotting crime, or ruffians swearing away innocent life for hire, or that general conspiracy against law and justice, which has filled

Ireland with police and military? No; the British Celts are as proverbial for peace as is their Irish brother for disturbance. The most orderly sailor who enters our ports is the Welshman, and our Queen yearly seeks the Scottish Highlands as the most quiet retreat in her kingdom.

You say that these British Celts are at least like the Irish, poor and indolent? We ask how mountaineers can well be otherwise. Is it on the stormy side of Snowdon or the Grampians you would look for wealth or bustling enterprise?—or is it *such* dreary moorlands you would compare with one of the finest islands of the sea? Why, it seems almost as necessary that the British Celts should be poor and slothful, as that the Irish should be wealthy and diligent; yet they have not a tithe of the sloth and poverty we find in Ireland. The traveller can testify how cultivation is creeping up their bleakest mountains, while with us the process is reversed, and the wilderness is creeping down upon our finest vales. And though in 1847 the potato failed with them as with us, yet who heard of their hills covered with the dead and dying—of millions granted them from the treasury—of months spent with their case in parliament—or swarms of their beggars disturbing the world?

How, then, can *race* explain the difficulty, when we find such difference in tribes of the same race? Yes, and strangest of all, in the same tribes at different periods. Time was when Wales and the

Highlands were the very home of blood and desolation. The Welsh mountains have witnessed tragedies which still form the theme of many a thrilling story; and those Scottish glens through which our Sovereign wanders unattended by a soldier, once rung with the clansmen's wildest yells. Now, surely any natural degeneracy of the race would exhibit much the same features at the same time in all its tribes; yet here we have two emerging from barbarism to civilization in spite of vast disadvantages; and the third, from having once been the light of Europe, fast sinking into ruin, despite all that can be done to save it.

So much for this groundless assertion. We now go farther, and boldly assert that the Irish, so far from being naturally degraded, possess qualities so admirable, that nothing but the foulest mismanagement could have hindered them from becoming one of the finest nations on the earth; and we feel the more at liberty to speak on this point, as none but an Irishman can truly comprehend the odd construction of the Irish mind. To most men it is a puzzle—and to the British a national contrast. They see before them a strange medley of faults and virtues, of blunders and cleverness, of the comic and the tragic; and they are bewildered amidst the nooks and corners of a mind so singular. Hence they are unable to discern between his natural qualities and his actual condition—between what he is and what he might be made; and because they see him begging and stealing, and robbing and murdering, they put him down as all but hopeless. Alas! they forget that in truth he has been "more sinned against than sinning," and have confounded the man with the malignant influences with which he is beset.

If you look even to his body—where will you find a hardier?—able on dry potatoes to work down the English laborer on his flesh meat and ale; and one cannot see his miserable diet without wondering how nature can manufacture such bone and sinew out of food so wretched! Yes, and within that robust frame dwells a spirit whose buoyant vivacity years of sorrow have not destroyed—of which his fun and frolics are but the irregular escapes, and which one cannot but think was mercifully given him to support him under woes which must have crushed a more gloomy and contemplative spirit.

If you look to his mind, he is at least as much celebrated for intelligence and wit, as for wildness and rags. Expressions to him the most commonplace, you hear detailed as gems by the delighted tourist; nor can we think their simile very much exaggerated who have compared his mind to the fragments of the diamond sparkling in the brilliancy of unpolished lustre. And even as to those more substantial qualities for which he usually gets less credit, where has he ever been carefully trained that he has not rewarded the cultivation? Shall we appeal to the revolution wrought by Lord George Hill in one of the most barbarous of our mountain regions?* or speak of the Connaught children who come to our industrial schools absolutely wild—needle and thimble being to them perfect mystery—and who in a few months become new beings, and execute work so fine and delicate as to have won a high place at the Great Exhibition. While as to more lofty pursuits of mind, though our country cannot boast many stars in the firmament of knowledge, she has at least shown what her sons could do were their advantages equal to those of others; and has given to philosophy, a Boyle—to literature, a Goldsmith—to eloquence, a Grattan, and to poetry, a Moore—to the senate, the immortal Burke, and to the field, the Hero of Waterloo.

Finally, if you look to our countrymen's heart, what fine traits of character you will often see bursting forth through all his degradation! Within his rude bosom lies the germ of many a noble quality which, if duly ripened, would make him a fine specimen of human nature. Hospitable to a proverb—generous to a fault—grateful, confiding, warm-hearted, and enjoying a world-wide renown for that reckless valor which seems scarce conscious of danger! Of this the peninsular war furnished scores of romantic instances; and the truth of O'Connell's doggerel none can dispute—

"On the field of Waterloo,
Duke Wellington would have looked blue,
If Paddy hadn't been there too."

* "Facts from Gweedore," by Lord George Hill.

We have noticed those heart-rending proofs of passionate tenderness which are daily furnished by our departing emigrants; and if any one is disposed in cruel coldness to hint that such affectionate grief is too strong to last, we appeal to the letters and remittances they are continually sending home, not to their parents and friends only, but often to their neighbors, to enable *them* also to emigrate. It appears from official papers that near £2,000,000 sterling have in the last three years been remitted from North America by these *poor* people. And a return lately made by the Post-office shows, that one third of all the letters coming weekly from America are destined for Ireland. Follow those letters to their destination! Imagine the sensation produced in each humble abode when the anxiously-expected epistle from some absent child arrives! The village neighbors flock in to hear it read; and as some one more learned than the rest reads aloud, mark the tears, not only of the old couple, for that is nothing, but of many a kind-hearted neighbor! It is full of inquiries after old acquaintances, and tender allusions to by-gone scenes, which, despite their occasional tinge of the ludicrous, do vast credit to the best feelings of our nature. In a word, the character of the Irish is so richly dramatic, as to have given rise to a distinct class of writers, such as Edgeworth, Lover, and Carleton. The bleak winds which beat on their half-naked forms may make their bodies more callous, but they leave their feelings as tender as ever; and those sensibilities which misfortune sometimes blunts in others, it often makes morbidly acute in them.

Still we own they have many faults; we only assert, and engage to prove, that these are the offspring of the unhappy circumstances in which they are placed; while we contend that many of them confirm the position we are establishing, and are the faults of a fine mind which has been poisoned or neglected. How many of our countrymen owe their present poverty to the very excess of their hospitality? How many, their turbulence, to that unsuspecting confidence in their advisers, which marks a generous mind? How many of their worst quarrels, to that warmth of temper which usually accompanies warmth of heart? And if, as is too justly alleged against our countrymen, there is as much mercury in his heels as there is wit in his head; if he is as fond of handling the shillelagh as the spade; it is owing much to that impulsive ardor of character which is as useful when well trained, as it is mischievous when ill directed. Nor should we omit to mention, that, being a sort of *living hyperbole*, he has in very many respects earned a reputation much worse than he deserves. When he is drunk, he makes the whole town know it; when provoked, he bawls and gesticulates as though he were frantic, and perhaps makes free with his neighbor's head; yet we who know him well assert, that in all this "pother" there is not so much real, and far less enduring wrath, than is often betrayed in another man's scowl.

Here, then, we find the elements of a noble race —a mind and heart of a structure as fine as it is singular, resembling a complicated but delicate musical instrument which is easily destroyed by a clumsy hand, but gives forth the finest tones when swept by a skilful performer. We have here a character peculiarly capable of great good or great evil —of the loftiest elevation or the lowest degradation —which, like their own rich soil, can produce nothing in common measure, but exhibits equal rankness in the weeds that infest it, and richness in the flowers that adorn it—a character, in short, which can be turned to the best or the worst account, and has been justly compared to fire, which when uncontrolled is the most destructive of elements, but skilfully managed, is the most useful, serving alike to propel the engine and kindle the incense of the altar!

And thus we demonstrate that Ireland's miseries can no more be traced to the race than to the country; that, on the contrary, the natural superiority of both proves that not only must the cause be sought in some other quarter, but that it must truly be one of dreadful malignity to have desolated so fair a land, and degraded so fine a people.

CHAPTER II.

THE POLITICAL.

We now approach a subject which contains perhaps the most popular solution of Ireland's wretchedness—the very *eureka* of multitudes.

For many years we have had two sets of rulers, the one in St. Stephen's, and the other in Corn Exchange; and we have had each charging the other with our country's woes, in terms generally more forcible than courteous. The grand text of the one has been—"the curse of British misrule;" and a favorite theme with the other—"the pest of Irish agitation." And if what the one party rings in our ears be true, the wrongs of Hungary are but trifles to ours; while if we are to listen to the other, such swarms of demagogues must needs destroy the finest land. Let us judge for a moment between parties so fierce, and statements so conflicting.

The Agitator.—It is true, Ireland has for ages been the hotbed of agitation. Inhabited since the days of Elizabeth by two distinct races, having little in common but the soil they tilled, regarding each other as aliens in blood and religion, and their feelings embittered by their relation as conquerors and conquered—the result has been, that party strife which has so long afflicted Ireland, and those swarms of agitators that have so long infested it. Hence it has been almost as much the scene of political conflict, as though this were the necessary condition of its being—a something which floated in the atmosphere and grew on the soil.

But what if it is those who denounce this agitation who are themselves in part to blame for its existence? Some real and more imaginary grievances are the agitator's stock in trade; and Britain has in times past furnished so much of the former, as has made him but too successful in palming off the latter. Nay, even her mode of redressing grievances has sometimes served his trade almost as much as her obstinate continuance of them. Wise and timely concession is death to the agitator; but her concessions have often been so tardy, and made with so bad a grace, as rather to have increased his power. She has too often led the Irish to think that she has granted them more from motives of fear than from a sense of justice. And when the agitator thus discovered that little could be got without clamoring—when he saw, or thought he saw, that turbulence fared better than loyalty, that the quiet petitioner was shoved aside, while the noisy blusterer obtained a ready hearing—no wonder that he pushed his trade and found it to flourish.

We must add our conviction that the evils of agitation are much overrated. It is error, not truth, which suffers most by it in the end. Even the worst form of it can only thrive on popular ignorance;

yet it tends of necessity to dispel the ignorance on which it thrives, and thus it sooner or later perishes by its own hand. We appeal to the career of the great Irish demagogue. Not only did he do much to emancipate the Irish mind, and, by inspiring the people with a love of civil liberty, awaken of necessity some longing for its twin sister, religious freedom; but it was his own teaching which mainly enabled them, at length, to see through his schemes, provoked that revolt which cost him his life, destroyed Irish agitation as a trade, and sent him down to the grave so little regretted, that you will now seldom hear pronounced, even by those who once worshipped him, the name of that prince of agitators, who, from the rock of Darrynane, once governed the empire. Irish agitation has thus committed suicide. O'Connell is no more: and where is now his vast train of followers? Young Ireland, that killed him, is also gone, having perished ignobly in a cabbage garden. Conciliation Hall is closed; Tara's Hill is now as silent as Tara's Halls. Even the priests, once omnipotent, already know that their new "Defence" agitation is doomed to be a failure. Our quick-sighted countrymen have learned wisdom. They have discovered their "Liberators" to be greater tyrants than those from whom they proposed to free them; so they are bent on emigration, not on agitation; their thoughts are in the land of the West.

Finally, agitation is sometimes a positive duty.

Constitutional agitation is the Briton's privilege, and, where grievances exist, the country's blessing; and if, in designing hands, it has been the parent of rebellion, it has, in upright hands, been the parent of progress. To it we are indebted for every political boon we have ever gained, from the triumph of Runnymede to our latest reforms. Our glorious Constitution itself is its child. And if Irish agitation is an evil, it has sometimes, we fear, been a necessary one. If at this moment, for instance, we see agitation rise in Ulster—a province as proverbial for peace as is the rest of Ireland for turbulence,—if we see amongst its foremost leaders, not the desperate adventurer who has been schooled in the club-room, but the quiet farmer who follows his team—if we see this man doing violence to all his tastes and habits, passing at once from the plough to the platform, and there reciting his tale of sufferings with an artlessness that proves its truth, and a feeling which proclaims their intenseness—above all, if we see him countenanced by those gospel ministers to whose labors it is owing that Ulster is the Goshen of Ireland, and amongst whose flocks those who denounce them as "reverend agitators" can alone sleep safely on their pillow—then must we own that there is surely some good cause for a phenomenon so singular; and we must charge the attendant evils of such agitation, not on those who *seek* redress, but on those who *refuse* it. If their story is false, it is easy to convict them of falsehood; but if true, it is the foulest wrong to call them incendiaries—the cruelest mockery to bid them be still—the vilest hypocrisy to denounce their strong language without breathing a whisper against the oppression which provokes it—and the basest insult to the gospel to ask its ministers to make it the despot's tool by preaching silent submission while the fruits of their pastoral toils are being blasted, the only fair province in Ireland is being desolated, and those who are the very salt of our country are being driven to other climes.

Having said this much on the general subject of agitation, we still most freely admit that it must have greatly injured the country; but to say that it has ruined it, is absurd. Agitation may produce national discontent, but where has it ever caused national dissolution? Besides it is those western regions which have been the least agitated that are the most distressed, and those midland districts which have suffered least, that have been the chief scenes of excitement; while it is well known, that years ago, when political agitation was at its height, the country was comparatively prosperous, and it is when its fires are almost extinguished that we have reached the lowest depths of misery.

Besides, agitation itself is not a primary evil, but owes its existence to other evils. It either springs from real grievances—and then not the agitator but the legislature is chargeable with its evils—or from imaginary grievances, and then they must be charged on the guilt of the demagogue or the ignorance of his dupes—causes which are moral, not political. With wise and just rulers there can be few grievances, and therefore little righteous agitation: with an enlightened and virtuous people there can be few dupes or deceivers, and hence little unrighteous agitation. Therefore, granting it, as we do most freely, to be one cause of our miseries, it is but a derivative one, and must itself be traced to some higher cause.

The Legislature.—Is our country's blood, then, on the hands of our rulers? Surely there must be good ground for the everlasting cry of "Sassenach oppression," which even our village children have learned to repeat. It can scarce be possible that the favorite theme of the Irish agitator, and the most fruitful source of Irish discontent, should prove, when examined, "like the baseless fabric of a vision." Let us see. The "curse" alleged must be found either in the constitution or the mode in which it is administered.

Is it the constitution you object to? Then would you have republicanism? So have France and Mexico; and there you have edifying specimens of liberty! Or absolute monarchy? So have Russia and Austria; and Africa contains not baser slavery than is imposed on those countries by the "beardless Nero," and the "northern bear." Or an ecclesiastical government? So has Rome; and if you wish a sample of a government at once diabolical and dastardly, committing the vilest crimes in the name of Jesus, read Nicolini's late History of the Pontificate of Pio Nono. Or a mixed government, combining, as far as possible, the benefits of the others without their evils? Why, this is what you are blessed with, if you only knew your blessings. Defects it has, like everything human; but these deserve not to be named in comparison to its perfections. It is the glory of England, the envy of Europe, the admiration of the world; and had Britain done no more for Ireland than to displace her barbarous Brechon laws with such a glorious code, that was a boon which deserved her eternal gratitude!

Is it, then, that Ireland is defrauded of the blessings of this constitution, and is the victim of unjust laws? Doubtless, in the best statute book, there is room for improvement, and, as we have hinted, we could suggest amendments in our own. But what true British subject can look this instant over Europe, and not feel thankful for his own immunities? While our countrymen have been roused to madness by the demagogue's artful tale of British wrongs, how carefully has he withheld the far longer list of British benefits? Grant that, in former days, England did not thoroughly act out the principles of liberty, civil and religious;—this was owing to the darkness from which the world was then but emerging; and the blame rests not with her, but the *authors of this darkness.* Grant that she imposed disabilities on the Roman Catholics;—if such acts of iniquity as the gunpowder plot convinced her that they could not be trusted with power, who but themselves were to blame for the loss of it? Or, granting that there once was ground for the charge of British misrule, on what do you rest your accusation now? Are we insufficiently represented in Parliament? We have 105 members, while Scotland has only 53. Is the suffrage too limited? For a long time, it embraced even 40*s*. freeholders, and, as is now universally admitted, this proved not a blessing but a curse, and led to that subdivision of land which has so greatly enhanced our calamities.

Is it, then, the legislative union which has wrought our country's ruin? Such has been the language of a thousand meetings, and the hottest bolts of "patriot" indignation have been launched against the very name of "that traitor, Castlereagh;" while repeal has been proclaimed the measure which would usher in the millennium of Ireland. Well, union is usually strength, not weakness. Scotland has felt the full force of the proverb since her parliament was transferred from Holyrood to Westminster; and how can the same measure prove Scotland's prosperity and Ireland's destruction? Besides, other stubborn facts interfere most rudely with our patriots' assertions; for it appears from the records of the Irish House of Commons, that trade had so grievously declined before the union, that College Green was beset with complaints on the subject;

while, according to returns from time to time ordered by the Imperial Parliament, our imports and exports have, since the union, greatly increased. Now if, as we are told, the southern provinces have declined since the union, of course this increase must have been chiefly confined to Ulster; and then comes the problem, how the union can be such a blessing to one province, and such a curse to the rest, especially when, instead of being the most favored by government, Ulster has been notoriously the most neglected of the four? In truth, a parliament in which so few were found proof against the "bribes" of Castlereagh, was, at best, but a doubtful blessing; nor, were all the ancient glories of College Green to be restored, could we expect an assembly of much purer patriots, if we are to judge by the specimens that often grace our hustings, and offer our country their senatorial services.

Again, we are told of the heartless treatment which Ireland receives at the hands of Britain. Nay, so far have base men reckoned on our people's ignorance, that they have assured them no country groans beneath such a load of taxation! Why, the taxes of Great Britain are, at least, thrice as numerous, comprising a long list, unknown in Ireland, of taxes on carriages, gigs, horses, dogs, servants, coachmen, heraldry, income, plate, &c.; and our only heavy imposts are our poor-rates, county-cess, and tithe-rent charge, all of which are expended among ourselves, and the severity of two of which is owing to our own poverty and crime. And as to oppressive laws, we ask on what page of our statute book are they contained? Or, where, alas! can you find amongst us those features of down-trodden greatness which oppression never fails to bring out, and which have made the Pole and Hungarian the admiration of the world? Is it such wretches as throng our jails, who constitute the victims of British oppression?—or such deeds as larceny and felony that compose our claims to the sympathy of nations? Misrule! such was the impression the attempted rebellion of 1848 made even on its own leaders, that they were heard to confess that their countrymen "did not deserve to be free."

The truth is, Ireland has been the object of the most pains-taking legislation; and whatever have been the sins of our rulers, it would be downright wrong to deny this. More time is each session spent on Irish affairs, than on all our colonial affairs together; and more of the public treasure has been lavished on Ireland than any other portion of the empire. Since 1800, 33 Committees of Parliament, and 21 Government Commissions have been appointed to inquire into the causes of our miseries, and the best means of their removal; and during the same period we have received £26,000,000 sterling in mere grants and advances.* £1,000,000 has been given to construct harbors for our commerce; £8,500,000 to encourage our manufactures; £8,000,000 to save

* Thom's Statistics, *passim.*

our people from the grave of famine; while our canals, railways, agriculture, and fisheries have all been nursed at the public expense. Nay, even our charitable institutions are largely supported by parliamentary grants.* Yet, while not a tithe of this kindness has been shown either to Ulster or Scotland, the southern demagogue has for years harped upon British neglect.

Where, then, can you find such political grievances as can at all account for our miseries; or how explain that our least favored province is the most prosperous, and its people the most loyal, though at least as able to detect, and ready to resist oppression as any of their countrymen? Does it not demonstrate how little our disease is connected with politics at all, that we have for years been growing worse, while our legislation has confessedly been growing better; until now, the country is at the point of dissolution, when according to our political empirics she should at least have been convalescent? Alas! if legislation could have blessed us, we should now have been the happiest of nations, for on no country's behalf have more statutes been framed—and our people are at length beginning to perceive this. They have seen how their "patriots" have all been strangely hushed in the hour of our deepest distress, when, if British misrule is its cause, their voice should have been louder than ever. And they are beginning to see that other motives may influence

* Thom's Statistics, 1852, p. 251.

an agitator besides those of pure-minded patriotism; that, after all, parliament can do little for a country if it will do nothing for itself; and that in order to prosperity, Ireland needs something far different from what agitation can extort, or legislation concede. Hence they are beginning to suspect that the grand cause of their evils is something in themselves rather than in the laws—something which follows the Irishman beyond his native shores, and makes him the same wretched being in every town in Britain; beyond the United Kingdom, and makes him the same byeword by the lakes of Canada, and on the plains of Australia; aye, beyond the "curse of British misrule" altogether, and makes the southern the chief inmate of American jails, while many a northern has reached the first rank amongst her citizens!

CHAPTER III.

THE SOCIAL.

Thus, the mystery of Ireland's woes seems but to deepen as we proceed. We have sought its solution in her physical state, but it is not there. We have examined her political state, neither is it there. Perhaps we shall be more successful in our present department of inquiry.

We cannot give the reader a better key to Ireland's social state, than to say that the clouds of feudalism still linger on her hills. Why they so linger after having gone up so generally off the face of Britain, shall hereafter be considered; it is enough now to state the fact. You not only see it in the extreme paucity of a middle class, that index of a country's progress; but you can still trace the old division into barons and serfs only too distinctly in the modern one of gentry and peasantry; and you have, of course in a milder form, the same haughty assumption in the one class, and the same servile submission in the other. This remark will prepare the reader for the following brief glance at Ireland's social state, under the simple classification of *habits* and *pursuits.*

Habits.—There is little which more distinguishes the upper classes of Ireland from those of Britain than extravagant habits, combined with foolish notions of rank and style. Inquire into the history of those decayed families which now fill the land, and you will find, that with many honorable exceptions, doubtless, they have for generations lived in a manner unsuited to their station, and incompatible with their means. Even so late as 60 years ago, high life in Ireland was little else than a round of fashionable dissipation; and the wildest escapades to be found in the works of Barrington and Lever, were, if not literally, at least in substance perpetrated. A host considered it discreditable if any of his guests were allowed to leave his table without needing help; and so deliberately did the guests themselves prepare for their fate, that they often wound up their watches before sitting down to dinner! As for fighting, Sir Lucius O'Trigger was the commonest character. No gentleman travelled without duelling pistols. His "marking irons," as they were called, were as indispensable an article as his razors; and doubtless sufficient ground was given for the squib which represented the morning orders at an hotel sometimes to be, "Pistols for two, and breakfast for *one!*" What, then, shall we say of other vices? It was the frequent boast of not a few of these *gentlemen*, how many females they had destroyed; and such moral nuisances were many of them, that absenteeism itself became a blessing, and the most important service they ever rendered their country was to die.

Alas! these habits have not all died with them. The improved tone of society at large forbids, of course, the same reckless wildness; but so far at least, as extravagant style is concerned, too many of our present gentry walk in the ways of their fathers. With many highly honorable exceptions, the same passion for display which has already beggared them, continues, though the means of indulging it has failed. Numbers are at this moment living at the expense of others, when no longer able to live at their own. And to judge by their conduct, one would think that they considered it the deepest dishonor for a gentleman to stoop to any kind of industry; more disgraceful to be a shopkeeper, than to be hopelessly indebted to one; and scarce so humiliating to borrow one's bread, as to earn it in some honest calling; while nothing is to them more incomprehensible than that English members of parliament should sometimes be proprietors of a warehouse!

Habits travel downwards; and those of the upper ranks have been aped by our scanty middle class. Men often retire from business and set up as "gentlemen," with less means than Englishmen generally commence on; and you will meet dozens in every southern town, driving about in total idleness, on "fortunes" which English farmers would scarce deem a competency. The same passion for style marks their very nomenclature;—a small trader is a merchant, and a shop a store; a plain cottage is a villa, and a common street a mall. Nor is it less observable in their domestic arrangements. Convenience usually yields to show;—if the drawing-room is well kept, it is not so much matter about the kitchen; and the back premises often sadly contrast with the lawn. The young gentlemen's ambition is to have a dog or a horse. The young ladies sit in the drawing-room and play the piano; and if one drop of blood of any ancient family can be traced in their veins, then, no matter how penniless they may be, the thriving "upstart" who aspires to their hand often meets a response more prompt than agreeable.

What, then, shall we say of our peasantry? You

need only enter one of those innumerable cabins which disfigure the face of our country, to get a glimpse of their condition. You enter and find sometimes two, but oftener one apartment; and there the pig and the family dwell harmoniously together. You look around and find a group of half-naked urchins, whose legs are encrusted with mire. You ask for the poor man's wardrobe—it is all on his back; and a sad specimen it usually is of "looped and windowed raggedness." You cannot help wondering how, when once out of his clothes, he can ever get into them again, or perhaps your wonder rather is how this can be a difficulty, there being so many entrances. Finally, you ask his history, and find that, from whatever cause, his entire class has for ages stood still on the borders of civilization; and that whole districts continue in a state of primitive barbarism, not much exceeded by the American Indians. You traverse, for instance, the entire west coast, from Donegal to Cork, an extent of 300 miles, and stretching the whole length of Ireland; and can scarce discover one sign of that upward tendency which distinguishes the man from the beast; but the same unchanging style of hut and habits continues through generations, as though their only guide really were the instinct of the lower creation.

Pursuits.—We have seen the sickly state of our husbandry, commerce, and manufacture, despite the rarest facilities—that perhaps in no country has nature done more, and art done less. Alas! every effect has its adequate cause. Let any one brought up in an English town, accustomed to its matchless habit of business, and the clock-work regularity of its establishments, pay a visit to any of our southern towns, and in what a different atmosphere he instantly finds himself! How forcibly he is struck with the air of idleness that pervades its streets; he is not less struck with the unbusiness-like appearance, and often positive slovenliness of its shops and offices. And, save where some Scotch house has chased it away, he finds much the same style of business, with all its attributes—its high prices, and second prices, and indifferent assortments—which prevailed in those "good old times," when the affairs of life jogged quietly on; when the goddess of pleasure shared the throne with the god of riches; and when the evening was the best part of the day. Nor let him be surprised to see the proprietor taking his drive during business hours, or hear of his going a-sporting once a-week or so. Least of all, let him wonder when he examines his ledgers, to find them fall short of his English notions of accuracy. And to all this let him add such a moral tone in society, that it is nothing rare for a clerk to abscond, or an employer more than once to fail, or even plain cheating itself to occur—and then let him say if our commercial decline is any great mystery.

Should any one pronounce this picture overdrawn, we assert that it is rather the reverse. Is it not notorious, that all over the south and west—(for we speak not of Ulster; its social state, we shall presently see, is as different from the rest of Ireland as its temporal)—our best houses, in most departments of trade, are Scotch and English; that, even now, *they* are flourishing when our own countrymen in the same business are melting away; and that it is to them we are mainly indebted for the little commercial character we possess? It is they who have compelled our own people to adopt their improved mode of business, and created a trade where none previously existed. To them we are largely indebted for a fish and pork trade; and there was not in the entire pasture county of Kerry a single butter market, till one was, some years ago, established by a Scotchman! Even our Irish employers themselves find it often necessary to employ Scotch or English servants. Are not our railways generally constructed, our fisheries conducted, our banks officered, nay, even our posts of gardener and land-steward, filled by strangers? Was there ever such folly as to blame all this on England, as some are so fond of doing? The tides of business obey the same laws with those of the ocean; and if we ourselves were what we ought to be, the whole power of England could not produce this state of things. Nothing, in fact, can make inferior articles long keep the market against superior ones. Natural laws are too strong for artificial restrictions; and if there is any conspiracy against us, it is not an English, but a world-wide conspiracy. The Dutchman undersells us in the London markets; the American undersells us in our own. Our hottest repealers themselves traverse England for goods which they might often get at home; and too well they know why—that, however humbling the truth, poor Ireland has dropped far behind in the world's commercial march.

But the chief interest in Ireland, is the *agricultural;* yet, though no people are more dependent on the farm, with none is the style of farming worse. No man seems to trust more to the mere *vis naturæ* than our peasant farmer. Subsoil ploughing he scarce ever heard of, and draining was rare until the late drainage bill was passed—he usually leaves the water to go as it came. His ploughing is bad, his fencing worse, and his spade, called a *loy*, seems as if made on purpose to disturb the ground as little as possible. His crop is usually left to struggle on as best it can against an army of weeds; and as if it were sacrilege so far to interfere with Nature's wildest productions as to cut them down, you will see thistles standing on the harvest ridge, the crops having been carefully *cut away around them*, and in windy Autumn's days, you will meet their winged seeds careering along the fields. As you go westward, things grow worse. In Mayo, you will see the limestone in the river beds, and the turf on their banks to burn it withal; yet it lies undisturbed, as though its use were unknown; and even so late as 1847, when Mr. Brannigan introduced turnips to

Ballinglen, so new were they to the peasantry, that they went by the name of "Brannigan's turnips."

You inquire the cause of such agricultural delinquency, and find that, as usual in Ireland, all men blame all men but themselves. The tenant declares that the rent is too high, and the landlord replies by threatening to raise it; the one protests that his landlord is a tyrant, and the other that his tenantry are sluggards: and each adduces so much in proof of his charge, that one is half inclined to believe them both. At all events, the truth seems to lie between them. We cannot believe the tenant to be the innocent martyr he represents himself, or that high rents are the sole cause of his wretchedness, else how is it that those tenants whose land is 1*s.* an acre, are usually as poor as those who pay 20*s.*? Indeed, it is quite a common remark, that this class never thrive until their rent is raised: and should we charge on the landlords all the poverty, even of those who pay the highest rents, their own broken fences and weed-grown fields would testify against us.

Still, we believe that the tenant's wretchedness is mainly chargeable on the landlord, or, rather, the wretched system of landlordism in Ireland, and that, of all the secondary and derivative causes of our miseries, this is the chief. The gentry being the monopolists of the soil, have always been able to let it to the peasantry on whatever terms they pleased; and the latter, having no other means of livelihood, have had no alternative but to accept their terms or starve. Such entire control presented temptations too strong for slender virtue. Such irresponsible power naturally led to tyranny; such complete monopoly to exorbitant rents; such easily acquired wealth, to extravagant living; and all together, to many of those evils in which both landlord and tenant are now hopelessly involved. Forgetting that property has its duties as well as its rights, many landlords lived as though they were born but to enjoy, *fruges consumere nati*, and, instead of seeking the elevation of their tenants, treated them as mere ministers of their pleasures, and supporters of their extravagance.

This conduct sowed the seeds of manifold evils; the events of the last thirty years have fearfully accelerated their growth; at length the terrible harvest has come, and landlordism now reaps as it sowed. Fifty years ago, the extravagance of our gentry was at its height, and their estates were becoming rapidly embarrassed. At the same period, the wars of Napoleon had raised farm produce to an artificial price. The opportunity was too tempting, and the landlord generally raised the rent in proportion. While the wars lasted, "times were good;" the farmer could pay, and the landlord lived accordingly: but ever since the peace of 1815, farm produce has been sinking in value, till now it is not one half its old *war price:* yet land has still continued at the old *war rent*, and in many cases risen far above it;—

that is, the farmer has as much, or more, rent to pay with but one half the means of paying it; and the result has, of course, been his rapid decline. In vain were the landlords entreated, for their own sakes, to lower the rents in time; in vain were they assured that they were "killing the goose which laid the golden egg;" in vain were they reminded that they were driving to America the very flower of their tenantry, and filling their places with a degraded class, many of whom would promise any rent and pay none. It was utterly vain. They had not the sense to foresee the future consequences, nor the firmness to withstand the present temptation, and so, allured by "a high bid," they drove off their substantial farmers to make way for a pauper tenantry; and now the day of reckoning has arrived.

These evils have been aggravated by various circumstances. One has been our system of "middlemen"—that "squireen" class, who, holding under the head landlord, sublet their property at rack-rents, and, instead of earning their bread with the sweat of their own brow, lived in idleness on the sweat of a down-trodden tenantry. Another, has been the oppressive exactions of unprincipled agents, with their grim train of *bailiffs* and *drivers*. Even so late as 1845, the "*Times* Commissioner" brought to light a system of iniquity, on the part of both middlemen and agents, which was scarcely credible. It has often been remarked, that whoever is poor, agents generally get rich; and could the "office" walls speak, the mystery would perhaps disappear; while, to say nothing of such oblations as eggs and butter, geese and turkeys, many are the more costly offerings with which a trembling tenantry are obliged to propitiate a middleman's favor.

But the crowning hardship is the tenant's liability to have the fruits of his improvements grasped by his landlord. If a peasant rents a common for 5*s.* an acre, and, by his own sole exertion, makes it in a few years worth 20*s.*, the landlord not unfrequently raises the rent to 20*s.*, and gives him his option to pay it or "quit." The present Tenant-Right agitation in Ulster owes its existence to these unrighteous exactions. The Ulster farmers are by far the most improving in Ireland. They found Ulster a desert; they have made it a garden. "Tenant-Right" simply means the tenant's right to the benefit of his *own* improvements. Besides its obvious justice, it was secured to them at the time of the "Plantation," and has ever since been the prevailing *usage* in Ulster. But the farmers have of late got some cause to think that the sooner it is made *law* the better; and nothing but the most short-sighted policy would resist a claim so righteous. That landlord must be blind who does not see that, if he would have his estates improved, it is by rewarding, not punishing the tenant for his industry. No man in his senses will make improvements in the prospect of being robbed of them, or taxed for them; and if this is the reward the Ulster landlords will confer upon tenantry who have made their position such an enviable contrast to that of Ireland's other landlords, let them rest assured that the same ruin awaits them which has now fallen upon these their brethren. In truth, it is manifest that no concession of mere tenant-right can now save them. A series of social changes has so altered our entire condition, that the relations of landlord and tenant must be completely readjusted to meet these altered circumstances. To resist such a measure seems to us like contending against fate, and, we fear, the longer it is deferred it will be the more sweeping when it comes.

Such, then, is a brief sketch of Ireland's social state. Well, the complicated cause of our wretchedness begins at length to unfold itself; for what else but social decay could flow from such social derangement? It surely requires no great sagacity to perceive that such habits must lead to want, and want to general disorganization, or that that country *must* decline, in which all classes, from the landlord to the peasant, so generally neglect the duties of their station? A country which wears such an air of idleness, that the Englishman, on first landing from his own busy home, almost fancies he has arrived on some holiday; whose style of business and farming is so bad, that he protests it would entail certain bankruptcy in Britain, and where the advent of a Scotchman is deemed a blessing to a neighborhood, and he makes a fortune on the spot where his predecessor starved. Nor can we have better proof of our position than the social superiority of Ulster. We have already seen its comparative prosperity; well, the least observant traveller who visits this province is struck with the diligence of the husbandman, the enterprise of the merchant, and the peaceful, plodding industry of all. There, all is frugality and simplicity—mothers, even of the first rank, attend closely to their households, instead of driving about in their carriages. There, idleness and style, instead of being deemed respectable, are despised; there, men take rank, not so much from what their fathers were, as from what they themselves *are;* and instead of the high-born profligate being respected, and the architect of his own fortune despised, *there* is practised the noble sentiment of the Roman, who, when taunted by a profligate patrician with his obscure birth, replied, "You owe all your greatness to others, I owe mine to myself."

But it is evident that Ireland's social state must itself be derivative; and, while one cause of our evils, must flow from higher causes. What can *these* be? is our next subject of inquiry.

CHAPTER IV.

THE MORAL.

Let us here premise, that *knowledge* and *virtue*, and *ignorance* and *vice*, are the chief causes of social elevation and degradation respectively. Enough of the former must raise any nation to the highest pinnacle of greatness; while enough of the latter must sink it to the lowest depths. What makes the chief difference between the savage and the sage but knowledge, or between the angel and the demon but virtue? The nation which has most of both must necessarily leave others behind. Scarce anything could keep down a people all light and virtue, and nothing could elevate a people all ignorance and vice. And this is so obvious, that let a wilderness be filled with the world's best benefactors, and it would soon become a paradise; then let these be succeeded by the worst malefactors, and it would quickly become a wilderness more terrible than at first; or let it be filled with succeeding generations, varying in their degrees of light and virtue, and all other things being equal, its condition would vary in exact proportion. How seldom does virtue find its way, even by mistake into a jail! And so rarely is knowledge itself found there, that for the four years ending 1850, the average annual proportion of prisoners in Ireland who could read and write, was not 18 per cent.* Let us see how far Ireland enjoys these blessings:—

KNOWLEDGE.—According to the census of 1841,

* Thom (1852), p. 201. It is this intimate connection of ignorance and vice which has induced us to class both under the one head of moral causes. Their powerful mutual influence will become more apparent as we proceed.

near 53 per cent. of the population of Ireland could *neither* read nor write; while only 26 per cent. could both read and write! Thus our educational statistics, at the very first glance, bring out the astounding fact, that 11 years ago three fourths of the people were devoid of the simplest rudiments of knowledge. You ask how can this be accounted for. Till the National Board was established, whole districts depended for their education on the Irish Hedge School—that matchless nursery of knowledge, whose site was a bog, whose forms were often the floor, whose slates and copy-books were sometimes the chalked walls and door, and whose school-books such select works as the "Irish Rapparees," and "Freny, the Robber;" while all was presided over by a pedagogue, compared to whom, Goldsmith's schoolmaster himself was a trifle.* What, then, was our learning when such was its seat? Even yet the National Board has a stupendous task before it. There are still whole districts into which scarce a book or a newspaper penetrates, and where you will find professional scribes who are employed by the people to write their letters for them to America.

We have already noticed the barbarism of our western coast. The numerous islands in particular, which so beautifully stud the bosom of the Atlantic, and seem designed, like smaller gems, to garnish the "emerald, set in the ring of the sea," are sunk in

* Report, Commissioners, Public Instruction, 1834.

such primitive ignorance, that when, some years ago, a boat from Tory island was driven by a storm on the mainland, the crew pulled leaves and branches off the trees to show as curiosities on their return !*

Their moral and religious ignorance is still more deplorable. It is quite notorious that thousands in Ireland never saw a Bible; never heard of the Trinity; know nothing of the Saviour but the name; and are so ignorant of the nature of vice and crime, as to be restrained from it chiefly through fear of the prison. To the question, "Who made you?" how often have our missionaries received the answer, "It was my mother, sir!" To the question, "Are you a sinner?" you will often get the reply, "No, indeed, sir!" We ourselves have often asked, "How many persons are there in the Godhead?" and have been answered, "I do not know, sir;" and in reply to the question, "Who is the Holy Ghost?" have been told by several that they never heard of a Holy Ghost! And should you express surprise at any of these answers, you are often silenced by the touching reply, "God help me, I never got the learning." God help them, indeed! and these are not savage heathens in the jungle, but our own *Christian* fellow-countrymen—of whom, even while we write, some are passing before the judgment throne!

Hence their amazing superstition. You will see

* Noel's Tour.

charms called "gospels," and "scapulars" tied round their necks, and fixed in their cabin roofs to keep away devils and fairies! If their cow takes ill, it is "fairy shot;" if their churn will not yield the butter, it is "blinked;" indeed, they seem as if they thought evil spirits had a peculiar fancy for a dairy, and had little else to do than play pranks with the milk and butter. Their superstitious minds have covered the land with holy wells, trees, lakes, and mountains, each having its patron saint—rivalling the ancient Greeks in their poetic creations of naiads, nereids, fauns, and hamadryads. You will sometimes see them, as they pass a holy well, take off their hats and begin to mutter as if addressing some spirit who resided in its waters. Most of these wells are endowed with miraculous powers, and are therefore frequented by many. Some cure the lame, and some the blind; others seem not particular, but extend equal relief to all diseases. And one well in Erris, most unworthy of its country, is so ungallant as to have an utter aversion to the entire female sex!*

If next we turn to that *fourth part* who *can* read and write, while very many are most highly educated, the attainments of the majority are, we fear, but slender. In 6 counties, and 74 towns, with populations ranging from 2,500 to 12,400 each, there was not in 1849 a single book-shop; and in the entire island there was, in proportion to the population,

* Gregg's Visit to Erris.

only one for every 9 which then existed in Scotland!* While, as to private libraries, it is said that in the greater part of Connaught, there do not exist as many books as would stock a book-shop in a small English town.† And we fear that even these would not be found of the most select kind—and that the library, so composed, would be one rather of entertaining than useful knowledge. Indeed, so low is our thirst for learning, that, except in a few towns, the trade of bookseller is bad; that of publisher worse; and that of author worst of all. The latter have almost always to look, and usually repair to England for a livelihood. We have not more than two or three magazines which deserve the name; and the majority of at least our western newspapers, while generally dearer than the *London Times*, are sorry samples of a country's literature. In truth, the *cacoethes scribendi* has never been a failing of the Irish. Nor can we say much more for the *suetudo legendi*. Our people are fonder of the newsroom than the library; and when they are found amongst the corridors of the latter, poetry too often carries it against philosophy—fiction against fact; and even Brown and Newton have generally to yield to the rival claims of Scott and Dickens.

In a word, if you make the experiment, you will find that even our best classes are as far behind the Scotch in substantial attainments, as they are before them in polite accomplishments. Hearken to the

* Colportage in Ireland, pp. 9, 10. † Ibid.

conversation in Scotch and Irish steamers, and you will often find the Scotch farmer to possess more solid information than the Irish landlord. On religious subjects especially, the Irish gentleman would find himself but a sorry match for many a shepherd on the Lammermuirs. Indeed, such is the thirst for learning in Scotland, that not only do youths who are destined for the merchant's desk usually attend the university, but we have known common tradesmen to work in their shops one half of the day, and attend the college classes the remainder. And though we cannot speak so favorably of the general attainments of the English, they have ever been remarkably distinguished above the Irish for the important quality of being thoroughly acquainted, each with his own business, no matter how little they may know beyond it.

Now, if thus it appears that the minds of the Irish are left for the most part as waste as their mountains, we ask, what *must* be the effect? Never was "knowledge power" so much as now. Education has, in fact, become the grand road to advancement; national greatness can now be attained no longer by arms, but by arts and sciences; and in the clear conviction of this, other nations are pushing on with all their might in the march of enlightenment. Who, then, can wonder if Ireland *stationary*, has been left by the world *progressive;* if ignorance, only matched in the dark ages, should have no chance in an age of pre-eminent light; and if the vast superiority of other countries in the whole field of industry, from the highest manufacture to the humblest trade, should have driven us out of even our own market? Surely the blindest can scarce help perceiving that nothing short of a standing miracle could have hindered the tides of prosperity from leaving such a land, and flowing to other shores.

VIRTUE.—Again, the amount of virtue amongst us the reader himself can estimate by the following facts and statistics. The number of troops stationed in Ireland now for many years is surprising:—the annual average of the last 8 years has been upwards of 25,000 men! Thus, to control 7,000,000 of professing Christians, it requires near one fourth of that magnificent army, which is found sufficient (our native Indian troops excepted) to control the greatest empire on which the sun ever shone; containing 156,000,000 of subjects and tributaries; of whom 120,000,000 are heathens and Mohammedans! And if to this military force, we add 13,000 constabulary and metropolitan police, we have in this small island a constant army of occupation of 38,000 men!*

You exclaim—*Can* such a force be required? at least must it not supersede the necessity of jails and gibbets? Alas! it is a country of prisons as well as garrisons. There are in Ireland 155 jails and bridewells; near 700 law courts, from assizes to petty sessions;† and 10,000 persons ministering to justice,

* Thom's Statistics, 1852, p. 185. † Ib. *passim.*

from the judge to the bailiff.* And *can* this array of tribunals be required? Enter any southern court whatever; mark the crowds who throng the building and hang round the door; see the piles of indictments, processes, and summonses; observe the prodigious mass of business transacted during one single term; and then you may form some conception of the gross amount of *law* going on continually over the land with all its disorganizing influences. Yes, and though weeks are frequently spent at the assizes of one single county, yet the business is often left unfinished, and special commissions are sometimes required to relieve the crowded prisons. In fact, our chief public buildings, in addition to *poorhouses*, are jails and courthouses; and our most flourishing business is that of lawyers and solicitors.

Again, in Great Britain, with thrice the population of Ireland, and this consisting largely of the depraved manufacturing classes, there were in 1850, only 31,281 *committals*, while there were in Ireland in the same year 33,326, or upwards of 3 to 1 !† Yet this gives no accurate idea of the proportions of *actual* crime in these two countries; for conspiracy against the laws is in many parts of Ireland so perfect, that even assassinations take place in open day, within view of scores of people; and not only do they not inform, but so screen the assassin that he often eludes the utmost vigilance of the police. Nor is a less mournful fact brought out by the relative pro-

* Census, '41. † Thom's Statistics, 1852, pp. 199, 201.

portion of *convictions.* The same conspiracy against law and justice appears in our very courts; scenes of perjury the most revolting are common on the witness table; and in party cases, the frequent expression even of jurors, before entering the box at all, is that they will "eat their boots" with hunger before they find against the prisoner! Hence the striking fact, that while in Britain, of the above 31,281 committals, there were 23,900 convictions, or nearly three fourths, of the 33,326 prisoners committed in Ireland, there were only 17,108 convicted, or not much over one half.*

Perhaps you exclaim—Surely this array of crime must at least have been of the *petty* kind! Alas! its character was as melancholy as its amount. One fifth, at least, of the above convictions were for offences of the highest class; while of the entire number convicted, there were no less than 1,858 sentenced to transportation, and 17 sentenced to death!† All this, too, in a year of unusual peace! Then what must have been the statistics of our disturbed years? In 1848, we had near 40,000 committals, almost 3,000 sentenced to transportation, and 60 sentenced to death! You say this was during the famine period? Alas! it was even so. Unawed by the wrath of Jehovah himself, as if made worse by those fearful judgments which He sent to make us better, the period of our greatest calamity was that of our most dreadful wickedness, and the work

* Thom's Statistics, pp. 199, 201. † Ibid

of blood went on most rapidly beneath the outstretched arm of the angel of death.

Now, if such an amount of crime loads our calendars, despite the vigilance of an omnipresent police, the bristling of 38,000 bayonets, and the dread array of courts and gibbets, it is surely impossible to resist the conviction that were this enormous pressure removed which keeps down the wild elements of vice and crime, they would instantly burst forth with resistless fury. Indeed, such has been somewhat the case, even notwithstanding the presence of this force; for what has been Ireland's whole history but that of a moral volcano of pent-up fires and periodical eruptions, with whole counties in constant disturbance, and the entire country in occasional rebellion? Therefore it is manifest that even the foregoing statistics give no clear idea of our actual condition. Such an amount of crime can only exist where the social mass is fearfully diseased; and when correctly viewed, merely serves, like ulcers on the surface, to show the depth and malignity of the internal disorder. And faithfulness compels us at once to say, that with many honorable exceptions, there is in all classes a want of that high moral tone on which social health so much depends, and from the absence of which crime and misery necessarily spring.

We have glanced at our prevailing habits of idleness, extravagance, and style. Now the history of such habits has ever proved that their unhappy victims will live, if they can, at the expense of others, when no longer able to live at their own, and not be over-scrupulous about the means they adopt to prolong the dire struggle for existence. And so you have, in our wretched land, the needy landlord racking the tenant, and the thriftless tenant evading his exactions;* the employer taking advantage of his servants and tradesmen, and these taking their revenge by general unfaithfulness and frequent combinations; in a word, such a state of dishonesty, that where any legal flaw is found in their bonds and contracts, nine out of every ten usually take advantage of it. This system of mutual wrong has, of course, propagated and spread, giving birth, on the one hand, to extortions, distraints, and ejectments, and, on the other, to secret scheming, open resistance, and frequent assassinations. And thus have matters gone on for many years, till the unavoidable crisis has at length arrived; yet you wonder at our country's prostration, and speak as if some enchanter's curse were mysteriously resting on her! A country where masters and mistresses must generally stand over their servants to prevent their work from being destroyed by carelessness or neglected through sloth; in whose very turnip fields you will see sheds erected, where men keep nightly watch against the thief and the robber; in whose markets firkins of butter have been seized for being partially filled with clay; in whose farm-yards constant vigilance is required to

* Inglis' Tour, p. 167. Indeed, these statements are confirmed by every author acquainted with Ireland.

save the fowls from disappearing; and where the employer must often search his men, as they leave his stores in the evening, to save himself from being robbed! A country which has long been proverbial as the "land of *jobbing*;" where exists an entire class called "Sunday men," from never being seen except on Sabbaths, because they cannot then be arrested for their debts; and where not only is the arm of Justice paralyzed, but even the hand of Charity so foully abused, that the paupers often steal the bedclothes of the poor-houses which keep them alive, and deeds were on all hands perpetrated in connection with the late government relief-money, which we would positively blush to record! Is it *such* a country you would expect to prosper? Why, unless the laws of Heaven were reversed, and vice, not virtue, was the basis of prosperity, the half of what we have stated would blast the fairest land; and yet we have not stated the half of what exists. And it is blindness, or something worse, to charge the fruits of our own misdeeds on a Parliament which, with all its erroneous legislation, has, at least, evinced some desire to save us from ourselves.

Does any one deny these fearful statements, or say that, even if true, they ought to be suppressed?

Alas, to deny them were absurd, and to suppress them were criminal. False delicacy has too long concealed what faithfulness should have disclosed; and now that our country is sinking so fast, it were monstrous treachery to cover up those malignant ulcers of which she is expiring, when her life depends upon faithful probing.

KNOWLEDGE AND VIRTUE IN ULSTER.—If our solution is the true one, then should Ulster, being the most prosperous, be also the most enlightened and virtuous part of Ireland. Now, by the census of 1841, the proportions of the population in *each* province who could neither read nor write, were—Ulster, 33 per cent.; Leinster, 38; Munster, 52; Connaught, 64. Thus, it appears that, of persons totally ignorant, there were then in Ulster fewer by one third than in Munster, and by one half than in Connaught. Not *less* difference is found in the *general* intelligence of those who can read and write; and *much more* in their *religious* knowledge—the northern child evincing an acquaintance with revealed truth not often found in the southern grandfather. Indeed, the great educational superiority of Ulster is clearly proved by the fact, that while Connaught almost exclusively depends on National Schools for education, and Ulster has many others besides, yet, with twice the population, the latter province contains thrice as many National Schools as the former.* And, though a large number of the youth of Ulster are educated at the Scotch universities, yet, during the session of 1849, the students attending the Belfast Queen's College amounted to 192; while, in that of Cork, there were 115; in that of Galway,

* Thom's Statistics, 1852, p. 197.

68; and of this latter number some of the most eminent were natives of Ulster.* While, as to industrial knowledge, we shall only add, that the south has been sending individuals to the north to learn the cultivation and manufacture of flax; and the National Board is obliged to employ northern females to teach their southern schools the sewed muslin manufacture.

The difference in moral character is still more remarkable. Of the 25,000 troops usually stationed in Ireland, scarce 3,000 are found in Ulster, and, except in its southern counties, even these are wholly unnecessary. Not a soldier is stationed between Belfast and Derry, a distance of 70 miles, embracing two most populous counties and various large towns. Of our 13,000 police, the number stationed in Ulster, in 1851, was 1,901, little more than a seventh of the force for a third of the population.† And our prison statistics prove that even these are comparatively unnecessary. Of our 33,326 committals in 1850, the number in Ulster was 5,260, not one sixth part.‡ Yet, considering how many crimes escape detection in the south, from the prevailing conspiracy against the laws, and how few, in the north, from the opposite cause, even this is too large a figure to represent the proportion of actual crime.

The *character* of crime shows a still more remarkable difference. At almost every northern as-

* Thom's Statistics, 1852, p. 193. † Ibid. p. 180.
‡ Ibid. p. 199.

sizes, the first sentence of the judge's opening address to the grand jury, is one of congratulation on the peace of their county, and the lightness of their calendar. Comparatively few are transported from Ulster; and capital crime occurs there so rarely, that of 23 executions which took place in Ireland in the years 1849 and 1850, only *two* occurred in Ulster.*

In short, the vast moral superiority of that province is seen on every hand. In many districts, the doors of the dwellings are seldom locked; in numbers of shops a child can safely deal; while the atrocities which are the rule elsewhere, are the exception in Ulster. There landlords are scarce ever shot, or murderers sheltered, or wretches known to swear away innocent life; while in most counties, assizes last a day or two, jails are half empty, and gibbets scarce ever required. During the assassinations of 1848, one threatening letter was sent to the county Derry, to a landlord of high respectability; and it came from *Connaught!* The excitement it created was intense—abundant proof of the novelty of the occurrence; and the people formed themselves into a guard, and kept sentry for weeks round the gentleman's demesne; yet some journals would persuade us that, for the last few years, Ulster has become a scene of agrarian disturbance!

Now, of course it is impossible fully to estimate the influence exerted on Ulster's prosperity by its

* Thom's Statistics, 1852, p. 200.

superior light and virtue; in the security of property, the influx of capital, the encouragement of enterprise, and, above all, that general elevation and success which are the sure fruits of education and morality. But some idea of its magnitude may be formed from the fact, that with one third of the population, Ulster's share of the police, jail, and poor-law expenses of Ireland, is, in round numbers, but one eighth!

CHAPTER V.

THE RELIGIOUS.

THUS far have we proceeded in unravelling the perplexed web of causes from which Ireland's miseries have sprung. Will the reader be kind enough to accompany us one step further? After the most careful estimate of the share which *various* alleged causes of our country's wretchedness have had in producing it, we have found the *chief* to be her MORAL DEGRADATION. But it is manifest that this cause must also be derivative; and we know of but two possible sources to which it can be traced:—some *radical defect* in the people themselves, or some *malignant influence* to which they are exposed. We have demonstrated that it is not the *former;* and we have hitherto failed in our search for the latter. We have seen that the Irish are neither cursed with Moorish ferocity nor Bœotian stupidity, and that neither in the country nor the laws can any such evil influence be found as will *at all* account for such fearful degradation. One other field of inquiry alone remains. Is the cause to be found in our Religious condition? One would naturally suppose that *religion*, professing, as it does, to mould and regulate our whole nature, so as best to fit us for earth and heaven, should exert on any people a paramount influence for *good*. Why has it not been so in Ireland? Has she not a sufficient supply of Christian ministers? 2,176 Established clergy, from the primate to the curate; 2,361 Roman Catholic clergy, with a large auxiliary staff of monks and nuns; and 624 Presbyterian, with 281 Independent, Methodist, and Baptist ministers?* Why, with such an army of ecclesiastics, Ireland *should be* "an island of saints;" and there must be *fearful guilt* somewhere, when it is more like an island of savages. Then, we solemnly cite them to trial, that we may see at whose door lies the tremendous guilt of having wrought such ruin on a land so fair. Our rule of judgment shall be that of One who cannot err—"YE SHALL KNOW THEM BY THEIR FRUITS"† :—One who appealed to his own *works* in proof of his divine commission;‡

* Thom's Statistics, 1852, pp. 386–392, 414–421, 422–429, 430–432. † Matthew vii. 15–20. ‡ John x. 37, 38.

disowns the church which cannot do the same;* proclaims all religions *imposture* that pretend to be from God and are not *like* God;† and declares that "in THIS the children of God are manifest, and the children of the devil—whosoever *doeth not righteousness* is *not* of God."‡

THE COINCIDENCE.—The two great religious systems of these kingdoms are the Protestant and Roman Catholic. It is clear from the above test, that whichever of these most fully promotes "that righteousness which exalteth a nation," gives the best proof of its divinity. And should it be found that one of them invariably exalts, and the other as invariably degrades a people, then is the one as certainly TRUE, and the other as certainly FALSE, as though the fact were proclaimed by an angel from heaven.

Now, if we compare our two islands, we find Great Britain the most happy country on earth, perhaps the most Protestant; and Ireland the most wretched, one of the most intensely Roman Catholic. Britain, that little spot which would scarce be missed if sunk beneath the waves, is the queen of nations, and her name a passport among remote barbarians; while Roman Catholic Ireland, in all respects fitted by the great Creator for sharing the glories of her sister isle, is as utterly degraded as the other is illustrious; and the name of Irishman a term of as deep contempt as that of Englishman is a title of honor. We find,

* John viii. 41, 44. † 1 John iv. 1-6. ‡ 1 John iii. 8, 10.

moreover, the most Protestant part of Great Britain —Scotland—the most enlightened and virtuous; and the most Roman Catholic parts of Ireland—Connaught and Munster—the most benighted and depraved. Except in a few Highland districts there is scarce a Roman Catholic in all Scotland who is not Irish, while, at least until 1847, only one fifth of Ireland's population was Protestant.* Yet the former is a land of authors, the latter not even a land of readers; the one is as much distinguished for its virtue as the other for its crime; and even a large portion of the crimes of the one is committed by Irish Roman Catholics, while a mere fraction of the crimes of the other is the work of Protestants.† And lest this difference might be thought to arise, in part at least, from the social or political state of these two nations, follow them through all their migratory wanderings and it is still the same. In every region you find the one filling the post of honor and trust, and the other sweeping the streets or carrying the hod; and while the Scotchman in

* According to the Report of the Commissioners of Public Instruction (1834), which contains our latest denominational census, we find that Ireland then contained 1,517,228 Protestants, and 6,427,712 Roman Catholics. Of Protestants there were:—Established Church, 853,064; Presbyterians, 642,356; Dissenters, 21,808; total, 1,517,228. From the same source we learn that the entire Presbyterian body, except about 4,300, are found in Ulster.

† This fact is forcibly brought out by the jail statistics of Scotland.

Ireland conducts our banks or warehouses, the Irishman in Scotland is found in the coal-pit or the prison!

If next we turn to Ireland itself, we find from the census of 1834, that in Ulster the Protestants then were to the Roman Catholics in round numbers as 11 to 19; in Leinster as 2 to 11; in Munster as 1 to 20; and in Connaught as 1 to 23.* Now, we have seen the immense difference between Protestant Ulster and Roman Catholic Munster and Connaught in their statistics of ignorance, crime, and poverty. The brevity of this work has alone hindered us from giving the statistics of Leinster. But any one who consults the same authorities from which we have taken those of the other three provinces, will find that *in all four* as is the Protestantism, so are the knowledge, virtue, and prosperity. To give one more sample—in the year 1848, there were, in round numbers, 3 persons receiving relief out of every 100 in Ulster; 7 in Leinster; 14 in Munster; and 19

* The Commissioners of Public Instruction have followed the ecclesiastical, and not the civil divisions of the island. Now, in their four ecclesiastical provinces, which, though not quite coincident with the four civil ones, are sufficiently so for our purpose, we find the religious denominations to stand thus:—Province of Armagh, 1,171,618 Protestants, and 1,955,123 Roman Catholics. Province of Dublin, 183,609 Protestants, and 1,063,681 Roman Catholics. Province of Cashel, 115,233 Protestants, and 2,220,340 Roman Catholics. Province of Tuam, 45,768 Protestants, and 1,188,568 Roman Catholics.

in Connaught! Here is a graduated scale singularly correspondent to the Protestantism of each province, and, excepting Connaught, the very reverse of what we were entitled to expect. For, besides other advantages, Leinster has long been the seat of government, and enjoyed the benefits of the "English pale;" not only is Munster the garden of Ireland, but its population are the oldest inhabitants of the land; while Ulster is a mere colony little more than 200 years old, and composed for the most part of a few Scotch adventurers, who were doomed to struggle for years against a host of difficulties.

If from the *provinces* we descend to the *counties*, we find the same proportions prevailing with singular exactness. To make this perfectly clear, we shall contrast a few of the most Protestant with a few of the most Roman Catholic counties. In Antrim, the Protestants are to the Roman Catholics nearly as 3 to 1; in Down, more than 2 to 1; in Derry, about 1 to 1; and in Donegal, 1 to 3;—while in Cork, they are 1 to 16; Limerick, 1 to 22; Kerry and Waterford, 1 to 23; Mayo and Galway, 1 to 24.* Now, mark how the *light* of each county is as its Protestantism, with only an exception which establishes the rule; Donegal being mountainous, without a single large town; while Cork and Limerick are full of populous towns, with

* Compare Report of Commissioners of Public Instruction, (1834.)

all their educational facilities. In 1841, the proportions who could neither read nor write, were—Antrim, 23 per cent.; Down, 27; Derry, 29; Limerick, 55; Donegal, 62; Cork, 68; Kerry, 72; Waterford, 73; Galway, 78; and Mayo, 80.* Thus in the most Roman Catholic counties we have four fifths of the people in total ignorance; in the most Protestant only one fifth; and in all, with the above exception, the ignorance increasing as the Protestantism diminishes! We might farther prove, that in all those counties those who can neither read nor write, are almost *all* Roman Catholics. Instance Donegal, the only county out of its place in the above scale; and according to a report of the Rev. E. M. Clarke, chaplain and local inspector, of 138 Protestants confined in Lifford jail in 1849, 91, or near three fourths, could read; while of 922 Roman Catholic prisoners, only 213, or not one fourth, could read.† Indeed, *all* those districts which are remarkable for their religious and general ignorance, such as the West Coast region above noticed, are those in which the Church of Rome has for ages held unbroken sway.

Nor is the contrast less remarkable in the *crime* than the ignorance of these counties. In the four Protestant counties of Antrim, Down, Derry, and Donegal, the gross number of committals, in 1848, was not in proportion to the population *one fourth*

* Extracted from Census of 1841.

† *Derry Standard*, February 21, 1850.

that of the four Roman Catholic counties of Kerry, Limerick, Galway, and Mayo; yet, of the latter, none but Limerick belong to the "disturbed districts."* Again, while from the prevailing conspiracy against justice in the latter, their convictions are not much over a *third* of their committals, in the former they are nearly *four fifths*. And there is really no comparison as to the *character* of the offences:—for example, of 69 criminals hanged in Ireland, in the 6 years ending 1850, 13 were executed in Limerick alone, only 4 were hanged in Ulster, and only 1 in any of the above Protestant counties—viz., in Donegal, the *least* Protestant. Finally, as a mere sample of their *temporal condition*, we find that, in the 4 Roman Catholic unions of Kanturk, Listowel, Castlebar, and Ballinrobe, there were, in 1848, TWELVE TIMES as many paupers relieved, in proportion to their population, as in the 4 Protestant unions of Larne, Kilkeel, Coleraine, and Newton Limavady. And the awful state of these unions may be conceived from the fact, that half the population of Listowel, and one third that of Castlebar and Ballinrobe, were at that period obliged to support the remainder!†

Lest any remnant of doubt should hang on the reader's mind as to the extent of the coincidence we are tracing; lest he should cherish the least suspicion that Ulster owes its superiority to some other

* Thom's Statistics, 1852, pp. 199, 200.

† Ibid., 1849, pp. 144–148.

cause which we are unable to discover or unwilling to disclose—let us turn for a moment to its own counties. While in Antrim, its most Protestant county, the per centage who cannot read or write is 23; in Cavan, its most Roman Catholic, it is 51. With a population a little over that of Derry, that county has annually twice as many committals, and not one third the proportionate number of convictions.* The number of police stationed in Derry in 1850 was 106, at the expense of £5,299; while in Cavan there were 396, at the cost of £16,985—over thrice the expense, and near four times the force.† In short, Cavan is notoriously the most turbulent county in Ulster, and constantly occupied by a large body of military; while the only troops in the entire county of Derry, are a depôt stationed in Londonderry city, whose services are scarcely ever required. From counties we might even descend to *parishes*. One of the richest in Antrim is the parish of Killagan, and one of the poorest, that of Cushendun; yet in the former the Protestants are to the Roman Catholics as 6 to 1, and in the latter as 1 to 9.‡ Do you say the northern Roman Catholic was driven back to the mountains by the Ulster settlers? Then we ask, What has so generally driven the southern Roman Catholic to the mountains too? By what other foes has he been pursued thither than those evil habits which compel men to retire

* Thom's Statistics, 1852, p. 199. † Ibid., p. 180.
‡ Ibid., p. 183.

before the advance of light and virtue? But not to dwell on this, go to some of our finest *plains*, where no stranger has disturbed the southern. In the diocese of Cashel, Roman Catholics are to Protestants in the enormous disproportion of 28 to 1; and that naturally luxuriant region has long been known as the place where the demon of murder holds his court, and those assassination clubs have existed where each deed of blood is deliberately planned. Do you impute these crimes to landlord oppression? We ask not why such oppression, often as intolerable in Ulster, occasions there so few dreadful crimes, and why these few are almost exclusively committed by *Roman Catholics;* but we take you at once to the *towns*, where no landlord can rack, but men rise or sink by their own conduct. Instance Belfast and Cork, in the former of which Roman Catholics are to Protestants as 1 to 2½, and in the latter as 5 to 1; and in the ten years ending 1851, the population of Belfast has increased 24,400, or near 33 per cent., and its trade and manufactures proportionally; while the population of Cork has in the same period increased 5,700, or not 5 per cent.; and even this consists for the most part of paupers, whom, during the last 5 years, want has driven in from the surrounding country! Nay, pass if you please through the *streets* of each town, and you will find that in *both*, and with the very same opportunities, the Protestants are the highest, and the Roman Catholics the lowest of the people.

We really must not weary the reader;—but as the last resistless proof of the fact we are establishing, examine the *individuals* of each persuasion, and you will find the Roman Catholics as a *class* everywhere the lowest in knowledge, virtue, and wealth,—the uneducated, the criminals, the servants of their own land. And this is so common as to be the subject of frequent remark amongst themselves. It is notorious that during the late famine, even in Ireland's most Protestant parts, the immense proportion of the *relieving* were Protestants, and of the *relieved*, Roman Catholics. The vast majority of our prisoners, even in Protestant districts, are Roman Catholics. And our poor-house, jail, and hospital statistics usually show, from twice to four times as many Romanist as Protestant inmates, in proportion to the denominations of each district. We have already seen the proportion in the Donegal jail,* and we find much the same in all the rest. On the 8th of May, 1850, there were in Derry, 41 Protestant and 118 Roman Catholic prisoners—being three times as many of the latter, in proportion to the population of the county; and on the 14th

* Mr. Clarke, in his Report, pronounces a high eulogium on "the admirable conduct of the Presbyterians of Donegal, as evinced by the fact, that of a body exceeding 40,000, only 26 were committed within the year." The design of this work prevents us from giving the poor-house, prison, and education statistics of the *various* Protestant denominations; but it is only justice to the Presbyterian body here to state, that these statistics assign the first place to them.

of May, in the same year, there were in Tralee jail 572 Roman Catholic and only 4 Protestant prisoners. In short, turn where you will, and the result is the same; you can generally tell the prevailing denomination from the appearance of every parish, every village, and almost every house in the land.

THE INFERENCE.—How is it possible to account for this? If Romanism be true and Protestantism false, Ireland's mystery was never half so dark as now; for, in all other cases, has truth exalted and error debased mankind: but here we have degradation the offspring of heaven, and elevation the child of hell. But only venture the supposition that Romanism is false and Protestantism true, and like some dissected map the most shapeless part of Ireland's puzzle falls into its place in a moment. Observe how it unfolds every mystery in our *physical* and *moral* state; and explains why the "Black North" is a garden, and the "Sunny South" a wilderness; why southern jails are crowded, and northern ones half empty; and why the southern, with naturally the finest parts, is yet so degraded. Mark how it solves our *political* enigmas; shows why Ulster flourishes and Munster declines beneath the same laws; and not only explains why the country grows worse as her legislation grows better, but demonstrates that it must be so, if our rulers have at the same time been encouraging Rome. See what light it throws on Ireland's *history;* explaining the well-known fact, that it was while her principles were Protestant she was the school of Europe, and that from the hour the sword of Henry and the treachery of Adrian forced her to bow at the Virgin's shrine, her glory departed, and she sunk into wretchedness. And observe how it accounts for the alternate fall and rise of the Celt and Saxon in the social scale ; nay, for the otherwise inexplicable shiftings on that scale, which we have noticed, of the Celtic tribes themselves ; explaining how the fall of Celtic Ireland dates from her submission to the Pope, and the rise of Saxon Britain from the hour she flung his yoke away ;* how the Celts of Britain continued Popish long after their Saxon brethren, and *just so long* did their mountains ring with the shouts of embattled clansmen ; and how, from the very moment the Reformation reached them, were their claymores sheathed, and their mountains echoed far other sounds.

Nay, the history of Europe is explained by the same key. Rome was in her zenith during those "dark ages" which men now blush to recall, and the darkness thickened the mightier she grew ; but the Reformation dawned, and with it rose the sun of

* We know that the Magna Charta, the Crusades, &c., had before the Reformation done much for England ; we only maintain that they were more *overruled* than designed for her good. The Magna Charta itself owed its existence more to the selfishness than the patriotism of the barons, and was meant to increase their own power rather than the people's freedom.

Europe. And mark how those countries *only* sprung to life which this Reformation visited. Germany, Holland, Britain, emerged at the same instant from Rome and misery; Spain and Italy retained their allegiance, and grew more wretched. Ay, and so uniform is this connection between Protestantism and prosperity, that it seems scarcely affected by climate, or soil, or race, or government, or any other usually modifying cause. On the mountains of Spain, and the plains of Italy; beneath the despotism of Austria, and the freedom of Switzerland; in the empire of Brazil, and the republic of Mexico; the same blight marks the dominion of Rome. While the same blessing rests on the realms of Protestantism, whether in bleak Scotland or genial England, or swampy Holland, or Alpine Switzerland, or the United States of America, or the remote isles of the Pacific.*

* The only exception which even Roman Catholics attempt to urge is that of Belgium. Suppose we admit it, "the exception proves the rule." But local causes may modify the influence of any religion. Such causes exist in Belgium; among which are freehold farms and a liberal constitution; and making due allowance for these, the condition of that country is the strongest confirmation of the fact we are establishing. The most prosperous part of Belgium is the most Protestant; the south-west, the most Roman Catholic, is styled from its misery the "Ireland of Belgium." The manufactures, for which that country gets credit, were introduced by the French Protestant refugees; while its general prosperity is much overrated, as is proved

And the most striking fact of all is, that the intenser the Romanism the blight is the deeper, and the purer the Protestantism the blessing is the greater. Either the law of moral influence is a delusion, or the more numerous the priests, they must, if their *system* is good, exert the greater influence for good, and a country's virtue will be as the number of *their* chapels. Now, in Scotland, the most virtuous land on earth, the priests of Rome scarcely exist; in Spain, the most debased, they are literally swarming; Rome, their headquarters, is a sink of iniquity; and the Irish, everywhere degraded, are everywhere the most intense Roman Catholics. Unless, therefore, you believe that God's religion would blast, and Satan's bless mankind; or that God, in aiming to raise fallen men, has failed of his aim and degraded them, and that Satan, in aiming to debase them, has failed of his aim and exalted them;—nay, unless you admit the horrid blasphemy, that in all ages the Holy One has been the patron of vice and the Evil One of virtue—that God and Satan have exchanged characters, and heaven and hell changed places—then is the Romish system weighed in the balance and found wanting. For on no land has the Sun of Righteousness ever risen without bathing it in floods of light and virtue; nor the clouds of error ever fallen without sinking it in

by the fact, that no country but Ireland was the scene of such horrors during the late potato failure.—(See *Edinburgh Witness*, Jan. 19, 1850.)

darkness and vice. Reader! is all this true—is the half of it true? Then, if you have any concern in the matter, are you bound by the most solemn obligations to accompany us while we inquire—Why is degradation the constant fruit of Romanism?

PART III.

THE GRAND CAUSE.

THE moral universe, like the material, is upheld by a few simple LAWS, on the observance of which its existence depends. These, like their Author, are infinitely wise and good; therefore, their violation must be incalculably disastrous; and the only possible mode of arresting such disaster when it occurs, is to restore the violated laws to their full sway again. All true religion rests on this proposition. And as our DEMONSTRATION shall be based on it, we beg the reader's special attention to it.

Two of these laws we have found to be *knowledge* and *virtue*. And it has often been demonstrated, that the law by which the stone falls and vapor ascends, is not more necessary to the material universe than these are to the moral.* But the sum of all *knowledge* is acquaintance with God and his works; and the sum of all *virtue*, because of all the commandments, is love to God and our neighbor.† And from these *all good springs*—whatever coun-

* See Dick's Christian Philosopher.

† Matthew xxii. 37–40.

try, whatever world has most of them, *must* be most prosperous, exalted, and happy.

Man was made under these laws, and *adapted* to them—with a mind to acquire knowledge, a conscience to practise virtue, and a heart to feel love. And, of course, as these *chief parts* of his being are improved or injured, must his *whole nature* be elevated or debased.

Now, the end of religion is just to train man in *obedience* to these laws. And the simplest possible test by which to know how far any religion is true or false, and therefore how far it is beneficial or pernicious, is to ascertain how far it accomplishes *this end.* Take a simple illustration:—

Science holds that place in the material world which *religion* does in the moral;—*it deals with the material laws.* Now, *true* science proceeds in strict obedience to these laws; explains every phenomenon by them, and therefore, like them, is beautifully self-consistent, unchanging, wise, and beneficial; while *false* science is based on ignorance or disregard of these laws, and hence is contradictory, fluctuating, absurd, and mischievous. Thus, true science explains eclipses and diseases, and regulates navigation and the healing art by the *laws* which govern the stars and the human body respectively, and is, therefore, the parent of manifold blessings; while false science, disregarding these laws, has given birth to astrology and quackery, and those endless superstitions, with all their absurdity and mischief, which have in all ages made millions the dupes of imposture, trembling at eclipses, consulting the stars, and using *charms* for the cure of diseases. Just in like manner *true* religion, *regulating our moral cure by the laws which govern our moral nature*, is beautifully self-consistent, wise, and benign, and is the great parent of happiness here and hereafter; while *false* religion, disregarding these laws, is absurd and mischievous, giving birth to those various superstitions which have in all ages led men to crouch before priests, and rely for salvation on the senseless mummeries of idolatry.

Try any false science by this test, and it is detected in an instant. But just by the same test do we detect a false religion. See, for instance, how, before its tremendous light, Paganism and Mohammedanism vanish like fogs before the morning sun. If, therefore, we find in the Romish system the *same* defiance of the laws of God and of man's nature, and the *same* inconsistency and absurdity, it *inevitably* follows that it must be equally false and pernicious.

Now, we solemnly charge that system with setting these laws as completely at defiance, as though its aim were to thwart them all;—with being the enemy of *knowledge*, *virtue*, and *love*, and thus entailing on its victims degradation and ruin; with attempting to eclipse the *mind*, corrupt the *conscience*, destroy the *heart*, debase the *whole nature*, and thus ruin man's *temporal state*, and blight his *eternal prospects*.

CHAPTER I.

ROME ECLIPSES THE MIND.

THE glory of our race is *mind.* It lifts us above the brutes and assimilates us to the angels. The religion, therefore, whose effect is to extinguish or *dull* this immortal spark, must be the enemy of God and man.

Now, mark the uniform conduct of Rome. She knows that "God is light," and Satan the prince of darkness; that the very first voice of Jehovah which echoed through chaos, was, "Let there be light," and that the arch-fiend's first utterance over this fair earth, was, "Let there be darkness;" and that accordingly God created man in "knowledge," and Satan has shrouded the world in ignorance. She knows, too, that the grand struggle of God's servants in all ages has been to banish this darkness, and of Satan's to deepen its gloom; insomuch, that from this their very titles are derived—the "powers of light"—the "powers of darkness."

Now, amongst which of these does she range herself? None knows better than that sagacious church, that "knowledge is power," and that the only possible way to elevate *mind* is to enlighten it. She knows, moreover, that God only needs to be known in order to be loved; that men hate him because they do not know Him; that religion is *therefore* called the knowledge of the Lord; and that the shortest way to bring on the millennium, is to "fill the earth with this knowledge." * She is well aware that it is because the arch-deceiver knows this too, that he has ever struggled to shroud the world in midnight; and hence, that to spread light is to *follow*, and to extinguish it is to *thwart* the laws of God and of man's nature. And she is equally aware that *truth* has everything to gain by the light, while it is only *imposture* that can profit by darkness; and therefore that all honest men love the light, while only Satan and his servants hate it—like the lurking assassin, and for the same reason. Yet in the full consciousness of all this—knowing that by opposing the light, she not only violates the laws of God and our nature, but exposes herself to the *very worst suspicions*, her whole history has been one dire struggle against it.

Religious Knowledge.—Shall we commence with her own beloved maxim, "Ignorance is the mother of devotion?" According to this matchless aphorism, He who gave us *reason* demands its extinction as the first requisite of worship; He who made us above the brutes frowns on our homage till we make ourselves equal to them; and He, whom to know is to love, so ill bears inspection, that the less we know Him we love Him the better! Why, it is not even an ingenious apology for delusion,

* Isaiah xi. 9.

and, except for its blasphemy, is really not worthy the old serpent. According to it, the most degraded savage must be the most devout, Christ's minister's the most godless, and Adam vastly improved by the fall. In a word, barbarism must be the best state, and civilization the worst; Paganism is the world's blessing, and Christianity its curse; the apostles *deserved* martyrdom, and their murderers canonization; the Prince of Light is the world's worst enemy, and the Prince of Darkness its truest friend! ! God has said, "My people perish for *lack* of knowledge." And so to make himself known He has hung out Creation, and written his Word; and on the wondrous cross has shown us "deity full robed," "in all his round of rays complete." Well, the universe gaze enraptured; heaven rings witn hallelujahs; earth is commanded to echo the news. Forth steps this system, and bids heaven and earth be hushed; burns the book which tells of his love—the only book God ever wrote; tears down the superscription which even a pagan put over the cross; and draws the pall of night over the world!

Now, fancy three thousand priests for ages enforcing this maxim in every corner of Ireland with a fierceness of which the following are but a few samples. The "greater excommunication" contains the most fearful torrent of curses that ever issued from the mouth of hell!* Any one so cursed is

* Of this hideous production, which would fill two pages of this book, we give the following specimens:—"May the

supposed to be thereby hopelessly damned. No one, on pain of the same doom, must speak to him, shelter him, or give him a morsel, though starving; and while the "curse" was still powerful in Ireland, you might have seen the people running away as the cursed individual approached, lest the earth should open and swallow them! Well, let any of their flocks send their children to an industrial school, to learn virtue, industry, and the fear of God, and this curse is levelled at their heads, accompanied by the most exciting harangues from the altar; the people are often urged to deeds of blood, and the priest sets the example with his horsewhip or cudgel. Even in the enlightened county Antrim, priest Walsh pronounced this curse on a poor miller for reading the Irish Bible to his neighbors. The priest of Achill commanded his flock to have pitchforks well sharpened, and, in case Mr. Nangle, or any of his agents entered their houses, one was to stand at the back door, and another at the front,

Father, who created man, curse him! May the Son, who suffered for us, curse him! May the Holy Ghost, who is given to us in baptism, curse him! May all the angels, and archangels, and saints, damn him! May the heavens, and earth, and all the holy things contained therein, damn him! May he be damned wherever he shall be! May he be cursed inwardly and outwardly! May he be cursed in the hair of his head! May he be cursed in his brains, temples, forehead, ears, eyebrows," &c. &c. Here follows a minute enumeration of every part of the body, to the very "toe-nails," and each is severally "damned"!!

to render escape impossible; while he uttered the most frightful imprecations on all who would even work for Mr. Nangle, which he described as working for the devil; and he "prayed that those who disobeyed his orders might not have a child that day twelvemonth, and that when they died they might have none to stretch them."* This pious example has been diligently followed elsewhere. A late devoted lady was, for keeping a farm school in the neighborhood of Milltown, county Kerry, the frequent subject of such altar abuse by the parish priest as we cannot pollute our pages with: her boys have been repeatedly cursed in the chapel, and assaulted on the roads; and twice, on the sabbath evenings after such denunciations, were a number of persons, including the writer, set on and stoned by the Milltown mob. While, on one occasion, at Ballymaciola, he and an entire congregation were attacked by priest Timlin and an infuriated rabble, and a number of persons were brutally beaten.

The chief object of all this deadly hatred is the Bible. When any of their flocks are suspected of the crime of stealing a little light from this blessed book, they frequently enter their houses and search the chest, the bed straw, the very rafters, for it; and when they have found it, they have been known to take it up in the tongs, lest it should pollute their fingers, fling it into the fire, and burn it to ashes!

* See Hon. and Rev. Baptist Noel's Tour in Ireland, pp. 171, 172.

THE BIBLE! that blessed volume, which suits every taste but a corrupt one; which teaches nothing but truth and virtue, and opposes nothing but error and sin; that emanation of God's own mind, and therefore pure as the mind that produced it; whose plain lessons no man can follow without becoming Godlike, and no country could obey without becoming an Eden; that book has ever been the object of Rome's relentless hate—cursed from the altar, burned by the hangman, and its readers butchered by thousands! What Pope has not hurled his anathemas against it? It was one of the last acts of the late pontiff, and one of the first acts of the present one, to write "Encyclical Letters" against it. Even the "liberal" Dr. Doyle compared Bible Societies, for mis chief, to Whiteboy societies, and the Bible itself to the works of Rousseau; and loudly extolled a certain man for having buried in the earth a Bible that had been given him! And not to weary the reader with proofs which we might furnish from every county, let them take the following sample of the harangues of the Irish priests against it. Preaching before Dr. M'Hale and a number of his clergy; and choosing, no doubt, the theme most grateful to sacerdotal ears, Friar Jennings thus exclaims:—"As the poison of Bible information is fast falling and spreading, in this parish particularly, you ought, by all means possible, to put a stop to the machinations of these heretics; for assuredly any one who practises the reading of the Bible will inevitably fall into everlasting destruction. Why would you permit persons who bring with them the worst of all pestilence, the infectious pestilence of the Bible, which would entail on yourselves and your children the everlasting ruin of your souls? They who send their children to schools where the Scriptures are read, do give their children bound in chains to the devil!"*

Is it strange that our country is filled with darkness and crime, whose very altars ring with such heaven-daring blasphemy? This blessed book is so pure and holy, that it is easy enough to account for the hatred which devils and wicked men feel against it. Hence it has ever been the chief ground of conflict between the servants of light and the legions of darkness. And in this fearful struggle we have ranged on one side, prophets and apostles, and the world's brightest worthies; and on the other, the entire brood of infidels and criminals, from Voltaire to the vilest wretch that ever rotted in the purlieus of vice. Well, here we have this "Church of God" leading this crusade against the book of God, and ranged with Paine against Paul, with Julian against Jesus, with the scum of the earth against its very salt. And what is the plea for this deadly hatred? Because it is obscure and misleads the people! So, then, the effect of a book all *truth* is to deceive, and of a volume all *divine* is to damn! And He who can neither err nor deceive, gave it to us in the full

* Protestant Penny Magazine, No. xxvii. p. 39.

foreknowledge that it would thus mislead us, and the better to insure our ruin, commands us to read it;* and His priests must step in to arrest the rash production, and save His cause from being destroyed by Himself! Why, if there was one shred of honesty in this plea, then should every chapel resound with expositions, and every parish teem with commentaries on it. Yet you will travel days without finding amongst their flocks even a Douay Bible with their own notes; and be tired of life ere you hear of a course of lectures on the gospel from a single altar. Nay, their own primate Cullen rages against those who would circulate it as "Bible hawkers," and their own organ, the "Tablet," raves about the places where it is circulated as "hells opened!" But this plea has not even the merit of ingenuity. No man can follow its plain directions without becoming virtuous; and this is to misunderstand it! The nursery child whose eye glistens delighted at its stories, unconsciously testifies that it has reached that highest climax of simplicity, plainness enough for the infant mind; and this is to be unintelligible! What if, after all, its real fault is this very simplicity? Had it been filled with such foolish jargon as the Breviary, or the Lives of Saints, it might not have been so much hated by those champions of plainness, who offer the very prayers of the altar in an unknown tongue. It is not the spots but the splendor of the morning sun

* John v. 39.

that makes him feared and shunned by the birds of night; and the Bible's true crime in the eyes of Rome, is not its obscurity but its celestial clearness.

Again, who can help admiring the matchless device of a CHRISTIAN MINISTRY, and the moral power of a gospel pulpit; or contrasting the Christ-like pastor with the pagan priest, and the divine service of the Christian church with the mummeries of a heathen fane? Mark that man of God, moving through his flock a living sample of holiness; on Sabbath teaching truth divine, and through the week exemplifying it:

> ——— "The man whose heart is warm,
> Whose hands are pure, whose doctrine and whose life
> Coincident, exhibit lucid proof
> That he is honest in the sacred cause."

Now, turn we from this charming picture to the Irish priest and altar. Taken usually from the lowest of the people, and often from turning the spit or tending cattle not their own, the Maynooth students are rude enough samples of the *lignum sacerdotis.* You would say they have but one chance of becoming educated men and gentlemen, and that is found in the college they attend. Well, that college is usually Maynooth. In its cells they are immured—their books a few monkish authors, their companions, youths as raw as themselves—and there, as best they can, they must form their manners on the one, and their minds on the other. There they are trained in the casuistries of Bailly, the subtleties of Delahogue, and the legends of Butler;—the first of these being a book so vile, that Napoleon himself prohibited its use; and if this is one of Rome's sacred books, what must be her profane ones? There they are taught that Torquemada was a saint, and A'Becket a martyr, and the world's brightest worthies detestable heretics. And, after a course of training, devised with fearful skill, to shrivel the mind and wither the heart, in which bigotry can scarce help blackening into fanaticism, forth they are poured like a fiery flood from this "spiritual vomitory," to spread ignorance and error through the land. Forth comes the scion of Maynooth—how different even from the "continental" priest!—a sad instance of the intoxicating effects of shallow draughts from the Pierian spring, to bluster and swagger through some hapless parish, and perhaps swear at and horsewhip some degraded flock.

You deem this picture colored? Could you only hear some of those gems of literature which issue from hundreds of Irish altars, you would condemn it for its dulness. If any hapless parishioner has failed to pay his dues, or otherwise incurred the wrath of his priest, woe to that person; for if anything can be said against his fair name, the congregation are most likely to be edified with it all. We have known even the under garments of the females to be attacked, for want of a better theme. If a landlord is to be denounced, or if an election is approaching in which an obnoxious candidate must be opposed, the work is done in the house of prayer, the better to screen the instigator from public justice. Who has not heard of the altar advice, once deliberately given to a congregation, to kidnap the Protestant electors and confine them until after the election? and "if," added the priest, "any one meets you and asks you what you are doing, tell them you are hunting corncrakes!" Another priest declared that the lady who kept the farm-school already noticed, was nightly visited by infernal spirits; another, that devils were swarming in the rafters of the house of a Scripture reader named Davern, and that he had seen them there himself; while a third assured his flock that Satan had been seen rising out of Lough Corrib—his whole body, from his "enormous head" to his "ponderous tail" being made of *stirabout*, and that therefore if they would not withdraw their children from Mr. Dallas's schools, they might in the stirabout they got there eat his "satanic majesty" himself unawares.* Such outrageous effusions are multitudes doomed to receive as their *Sabbath* instructions—not even "stones" instead of "bread," but "serpents" instead of "fish." That blessed engine, *the pulpit*, is perverted into one of mischief; the very conduits of the waters of life are thus by Satan seized and poisoned; and yet you

* Gregg's Visit to Connemara, p. 13.

wonder how our countrymen's hearts are so depraved, and their minds so degraded.

But even these are trifling samples. A flourishing Presbyterian mission exists in Mayo. During the horrors of 1847, the priest of the district assured the people that the famine was sent them as a judgment for tolerating the "missionaries." One of them reminded his flock that it was the *north* wind which usually blasted their potato stalks; and declared that not a single potato would grow in Connaught till the "northern heretics" were expelled. The curate of Ballycastle asserted that "not till pearls would grow in his boots," would they otherwise expect the potatoes to return. Another declared from the altar that Mr. Brannigan was not a human being, but "one of the fallen angels" who had assumed the appearance of a man; and threatened that unless the people removed their children from the mission schools, he would turn one half of them "into hares, and the other into hounds, and thus amuse the country gentlemen with a first-rate hunt." And such fears did the poor people entertain, lest this metamorphose should actually take place, that they were only induced to let their children remain at the schools by Mr. Brannigan promising, that if the priest turned them into hounds and hares, he would restore them to the human form!* You say such cases are rare—we assert they are of

* Mr. Brannigan's speech before the Irish General Assembly in 1847.

constant occurrence; and we are only amazed at the ignorance which at this time of day would question their prevalence. Why, miracles themselves are every-day events amongst us; and what wonder, if, when France is blessed with its Rose Tamisiers, and Italy with its winking virgins, "Catholic Ireland" should be vouchsafed some celestial manifestations? You say the priests do not attempt such things in England? What! amongst such obstinate heretics, who would only laugh and cry delusion!—who sneer even at those miracles which Newman himself has just countersigned; and won't so much as believe that St. Anthony *did* sail to Russia on a mill-stone, and St. Denis, when decapitated, carried his head in his hand for miles! But Ireland is a land of the *faithful*. And so she is honored with such miracles as the "Estatica" of Youghal, and the devil cast out of men in the shape of a crow! And from Lough Derg to Googan Barra, from Croagh Patrick to Carrigaline she is covered with wells and hills, over which, of course, priests are the presiding geniuses, and which dispense blessings of every kind. In these the blind receive their sight, the lame walk; every form of malady flies; and when the cure fails, want of faith is of course the reason. What, though other lands rejoice in their protecting relics; though to oblige the faithful, the angel Gabriel has given a feather from his wing; the Virgin Mary a bottle of her milk; and the blessed Saviour has so multiplied his coat, that you have one at Treves, another at Rome, and half-a-dozen elsewhere; and each apostle has kindly left his head in so many different places, that if all his heads were collected, he would have at least as many as the great Red Dragon:*—what, though by reason doubtless of our propinquity to heretic England, we are denied such blessings, and have not so much as an apostolic toe-nail, or rotten tooth to bow down to,—with our miracle-working priests, we can manage to get on without them. If our fishermen want a good fishing season, they have but to send for the priest; and for the small charge of 2*s.* for blessing a boat, and 2*s.* 6*d.* for blessing a net, they may have as many miraculous draughts as they please. When a pig or a cow takes ill, let the priest be paid for saying a mass or two, and if the owner has faith enough, the animal is sure to recover. Nay, if you want every form of goblin kept at a respectful distance, only get some "holy water" or "blessed clay" from the priest; and there is not an inhabitant of the infernal world that will not fly before you!

Such are a few specimens of the teachings and practices of our Irish priests. And now, we ask, what can you produce worse amongst the jugglers of India, or the fetish priests of Africa? Yet these are but *specimens*—we are prepared with many as bad, if challenged to produce them. To what utter prostration must these men have reduced their people's minds, before they could believe or tolerate

* Seymour's Pilgrimage to Rome.

such imposture! And if Rome can so besot and *kill* the finest mind as to have in a few years transformed Newman himself into a devout believer in her most drivelling legends, what *must* be the effect on our countrymen of a system which thus at once excludes the truth and teaches such impudent falsehoods? Or what mind could help sinking into utter decrepitude when thus deprived of its proper aliment, and fed instead on a compound of trash and poison, such as never yet has failed to benight and stupefy the finest race that has ever been exposed to its blasting power?

SECULAR KNOWLEDGE.—We have seen that Ireland does not know her alphabet, and that in every parish the ignorance deepens as Rome prevails. Now, the omnipotence of the priesthood is their own loudest boast. Until very lately, they ruled the country—the government itself was obedient to their will—and from the centre of their respective parishes they were virtually able to look around and exclaim, "I am monarch of all I survey." Then surely no one will doubt that such men, who could drive their people like sheep to the hustings, and through the worst of the famine keep the Repeal chest full, could have planted the country thick with seminaries, and made Ireland the glory instead of the shame of the age. When have they ever once so employed their powers? They have not been slow to wield them in other directions; but where are the libraries they have formed, or the lectures they have founded? They have raised millions for political objects; how much have they raised for literary ones? They have formed scores of societies for agitation and mischief; point out one they have ever projected for the mental improvement of the masses? Why, all that has ever been done to elevate their own people has been effected by Protestants; and the only share the priests have had in each movement, has been to give it their most determined opposition. When an effort has been made by industrial schools to send a few rays of light into those benighted western regions, of which for ages they have held undisturbed possession, they manifest a fury which proves but too clearly how they "hate its beams," and tremble at the approach of the schoolmaster. One female teacher the author saw in a dangerous fever, brought on by a priest entering her school, and flogging the terrified children. Lately a Ballina priest was prosecuted for beating a poor widow on the head because her child attended an industrial school; and you may see, in a late "*Tyrawley Herald*," a long letter from his pen in defence, and even laudation, of the horsewhip, as one of the choicest implements of ecclesiastical discipline. And when a Scotch merchant established a similar school in Westport, from which the Bible was wholly excluded, the priests never rested till they destroyed it. National schools have been offered them, giving them "complete control," yet numbers have refused to accept them: many who at first adopted them, did so in a great measure out of opposition to those Protestant ministers who were unfriendly to the National Board; the more sagacious have long seen that these schools are springing a mine beneath their feet, and would gladly close them if they could; and as the best proof of this, every means are employed, from the thunders of the Vatican to the decrees of Thurles, to destroy those Queen's Colleges, which are founded on the *very same principles.*

You reply, there are many exceptions. Of course there are; yet, perhaps, not so many as you think. Do you not observe, kind reader, that our few priestly patrons of learning are chiefly found in Protestant districts—that their schools are frequently commenced *after* the Protestant ones, and as frequently cease when, from any cause, the latter are given up; that we never heard a word of a Popish University till *after* the Queen's Colleges were established; and that some of the worst enemies of our industrial schools are now establishing similar ones, as the only hope left them of wiling their children away from us? Yes; and if the Ulster Roman Catholic is more enlightened than his Connaught brother, think you it is Popery he has to thank for it? Can you really doubt the doom that would have befallen him, had he been cradled in those western regions where Popery reigns, and with it mental "chaos and old night;" or be at any loss to know what the Connaught priests would do for Ulster, did they possess the power?

But, of course, it is not in these islands, where Rome's constant restlessness proves how fettered she feels, that you are to look for her genuine character. Go to those dominions where she "sits a queen," and the prince does homage to the priest; and where has she ever gained the ascendency that her first step has not been to *extinguish the lights?* Go to her capital, and see the vast machinery there constantly employed to stifle the free utterances of mind. Behold that "conclave of owls," the Congregation of the Index, ready to pounce on every author who would dare think for himself, and consign him to the Inquisition for the good of his soul.

By that ghostly tribunal has the traveller's portmanteau been ransacked. In their expurgatory and prohibitory index, the first book proscribed is the Word of God! And while you search it in vain for the vilest productions, you see in its dark catalogue such matchless works as those of Locke and Bacon, Addison and Hale, Cowper and Young, Mosheim and Robertson! Instructive contrast, truly, between Rome and England! Earth's most illustrious authors the one rears and the other proscribes. True, painting and sculpture have flourished under Rome, and there is a good reason. Such men as Raphael and Angelo were this giant enslaver's best servants, by filling her cathedrals with that charming "drapery," which spell-binds the ignorant devotee; for none knows better than Rome how to speak to the senses by the statued aisle, and the painted window, and the Gothic edifice. Painting and sculpture were therefore smiled on by Rome; but under such patronage, they have been well compared to beautiful captives chained to the chariot-wheels of some Ethiopian divinity.* But look to the history of other sciences, and Rome has been little better than their jailor. How often have her police mounted guard at the astronomer's door, and watched even the inspirations of the poet! It was this infallible church which persecuted Harvey for discovering the circulation of the blood; beat Prinella with rods for saying the stars would not fall; and seven times tortured Camparella for asserting there was a multitude of worlds. Yet this is the church which Paul Cullen has had the effrontery, in his Drogheda manifesto, to pronounce the very light and civilizer of nations!—a church which, in the name of Paul, imprisoned Columbus for saying there was a new world; and, in the name of Joshua, imprisoned Galileo for the blasphemous assertion that the earth moved. Why, she has been the grand impediment to the world's progress. Long was medicine doomed to see inoculation classed among the mortal sins; long had surgery to beware of making one heretical incision; spectre monks have haunted the geologist in the bowels of the earth, and dogged the geographer

* Wylie on the Papacy.

on its surface :—the earth herself durst not go round until she got leave from the Pope; and had Georgium Sidus appeared but a century sooner than he did, he would no doubt have been anathematized for his profane intrusion. In comparison to Rome, infidelity is a patron of light:—the disciples of Voltaire at least *think*—those of "the church" must simply believe; infidel France is a land of authors—Popish Spain a land of ignorance. Mohammedanism itself is more friendly to learning—the arts flourished in Arabia, and Spain owed her greatness to the Moors. Nay, even Paganism cries out against the injustice of being here classed with Popery:—Rome, once the seat of learning, is now its sepulchre; —the muses have long fled from their ancient Italian haunts, and in every part of that classic land the stranger meets the *ruins* of Pagan greatness; and the Forum, which once rung with the inspirations of Tully, now resounds with the babble of ignorant monks.

Such, then, is the system beneath which Ireland groans,—a system which, for darkness, leaves heathenism behind, makes the office of *teacher* a burlesque on the name, and gives the infidel ground to say, that the mythology of Greece or Egypt is more friendly to knowledge than the religion of Jesus, and that in this respect Peter can but ill compare with Osiris or Olympian Jove. Surely, then, we have sufficiently accounted for Ireland's ignorance. Beneath a system which has for centuries "squatted like a night hag" on the energies of Europe, is it any wonder she should suffer so deep an eclipse?—a system which, wherever it has swayed its sable sceptre, has turned back the sunbeams of light on the dials of the world! And lest there should remain the least doubt on the subject, she has herself of late been kindly doing much to help the feeblest faith. Those "dark ages," which men blush to remember, she now openly parades as the very glory of history. The most peerless volumes of modern times, she avows her desire to supersede with the fables of mediæval monks. Her long-buried trumpery is exhumed; her obsolete calendars are reproduced; her silliest fooleries ostentatiously paraded; and St. Lawrence O'Toole is invoked in her public gatherings. Yes, and it is the moment when the whole world is rushing on at its highest speed, amidst the blaze of the nineteenth century, that her priests, like creatures of night, would choose to crawl back into the dungeons of the twelfth, and are doing their very utmost to drag the nations after them.

CHAPTER II.

ROME CORRUPTS THE CONSCIENCE.

We have proved that sin *must* bring ruin, and virtue prosperity. It was sin that blasted paradise; that scathed the earth; that burned up Sodom;

that drowned the world; that kindled hell; above all, that crucified the Saviour. Sin is that hideous thing which has turned angels into demons; comes sounding up from the depths of hell in the wailings of the lost; and could not be forgiven till the sword of justice was quenched in the bosom of mercy, and the Lord of glory had borne such punishment as none but Omnipotence could inflict—or bear. No wonder, truly, if a God *all virtue* should evince his supreme abhorrence of a thing so dreadful; and if his entire administration should aim at its destruction. So to arrest this fell thing all providence and grace conspire: but to spread it with all its miseries is Satan's constant aim. Therefore, the religion which conduces most to virtue, must most accord with the laws of God and the interests of man; while that which would relax the obligations of the divine law, must needs be a traitor to God, and a curse to man.

Now, what has been the tendency of Rome? Remember that virtue is man's normal state, and vice his abnormal; the one his healthy condition, the other his disease; the one, in short, his greatest blessing, and the other his greatest curse. Therefore, to be absolved from virtue were his greatest calamity, and the religion that would pretend to absolve from it, must be his worst foe. And yet the grand aim of Rome's theology seems to be, to get rid of that intolerable burden, virtue, which forms the heaven of saints and angels.

Her Principles.—First, The doctrine of *venial* sins proclaims the vast majority of man's transgressions to be undeserving of a hell at all. A little of penance or of purgatory suffices to expiate them, and even these can be vastly mitigated by prayers and payments. Then as to the few *mortal* sins which remain, the transgressor need feel no uneasiness; for his church has provided so many facilities of pardon, that not even the vilest wretch can perish, who is not bent on his own destruction. As oft as he pleases he can repair to the confessional, and return as pure as the virgin snow. Nor is it at the confessional merely he may be cleansed; all along the road of life, fountains of purification are placed at convenient distances. Scarce has he emerged from the womb, when baptism makes him an "infant cherub." Confirmation in due time cleanses the "sins of his youth." Every Sunday he may partake of the eucharist; and no sooner does he swallow the "wafer-god," than his title to the skies is renewed. And as his whole way through life is thus carefully guarded, so at the hour of death extreme unction comes "to lubricate his passage into eternity." Nay, lest by possibility these numerous safeguards should prove insufficient, the realms of purgatory stretch away beyond the grave. Moreover, not only may the sinner obtain pardon for *past*, but license for *future* sins. From the days of Tetzel, who made Europe an indulgence-shop, the privilege of committing the blackest crimes has been bought at Rome's spiritual bazaar. Simon Magus, in his "iniquity," thought to purchase the gift of God with money; but here Simon Peter is made to leave him far behind, by selling sin itself for gold. The commandments of God have been set up to auction, and the luxury of breaking them sold to the highest bidder. We ask, What must needs be the effect of such a system, by which poor human nature is not even left to its own corrupt tendencies, but God himself is made to hold out premiums and incentives to sin? How is it possible for Popish lands to escape being red with crime, and foul with pollution? Some wretch is tempted to do a deed of blood; while yet he hesitates, conscience remonstrates, reason condemns, and the looming gibbet grimly frowns on the half-formed design. But, amidst this array of stern remonstrants, one kind friend appears, and whispers a more accommodating morality—tells him, that if man is severe, God at least is indulgent, and has empowered *him* to pardon the darkest crimes that ever judge condemned, and send to heaven the foulest criminal that ever justice sent to the gallows. Is this a colored picture? Then is all history a fable. Deeds have been done beneath Rome's fostering shade, from which even corrupt nature recoils; the civil power has often had to protect public virtue from the ecclesiastical; and iniquity has often fled to the priest for shelter from the policeman, and found a sanctuary by the altar from the terrors of the bench.

You say the priest admonishes the confessor?—what cares he for all his lectures if pardon forms the closing sentence? Now, surely this alone would sufficiently account for Ireland's crowded jails and loaded calendars. But lest we should wrong this system, let us turn for a moment from its principles to its practice.

Her Priesthood.—If there is any good in a religion, it will, of course, be found in its ministers. They are at once its exponents and examples. In them it lives and breathes as its visible embodiment. And if, in all times and places, the majority of them have been good or bad, this alone stamps the character of the system; and ever must, till grapes grow on thorns, and figs on thistles. Besides, it is reasonable to think that Christ's ministers should be Christ-like—that the servants of the Holy One should themselves be holy—especially if their very work is the spread of holiness. Would it not be monstrous to suppose that the thrice-holy Jehovah, "who cannot even look upon sin," would freely admit its approach to his *altar*, and appoint, as "*ensamples* to his flock," men who are a disgrace to human nature? Do we not find, on the contrary, that his prophets and apostles were men of the most heavenly minds, "full of faith and of the Holy Ghost?"

Now, what is the character of the Irish priest? Surely *he* must be the purest of men who is admitted daily to God's inmost pavilion, to learn the secrets of the invisible world; to whom are entrusted the keys, and even the thunders of heaven; nay, who multiplies at will the body, soul, and divinity of his Maker. At least, of all ministers he *should* be the most spotless. The Roman Catholic has no other evidence but his word of the existence of a purgatory, whether his parent is there, whether he is escaping, or when he escapes; nor no other guarantee but his faithfulness for the right performance of those ceremonies on which his own eternal safety hangs. All depends upon the priest;—the divine authority of the "church" on his veracity—the salvation of the people on his fidelity. In a word, on that man's single shoulders rest the tremendous responsibilities which attach to the keepership of the gates of heaven. Would you not expect such a man to be as bright a saint as Noah, Daniel, or Job—to be the very image and reflection of Christ himself? Well, we have already seen a little of his character—how he can handle the horsewhip, and burn the Bible. And let the reader remember, that of his conduct in these matters we have given the most meagre samples. Such an everyday affair, for instance, is priestly opposition to the Bible, that if you ask the children of our mission-schools who hates it most, they answer, "The devil;" and if you ask, Who next to the devil, they at once reply, "The priest!"* Even the American ambassador,

* Gregg's "Visit to Erris," p. 34.

on his late visit of kindness, could not allude to the blessings that volume had conferred on his own glorious country, but forth comes a growl from St. Jarlaths, and the Popish papers suppress the sentiment.

But we have other charges still to prefer. There are few precepts of the decalogue with which the Irish priest has not taken liberties. Profane swearing, that lowest of vices confined to the very *canaille*, that vernacular of the ring and the cock-pit, is by no means uncommon amongst them. One of our missionaries, who met a priest on a Relief committee in 1847, was obliged to threaten him with exposure if he did not desist from blaspheming; and never was it the author's lot to listen to such a torrent of oaths as Priest Timlin poured forth during the riot at Ballymaciola. Yes, and though his entire conduct on that occasion was the theme of every newspaper, not a whisper of disapproval was ever known to be breathed by priest or bishop over broad Ireland. His brethren clung around him during his whole trial; and to this hour he rejoices in the undiminished sunshine of his own diocesan's favor.

We fear we can say as little for the temperance of the Irish priesthood. Indeed, the "jolly priest" is a stereotyped phrase amongst us; and the scenes which are sometimes enacted amongst these reverend symposiasts, are said to be of the most extraordinary description. On such occasions, not much respect is shown for the glasses or decanters, and sometimes little more for each other. We have it on the best authority, that a dance on the table is nothing new, and that even to be under the table, is by no means uncommon. Nor do they always confine themselves to midnight convivialities; the sun often looks on their frailties; and their flocks have occasionally to help them home from a fair. In the open street of Killalla, one of them in this deplorable state got hold of the Rev. Mr. Rogers, and actually kissed him, as the preface to some request he was going to make!

Again, a disregard of truth has been an old feature of Rome. To her belongs an entire order, who have "reduced scheming to a system, and wear the mask by rule;" who unblushingly avow that not only truth, but every other moral obligation, must yield to the "interests of the church:" and the immortal Pascal has taught us how well they have exemplified this iniquitous doctrine. There is not a crime in the dark lists of perdition, that the "Society of *Jesus*" have not over and over again committed, for the glory of God and the good of men's souls! Yet the Jesuits are Rome's best-beloved agents; and numberless bulls and decrees demonstrate how generally she has practised their tenets. That meanest of vices, lying,—that grand auxiliary of all other vices; of which the Devil is, by pre-eminence, called "the father;" and to be charged with which even worldly men count the foulest insult; has been the favorite vice of the infallible church. From her earliest days to this very hour, when she has just absolved Joseph of Austria and Ferdinand of Naples from their most solemn oaths to their subjects, oaths have been but straws to Rome; she has laughed at the most sacred pledges, and in almost all her standards, from the decrees of the Lateran to the class-books of Maynooth, has openly taught that truth must never stand in the way of the "church's" interests. Here is, perhaps, the worst feature of the system, indicating but too clearly its paternity. You see it in its every doctrine—enough of truth to make its lies go down with the ignorant. You see it in all its practice—seldom the flat lie, but one masked beneath some shuffle or quibble, designed as a loophole in case of detection. Instance her denial, in the face of all fact, that she forbids the use of the Scriptures, on the miserable plea, that any one may read them who has a license from his priest! Instance the pitiful Jesuitism of the Popish bishop of Clifton, in the case of Miss Talbot, and of Wiseman himself, in the matter of the cardinal's oath, as thoroughly exposed by Dr. Cumming. Indeed, the brazen audacity with which the Popish priests can put forth the grossest untruths, could scarcely be credited by those who do not know them. Priest Walsh, of the glens of Antrim, cursed from the altar the miller already noticed, and several others, for acting as Irish teachers; and yet, immediately after, proclaimed through all Scotland that there was not an Irish teacher in that whole neighborhood! In the case of the Miltown riots, not only did the parish priest publish in the papers the grossest untruths; but the attorney for the defence, who himself had no peculiar interest in the matter, sent the *Cork Examiner* a report of the trial, containing at least FIFTY falsehoods, and in which, besides a long speech from himself which had never been spoken, he makes several witnesses depose to the reverse of what they actually did swear. Yet even these are but trifles. It is a common remark in Ireland, that no Popish jury will convict a Popish priest, nor Roman Catholic witness testify against him; and not much wonder, if he can send them to heaven or hell at his pleasure. In the trial of Priest Timlin, one unhappy wretch, when being sworn, was detected putting the book to his chin, in the belief that, if he could avoid *kissing* it, he was not sworn at all. Another swore, first, that he could speak no English, then, that Mr. Johnston, who could speak no Irish, had a long conversation with him about attending the service at Ballymaciola! The charge against the priest was established so clearly, that the barrister, himself a Roman Catholic, while charging the jury, administered to him the severest castigation, assuming, as a matter of course, that he would be convicted; yet the jury, in the full knowledge of all the facts before they entered the box at all—for the outrage took place in the neighborhood—at once acquitted the prisoner. Nay, what is still more instructive, this was universally expected before the trial commenced at all. "As soon as I see who the jury are," said a Roman Catholic attorney, engaged in the prosecution, to the author, "I'll tell you whether you'll get a verdict;" and the instant they were sworn he whispered again, "You may make up your mind you'll get no verdict!"

It is needless here to speak of the blessings of the Sabbath—that heavenly institution so worthy of God and beneficial to man. It is enough to say, that wherever it is abolished, true religion expires. The system, therefore, that would destroy or weaken its obligations deals a fatal stab to the best interests of man. Yet by the priesthood of Ireland the first day of the week is made the hack of the other six. If there is to be any political meeting, the Sabbath is preferred as being an idle day. At a great "Sunday Demonstration" held in Tipperary in 1847, Archdeacon Laffan ridiculed the *hypocrisy* of some who had sufficient conscience left to decline attending on that day. And the largest procession we ever beheld, got up to welcome O'Connell to Cork after his victory in the State prosecutions, and reckoned to contain seventy thousand individuals, took place on the Lord's day, by the appointment of the priests; and in order to give the entire day to it, they announced on the previous Sabbath, that mass usually over at noon would that day end at eight in the morning. We have seen a priest in Connaught coolly superintending his laborers in the field on the

Sabbath. And another in the same province, not only publicly advertised the auction of his crops for that day, but actually held a raffle in his chapel after "Sunday mass," having previously distributed lottery tickets of which the following is a copy:—"To be raffled by the Rev. Arthur O'Dwyer at Athenry, on Sunday the 18th of May, 1851, a beautiful lever watch. The proceeds of the raffle to go to the repairs of the Newcastle chapel. Tickets, one shilling each!!"

So much has been said by others on priestly violations of the seventh commandment, that we are disposed to omit that branch of our mournful subject. The first revealed remark ever made on man by God was, "It is not good for man to be alone," and all experience proclaims its infinite justness. We cannot imagine a more satanic device than that which cuts off the Romish clergy from the softening and refining intercourse of woman. But if there is anything in their church worse than celibacy, it is the diabolic contrivance of the confessional. That single device sends its blasting influence in all directions, and in none more fearfully than in that of the priest himself. Oh, how that man is to be pitied who is continually exposed to the corruptions of the confession-box, and whose mind is the very cesspool into which the abominations of a whole parish are constantly running! But if even one of these devices is so dreadful, what must be the combined influence of *both?* Think of a young, full, hot-blooded priest daily encountering in his confession-box trembling youth and beauty, perhaps some one in particular, the poison of whose eyes he may have unconsciously imbibed, and whom, if he dare, he would make his virtuous wife. "I will suppose him a saint—unable to fly, he apparently groans, sighs, recommends himself to God; but if he is only a man, he shudders, desires, and already without knowing it, perhaps he hopes. She arrives, kneels down at his knees before him, whose heart palpitates. You are young, or you have been so; between ourselves, what do you think of such a situation? Alone most of the time, and having these walls, these vaulted roofs as sole witnesses, they talk—of what? Alas, of all that is not innocent. They talk or rather murmur in low voice, and their lips approach each other, and their breaths mingle. This lasts for an hour or more, and is often renewed."* And the subject of conversation, such as could not elsewhere be hinted at! The priest *bound* to put suggestive questions enough to pollute even angelic purity, and the penitent bound to *answer* them; the Romish doctors having ruled that concealment from a motive "so vain" as modesty "would be sacrilege."† All

* Paul Lewis Courrier.

† Not only Dens but Delahogue and Bailly, *Maynooth's recognized class-books*, contain questions so execrable that no man of the least delicacy could repeat them. Dens, vols. i., iv., vii., *passim;* Bailly, ii. pp. 228, 229, iv. p. 483; Delahogue, Tract. De Pen., pp. 164, 169.

this done in the name of holiness! Why, to say that corrupt nature could stand such an ordeal, outrages common sense. To say that it *has* done so belies all history. From the pontiff to the coadjutor, the priesthood of Rome have in all ages revelled in debauchery. The Vatican has been turned into a seraglio; and as for the humble curé, his flock has often compelled him to live in concubinage as a protection to society! While nunneries—those "sacred retreats" from which, according to M'Hale, "the odor of sanctity and virtue is diffused"—have ever been such scenes of pollution, that even so late as 1845, Mr. Seymour found that four nuns were *enceinte* in one convent at Rome.* Can we imagine then, that the *Irish* priest, his brethren's equal in all other vices, should be their superior in this alone? Alas, despite a system of secrecy fearfully perfect, their impurity too often transpires. But for the sake of a country which, notwithstanding their corrupting influence, still bears a high character for chastity, we refuse to lift the veil.

In truth, we are weary of the subject, and shall only add, that on the Irish priesthood are directly chargeable many of those outrages which disgrace our country. Many a man besides Major Mahon has proved the victim of altar harangues; and while the wretched dupes of priestly instigation have perished on the scaffold, and now sleep in the grave of infamy, those who in heaven's eyes are the *real* mur-

* Pilgrimage to Rome, p. 187.

derers still walk at large and disturb the country. Our missionaries are often obliged to prosecute their poor dupes for outrage; and yet while doing so, are painfully sensible that they are not touching the real culprits; they feel the presence of the priest like the great tempter in every scene of riot they encounter, yet like him he is invisible and eludes their grasp! Keeping always out of "shot range" himself, *his* part is to instigate—that of his *flock* to do and suffer. Instance the abortive rebellion of 1848. For with all their zeal, the Irish priests have never shown much taste for fines and imprisonments, and seem in no wise ambitious for the honors of martyrdom. Assassination itself, they have all but lauded. Archdeacon Laffan, in the meeting aforementioned, pronounced "John Bull" too great a coward to shoot a man from behind a hedge; and when the altar denunciations of '47 became so frequent as to engage the attention of parliament, and draw forth some letters to M'Hale from English noblemen, he not only defended his priests in characteristic terms, but called on one of the writers to put on sackcloth for daring to interfere, and to "weep between the porch and the altar." Now, who that considers the power of the priesthood can wonder at the crimes which follow such conduct, or doubt that if they so pleased our country would enjoy tranquillity? It was in this full conviction that when, in the above-mentioned year, a certain district began to be disturbed, some of the people met and resolved, that if any belonging to it was shot, they would shoot the priest by way of reprisal. The effect was surprising. No more thunder pealed from the altar—no more threatening letters reached the post-office—the happiest change seemed to have come over priest and people—and tranquillity reigned in the parish!

Such, then, is a brief sketch of the Irish priesthood. We have no doubt its correctness will be impugned: but this will only be an additional proof of our charge, that Rome will deny anything when it suits her purpose. In ignorant circles, her priests have been known to deny the existence of the Inquisition, and to pronounce the Bartholomew massacre a vile slander. Doubtless many of the Irish priests are moral men, especially in Protestant districts; for Rome distributes her troops with consummate skill; and as she has ever had her Murrays for the court, and her M'Hales for the mob, so has she always assigned her more upright priests to the Protestant localities, and those of more dubious character to the Popish. But to the foregoing statements we defy contradiction, and none know this better than themselves. Why *should* this sketch be deemed incorrect? Are the priesthood of any other land much better; and are they not *worse* where the shade of Popery is the deepest? Rome, its capital, has ever been a den of priestly corruption, and the "Vicars of Christ" have been foremost in guilt. Baronius, himself a cardinal, declares that they "were not pontiffs, but monsters;" and proves the charge by facts with which we must not pollute our pages. In the "church's" palmiest days, the priests enjoyed exemption from the dominion of the laws, and verily they required it; for crimes that would shock the modern criminal daily stained their hands; while such monsters as Alexander VI. and Cæsar Borgia made the palace of the pontiffs a sink of abomination, in which incest, sodomy, and murder were of frequent occurrence.

THE PEOPLE.—If such are the pastors, what must be their flocks? No stream rises higher than its fountain; and the inspired aphorism, "Like people like priest," is sustained by all experience. Indeed, it is pre-eminently true of the Church of Rome; for while in other churches the pastor is only one instrument of grace, in her he is its sole dispenser—the only channel of the waters of life; and if that channel is poisoned, his flock have no chance of escape. In our chapter on Ireland's Moral State, we have seen how sadly this is verified in her case. And will the kind reader pardon us if, for the sake of a people who have so long borne the blame which should have rested on their blind guides, we decline returning to the subject, farther than by giving two examples—the one of the frequency, the other of the atrocity, of crime amongst us? He will remember that the district of Cashel is amongst the most Popish in Ireland. A few years ago, the following paragraph appeared in the papers under the *usual* heading, "State of the Country:"—"THE CASHEL BENCH OF MAGISTRATES.—The following have been the gentlemen who, within the last few years, usually attended this bench:—R. Long, father shot, himself twice fired at; W. Murphy, father shot; S. Cooper, brother shot; Leonard Keatinge, nephew of Mr. Scully, shot; E. Scully, cousin of Mr. Scully, shot; Godfrey Taylor, cousin, Mr. Clarke, shot; William Rowe, shot: C. Clark, brother shot; nephew, Mr. Rowe, shot!" Again, amongst the cases tried by the special commission of 1847, was that of a party who went to the house of a man named Hourigan, in order to shoot him. He was absent; but the ruffians, instead of retiring and waiting for another opportunity, shot his wife dead in the kitchen. A child lay dying in the room; they entered, dragged him out of bed, held him up against the wall, and—unmoved by the pleadings of terror, unsoftened by the pallor of sickness, unawed by the presence of death—they presented a pistol, and shot him dead on the spot!!

Perhaps you say, such wretches, though professed Roman Catholics, were without the pale of their church. Suppose we granted this, it would only prove what all history confirms, that there is a point in Rome's demoralizing course at which she loses hold of her own votaries—that in her dreadful process of social putrefaction there is a stage at which portion after portion sloughs and comes off. The brigands and *sbirri* that infest the towns and mountains of Italy herself are terrible proofs of this truth. But we cannot grant even this supposition, for crimes have been sometimes concocted on the way from the chapel. Nay, devotion and murder have occasionally so closely followed each other, that, like the Thug of India, the assassin has prepared for the deed by repairing to the altar, and, as Mr. Nolan has proved, often confessed to the priest the meditated crime, and *thence departed* to commit it; and to crown all, the priest's vow of secrecy has hindered him from giving the doomed victim the least intimation of his danger.* Besides, it is notorious that most of all our petty offences—larcenies, for instance—are the work of mass-going Roman Catholics, and are duly confessed to the priest; yet, though we are told Rome always requires the penitent to restore the stolen property, how few cases of restitution are ever heard of amongst thousands of cases of theft! The only parties who seem to profit by the trade, are the thief who steals and the priest who forgives him.

Such are the moral fruits of Popery! Hedged round with malign influences,—kept in such ignorance that many of their sins they do not even know to be such, you would say vice was with our countrymen a thing of moral necessity. And *can* it be equity to assert the "majesty of British law" on such degraded creatures, and pass by the men who are

* See several fearful cases of this kind in Rev. L. J. Nolan's pamphlet. Dublin: 1838.

chargeable with this degradation? Oh, one would think mere humanity would hasten to the rescue of a people so trampled beneath the feet of the Beast. The wail of the emigrant who is torn from his home appeals to Christian pity against it. Every bugle that sounds from its hundred barracks tells heaven and earth of the ruin it has wrought. The blood alike of murdered and murderer cries to heaven for vengeance on it. The dying groans of multitudes, as they rise on the wintry winds, tell of its dreadful havoc. The throes of an expiring country bear awful testimony to its deadly venom. And, oh, what thousands of ruined souls will rise up in judgment against it at the last!

CHAPTER III.

ROME DESTROYS THE HEART.

MAN has a heart; and what a dismal world it would be if he had not! Now, mark how wonderfully the God who made it adapts his laws to it, or rather it to them. "God is love," and his religion is love. Its grand theme is—"God *so* loved the world," &c. Its divine founder is the loving Saviour, "who loved us, and gave himself for us." Its great command is—love one another; and its heavenly influence such, that none can fully practise it without becoming angels of kindness. On the other hand, all false systems are cruel as their author. Their gods are demons; their rites often tortures; their priests oppressors; their arguments, the sword; while their code often teaches men to expiate their crimes by crimes still greater, and their dark domains are "full of the habitations of cruelty."

If, therefore, we find that Rome withers the heart; if, instead of inspiring *love*, she has rather proved its very sepulchre, mingling blood itself with her sacrifices; if hers is a god who delights in the pilgrim's blistered feet and bleeding knees, a service which has borrowed many of the tortures of paganism, and a spirit which transforms men, not only stones, but demons—then again is she convicted as the enemy of God and man.

Love to God.—Love to God is the "first commandment;" that church therefore cannot be His which makes it not her first object. Now, a very simple test of a church's real spirit, is her treatment of His "means of grace:" instance the Bible—the Sabbath—and prayer. The child, in proportion as he loves his parent, will of course love to hear from him, to visit him, and to linger in his presence. Well, we have seen how Rome treats the Divine Word. So frequent are her Bible burnings, that almost every paper gives some fresh instances. In the "*Mayo Constitution*" of the 25th November, 1851, the Rev. Mr. Townsend of Ballyovee, reports the burning of two Testaments in his own presence by a monk, and adds, that "the ruffian thrust the burning book into his face, triumphing over his dark deed of iniquity, and calling it a 'damnable' and 'heretical' book." The Bible! that divine message of love from our Father in the skies, pored over by thousands with tears of ecstasy! Oh, fancy a son hunting like a demon for his father's letters, then making a bonfire of them, raving the while against all who dare murmur disapproval, and yet pretending to love that father!

We have also seen how Rome treats the Sabbath. That blessed day, so ardently loved by every true saint, is to her so irksome that she cannot even pay it a decent outward respect. It is to her such a bore, that it is generally over by noon,—that is, when the mass is concluded,—and the remainder of the day is given up to amusement. In purely Popish countries, the evening is spent in fêtes and theatricals; in our *own*, often in dancing and card-playing—the priests themselves mingling in the scene. And one of them who was lately rebuked for this profanation, coolly replied, that rest and recreation were the very design of that day, and a "little innocent amusement" he saw no harm in! Was there ever clearer proof of Rome's spirit than this? The wicked say, "When will the Sabbath be gone?" the believer says, "When will it return?" and each following his tastes, spends it, the one in his Father's service, and the other in *his*. Yet here is a "church of God" which has ever taken the lead in the ranks of Sabbath-breakers.

Take one other example. Prayer, the saint's delight, is Rome's most usual penance. At every confession prayers are dealt out by Papal Rome, as stripes used to be by Rome Pagan, in tens, twenties, thirties, and with a similar object. So that you will see thousands of penitents rhyming over their *paters* and *aves* with all possible speed, as though trying how soon they could get done with the task; and that they may not utter one prayer beyond the prescribed number, keeping the exact "count" upon their beads—an invention contrived for this very purpose. Communion with God, then, is the penance of Rome; and it is this *feeling* of penance—itself a sin most monstrous—which is designed as satisfaction for all other sins! Only fancy a child deeming converse with his parent his greatest punishment, and counting this dreadfully unnatural feeling a merit in his parent's eyes!

Then it is a system of *merchandise* as well as *slavery*. That God who *gives* everything; "who gave his only begotten Son," "without money and without price," and commands his ministers "freely to give as they have freely received," is represented as making his own house a "house of merchandise," and giving nothing without a *quid pro quo*. Salvation itself is made a system of traffic, in which gold is the currency, grace the commodity, the altar the shop, and the priest the salesman. For to Rome belongs the glory of the discovery, that in heaven as on earth, "*money* answereth all things." Without it you need expect little, but with it men have got indulgences to murder their own parents; and so accustomed are the people to pay it on all occasions, that they have sometimes asked our missionaries when about to pray with them—"But, sir, what will you charge us?" When a chapel is to be repaired, the gates are often shut on the Sunday morning with sentinels stationed at them, and none allowed to enter who do not first pay; the priest himself perhaps superintending the scene with cudgel in hand, and freely employing it against such as would pass without contributing.* At baptisms, the priest receives from 2*s.* 6*d.* to 5*s.*; at weddings, from £1 to £20; and often as much at each funeral for masses for the soul of the departed. In these cases a plate goes round, the priest often accompanying it; if each contributor gives not according to his supposed means, he is often most liberally abused; and so shameful are the scenes of this nature, which are frequently enacted at the very grave, that they have by the vulgar been called "canting the corpse." In short, be the service what it may, whether at the baptismal font, the hymeneal altar, the dying bed, or the gloomy grave, the horseleech is there, crying, "Give, give." On every mile of the road of life there is a toll-gate, ay, and beyond it too. As has

* Mr. Inglis was eye-witness to a scene of this very description in Cahir. (See Tour, 1834.)

been truly said, their people pay for coming into the world, pay for passing through it, pay for going out of it, and pay after they leave it! And so lucrative is this last device alone to an avaricious priesthood, that purgatory has been sarcastically termed, "the fire that makes their pot boil." Oh, Simon Magus was discovered to be "in the gall of bitterness" for "supposing that the gift of God could be purchased with money," but here are professed successors of the apostle who detected him, who will not part with it except for money! The spirit of Christian love prompts even the *layman* to "do good to all as he has opportunity," but here are ministers who disregard such opportunities as are not golden ones. Dear reader, do you doubt the truth of this charge? We can hardly wonder that you do; and yet, alas! it is too well sustained. The present wonderful openings in Connaught were in some measure caused by this very circumstance; for, during the famine, the priests, in numbers of cases, would not take the trouble of crossing a few fields to anoint the dying, because they had no money to pay them! And this is the religion of the God of love! Why, humanity would frown the wretch out of society who would refuse to save a drowning man unless paid for his trouble; but here are men, who profess to be able to save souls to any extent, yet will let them perish to any extent unless their purse is replenished by the transaction, and who thus prove themselves impostors, who do not believe in their own masses, or wretches who will not offer them.

Once more, it is a religion of *cruelty;* proceeding throughout on the assumption that God demands, not the sanctification, but the sacrifice, of the nature he has given us, and representing him as delighting in such tortures as are presented to Juggernaut or Kali. With Rome the degree of sanctity is always measured by that of voluntary suffering; and she holds up to our admiration such devotees as Hardwigg of Poland and Margaret of Hungary, because they so mangled their bodies that "they could scarce be recognized." Read the lives of her saints; see how the biographer kindles into ecstacy as he tells you how one mangled his body with scourges, another rolled himself in thorns, a third nailed himself on a cross, and a fourth burned himself in the fire. Or visit some of her holiest scenes of devotion—Lough Derg, for example. See that group of pilgrims approaching it; it is a bright autumn afternoon, but there is a gloom on their brow, strangely contrasting with the sunshine around them—say, is it the spirit of him who exclaimed, "I joyed when they said unto me, Let us go unto the house of God?" They approach that dismal lake, surrounded with dreary bogs, and selected with Rome's usual skill to impress the mind with gloom. Arrived at that stygian water, they are ferried across to Station Island, and there undergo a course of self-inflictions, not much exceeded at the island of Gonga Sagor.

And is *this* the sweet service of the God of love? Think you that poor devotee, who has finished his last round at Patrick's Purgatory, with his clothes all torn and draggled, his knees all cut and bleeding, can dream that that Saviour, who delights in this unmeaning torture, is the same with him who yearned over the widow of Nain, and wept by the grave of Lazarus? And yet even this is little; he is taught that this same Saviour has prepared for him another purgatory, of which Patrick's is a feeble type; where, according to the best authorities, some are transfixed with red-hot nails, others lashed by devils with dreadful whips, others gnawed by fiery serpents with ignited teeth, others pierced with the flaming stings of burning serpents, and others still shot out of belching volcanoes, and received back into their burning craters, to be shot out again and again!! Such a saviour he may *dread;* we ask, can he possibly *love* him? Oh, what a hideous caricature of that blessed Emmanuel, who suffered in our *stead!* Yet to these torments he consigns his own children for those transgressions which, but for his own licenses to sin, they might never have committed! ay, and the period of their torment there he makes to depend much on the length of their purse. The poor may burn on in those flames—the rich may escape in a month. Their priests could pray them *all* out, but will not, unless paid for it, and that by Christ's command!! And yet you wonder, reader, at the irreligion of our hapless countrymen, to whom the God of love is thus presented as the God of cruelty—the heavenly countenance of the Prince of Peace distorted into the face of a demon—the Sun of Righteousness overspread with the lurid hue of an eclipse—and by the same act, the glorious cross veiled from their trembling gaze and such purgatorial horrors presented in its stead.

Love to Man.—The religion of Jesus makes us kind. To use the words of the prophet, it turns the wolf into the lamb. Shedding its kindly influences over the whole face of society, it stills the stormiest elements of life; and makes the flowers of social happiness, so often laid prostrate by the tempests of human passion, to raise their drooping heads and exhale a sweeter perfume. And even War, that cursed demon that Christianity is destined ultimately to destroy, it meantime half disarms; distils some drops of mercy into the poisoned cup he holds; and half quenches the firebrands he flings around. In a word, beneath its heavenly sway hearts cease to bleed, and tears to fall; a thousand streams of relief flow, as if by enchantment, through the haunts of misery; and the downcast mourner looks up and smiles.

Has this been the influence of Rome—that church which trusts *so much* to her "good works," and keeps a treasury of supererogatory grace? Alas! she has done less to relieve human wretchedness, and more to create it, than all the other churches in Christendom; and while we find within her bosom a Bonner, a Beaton, a Cortez, and an Alva, in vain do we search for a Clarkson, a Wilberforce, or a Howard.

The same spirit of cruelty which fancies the Most High to take pleasure in tortures, is exhibited even to the lower creation. We refer not merely to the bull-baiting scenes of Popish Spain, which even Andalusian ladies delight to visit; we would only ask you to examine the torn backs of the donkeys and horses at any of our southern fairs, and then attempt if you dare to enforce the act against cruelty to animals. Nor is this want of feeling less displayed by the children of Rome in their dealings with one another. Roman Catholic servants will generally tell you that they prefer Protestant masters to those of their own persuasion, and assign the reason that they are kinder to them when in health, and far more tender in sickness. Ask their own poor whether they get most relief from Protestant or Roman Catholic,—from the parson or the priest? Often have we ourselves asked them why they do not go to their own clergyman for alms, and been answered, "God help us, we need not go to him." We have made careful inquiry at some of the principal hospitals in Ireland, and the results have in this respect proved truly instructive. In the north and south infirmaries of Cork, the vast majority of the inmates are Roman Catholics, and of the contributors, Protestants, in proportion to their respective populations in the city and county; while one of the directors of the Belfast Hospital lately characterized it as "a Protestant Hospital for Roman Catholic inmates." It is in vain to attempt to ascribe this difference in any respect to recent calamities, for it has always existed. In 1834, Mr. Inglis found 2,145 persons on the books of the Dublin Mendicity Society House, of whom only 200 were Protestants; and though the vast majority of the inhabitants of that city are Roman Catholics, he states, that for every pound subscribed by them, there were £50 subscribed by Protestants. It is equally vain to plead that Roman Catholics are usually poor—if the church of Rome so impoverishes a people as to make them a public burden, is she not all the more bound to give them what relief she herself can afford? Yet, even during the period of the famine, when every drain of selfishness should surely have been stopped to swell the streams of charity, the vast proportion of the relieved were Roman Catholics, and of the relieving, Protestants; and while the Protestant *laborers* of Ulster and Britain were sending their wages to the famished south, it was the topic of public remark, that balls and entertainments were going on as usual in several southern towns, though paupers were nightly dying in their streets!

We have already shown how little the priests seem to comprehend the Divine aphorism, "It is more blessed to give than to receive;" but the cases of extortion we have noticed are such as are sanctioned by the *church*. Sometimes, however, the priests carry on a little spiritual foraging on their own authority. Even in Ulster, we have often seen the small farmers driving to the priests haggard their half-load of corn, under the name of the "priest's stook." In Connaught, a similar tax is levied, called the "priest's '*bart*.'" At the various "stations" for confession which are held in different parts of each parish, a "treat," as it is termed, must be given to the priest; and the poor people have been known to sell their pig, in order thus to entertain him! Such a burden is this felt, that if any of the flock are suspected of Bible-reading, or other heretical practices, he often, by way of punishment, appoints stations at their houses; and so intolerable has the custom grown of late, that in some dioceses, a breakfast has, by the bishop's orders, been substituted for a dinner; while owing, doubtless, to the waning influence of the priests, the Synod of Thurles has found it necessary to discountenance the practice altogether. During the late famine—when the Hindoos of Calcutta and the Copts of Alexandria were sending relief to Ireland—its own priests, in many cases, not only left the people to perish, but robbed them of the alms bestowed by heathen and Mohammedan charity. One priest made large sums by selling holy salt to cure the potato disease, and many gave their last sixpence to purchase this specific; others sold the relief-tickets with which they were intrusted for gratuitous distribution; while several gave them to the people on condition that the first relief procured should be brought to them, as payment of arrear-dues!* Of some, it was reported that they never gave a satisfactory account of the relief which was entrusted to their care; and such currency did these rumors gain, that those who had first entrusted them therewith, soon thought it better to commit it to other hands. And Dr. M'Hale himself, while appealing through the papers to public sympathy on behalf of the starving masses around him, was convicted by the relieving officer as a defaulter in the payment of his own poor-rates! The author, while in Connaught in the winter of 1848, was as much struck with the fulness of the priests' haggards as with the emptiness of their people's; and, as an explanation of the phenomenon, a brother missionary related the following anecdote:—In the neighborhood of Westport, dwelt a poor man who supported a family on five acres of land. When the potato failed in 1847, his all was destroyed, save a small patch of oats, which amounted, when reaped, to sixty sheaves. The priest came round for his "bart." The wretched man pointed imploringly to his wife and family. You say, surely the priest gave him something; at least, it is impossible he could have asked him for anything; and, for the sake of our common humanity, one would fain so believe. But, deaf to every entreaty, dead to every feeling, he commanded his servant to count into his cart

* Ireland in 1846, pp. 174-176.

20 sheaves of the 60, and then he marched off with his booty!! Yet these men, who have only themselves to support, are the professed ministers of Him who "was rich, yet for our sakes became poor," and from his great tribunal will proclaim to the wicked, "I was an hungered, and ye gave me *no* meat," &c. No wonder the remark should be common amongst their flocks, that "a priest's money *never wears well.*" Yet this is the system which purchases heaven by liberality and love—has whole orders bearing such musical names as "Christian Brothers" and "Sisters of Mercy"—and especially boasts its convents as sanctuaries of heavenly charity! Well, we shall presently take a peep into these sacred retreats, and shall only now remind the reader, that such cases as those of Miss Talbot, the Misses M'Carthy, and Maria Monk, show that, within the abodes of celestial love, there is pretty frequently betrayed a hankering for the gold that perisheth,—ay, and various *other* passions of a *terrestrial* type!

Yet this is but lingering on the threshold of our theme. If you wish to see the inmost soul of Rome, consult the records of persecution. The only weapon Christianity knows, is the "truth in love." Besides, its Author knows that *mind* may be convinced, but cannot be coerced; that force may make hypocrites, but never true Christians; that the heart can only be won by kindness, and to attempt to force affection, is only to create disgust. Two individuals compete for your heart; one of them imprisons, tortures, burns you; you can scarce help abhorring him. The other yearns over you, showers kindness on you, lives for you, dies for you; can you refrain from loving him? As acts the latter, so acts Christ—according to the laws of God and of our nature. As acts the former, so does Rome—these laws seem to give her small concern. We will not insult the reader by proving, for the thousandth time, that her *tenets* are persecuting. We wonder why others are at so much pains to do this, because, forsooth, Rome denies it. We look to her *whole career*, their best commentary, and find it to be one of blood. The boot and thumb-screw have been her favorite arguments; and, as a living writer has calculated, she has shed more holy blood than all the gibbets on earth have shed of felon blood! Look to the Irish massacre of 1641, planned by the priests in Multifarnhan Abbey, in which 60,000 Protestants perished amidst their murderers' exulting yells.* Witness the rebellion of 1798, which, at first wearing a political aspect, soon became in many parts little else than a butchery of Protestants, under the direction of the priesthood. Or look to other lands; and is there a country in Europe whose soil has not been fattened with the blood, whose air has not been rent with the groans of Rome's victims? Pope Julius caused, in seven years, the slaughter of 200,000 Christians; 100,000 fell in the Bartholomew massacre; 100,000 in the butcheries of the Waldenses and Albigenses;

* Some say 100,000.

1,500,000 Jews, and 3,000,000 of Moors, were slaughtered in Spain; 15,000,000 in South America and Cuba; while the cold-blooded butcheries of the Dutch by the Duke of Alva, of the English by Bloody Mary, and of the Spanish and Italians by the "HOLY Inquisition," are familiar to all our readers. The latter infernal tribunal has destroyed, in Spain alone, 2,000,000 of lives;* while Rome is calculated to have shed, in all, the blood of 68,000,000 of the human race!!

Yet this brief summary gives no such conceptions of the character of Rome, as the circumstances under which these butcheries were effected. You see her popes and cardinals coolly plotting the extermination of whole countries, and then chanting *Te Deums* when their schemes have succeeded; and you see them executing their plots with a refinement of cruelty, of which only hell seemed capable. Who can read of the engines of torture by which myriads were tormented in the dungeons of the Inquisition, without fancying himself in the prisons of the damned, and surrounded by the fiends of perdition? Yet these horrors were matters of jest to the inquisitors themselves. "Give me a Jew," said Azzerro, the inquisitorial butcher of Cordova, "and I will show you in my crucible a residuum of ashes!" And the most revolting feature of the case is, that these atrocities have all been perpetrated in the name of Jesus, and for the love of God! The female martyr, whilst

* Llorentes' History of the Inquisition.

being torn to pieces by these monsters, was ever and anon greeted with these words,—"Beloved sister, recant." Heaven's blessing has been invoked on their most shocking butcheries, and their victim's groans have been drowned by their chants and hallelujahs. When the edict of Nantes was revoked in the face of the most solemn oaths, thereby effecting the ruin of myriads, a hoary-headed wretch exclaimed, "Lord, now lettest thou thy servant depart in peace, for mine eyes have seen thy salvation!!" Yes, in the name of RELIGION deeds have been done at which humanity shudders; and the rude soldier has wept over the innocents his priest has forced him to slaughter. And *such* a system of blood you must believe to be divine, such fiendish cruelty to spring from heavenly love, and deeds that would disgrace the bloodiest idol, we must father on the meek and gentle Jesus! Oh, think of that "Lamb of God" careering through the world with a sword in one hand, and a crucifix in the other; followed by a train of inquisitors, bearing such instruments of torture as Indians never dreamt of!!

You say she is changed? Then produce the man who has heard her lamentations over the holy blood she has shed. Changed! What bloody decree has she been known to revoke—what fiendish butchery to deplore? Were we not told the other day by her own organ, *L'Univers*, that another Bartholomew massacre had now become necessary? Changed! Witness in proof the scenes of Madeira and those of

Tahiti—Tahiti, that little isle in the distant Pacific, transformed by gospel missionaries from an island of savages to one of saints, Rome beheld from afar, like Satan eyeing Paradise, and never ceased her intrigues till it lay torn and bleeding at her feet. Changed ! Witness the Inquisition at Rome, unveiled by the revolution of 1849 to the gaze and execration of Europe, with its concealed traps, deep wells, quick-lime pits, &c.; and which was restored to its ancient vigor the instant the Pope returned. There *is* a change, we own, from the tiger in the forest to the tiger in the cage; but he must be judicially blind, who does not see, from all her late proceedings, that she only wants the power in order to bring back the days of Smithfield. Have we not given sufficient proof of her spirit amongst ourselves in the scenes of Achill, of Ballymaciola, of Milltown, and of Dingle? "I have told all my people," exclaimed priest Connolly, "to hiss, shout, and insult them in every way they can, *so as not actually* to break the law." Sufficiently intelligible! If the law but sanctioned an *auto-da-fé*, can we doubt that this gentleman would soon let us have one? And if such persecutions abound despite the protection of Victoria, what might we expect were another Mary raised to the throne?

Such, then, is the system which borrows the name of the God of love! And of the manifold mysteries which enwrap his providence, perhaps the most inexplicable is that he has so long endured a church which has revelled for ages in the blood of his saints, and far outdone the cruelties of Attila and Nero. Who can wonder that the glorified martyrs seem restless and impatient beneath the altar, and cry, "How long, O Lord, holy and true, dost thou not judge and avenge our blood on them that dwell on the earth?" How often amongst ourselves has Rome dried up like a scorching sirocco, the streams of social kindness, and fulfilling to the letter the apocalyptic prediction, forbidden her people to "buy or sell" to our missionaries? How often has she sought to freeze the springs of the Irish heart, and forbidden the people "to give the missionaries a drink of water," insomuch, that they have sometimes, in a manner truly characteristic, evaded the stern command by giving them a drink of *milk!* Yet by some they are deemed savages, whilst scarce a whisper of censure is breathed against that church which thus labors to instil into their souls its scorpion venom, and make hatred of Protestants the chief article of their creed;—a church which, wherever she has the power, rends into shreds nature's tenderest ties, and sets the parent against the child, and the child against the parent; and which seems to have become more wicked with advancing years, till now in her growing decrepitude she is gnashing her broken fangs at the young buoyant Spirit of light and liberty that is shaking its wings over Europe, and till those who erst were her credulous apologists, would gladly join in the jubilant shout which shall ere long ring to heaven—"Babylon is fallen, is fallen!"

CHAPTER IV.

ROME DEBASES THE WHOLE NATURE.

Thus have we demonstrated the blighting influence of Rome on the three chief parts of man's nature. But there are various qualities essential to human progress, which spring from these as branches from the stem, and on which the character of Popery is singularly displayed. As when the tree is lightning-struck, the blasting influence is seen on every leaf and twig, such is the scathing effect of Popery, not on the chief parts only, but on the minutest ramifications of the character and conduct. We can only trouble the reader with a very few examples.

The Devices.—Mark how the whole tendency of Popery is to paralyze the energies and blight the better qualities of man. What so certain to beget mental inertness in *all* the affairs of life, as the dreadful device of keeping him in a state of mental torpor in regard to its grand concern, religion? Will the intellect which is always thrown into a mesmeric sleep at the altar, not feel the deadening effect in the world? Can the mind which is pinioned one half its time use its wings so expertly the remainder; or a man who is a mere machine to-day, become by his simple volition a philosopher to-morrow? Then the whole tendency of Popery is to make its victims *social* cripples, and their life a prolonged childhood. From their cradles to their graves they are dependent on their priest; he thinks for them, prays for them, shrives them, anoints them, manages all their eternal concerns, and interferes pretty freely with their temporal also. They must not even use their senses but as he directs; for when he tells them bread is no longer bread, they must believe him. And thus their whole training makes them helpless creatures; they acquire of necessity the habit of dependence; and accustomed to confide to other hands their eternal all, *the greater* interest, they come but too naturally to confide their temporal all, *the less*. How sadly exemplified in the case of our countrymen! If they want their rivers deepened, their harbors improved, their very land drained, they look elsewhere for assistance. Hospitals are established—they look to parliament to support them; trade is decaying—they look to parliament to relieve them; the potato fails—they look to parliament to feed them; they want a Galway Packet Station, and look first to England, then to America. Nay, they cannot even get up a rebellion without seeking foreign aid: in 1798, Wolfe Tone presents himself before the

French Directory; in 1848, Smith O'Brien waits on Lamartine. And thus our poor country lies a paralytic on the world's highway, crying to all nations to come and help her along!

Look farther to the havoc which Rome works on one's *spirit* of independence. Such are the terrible conditions imposed by this giant enslaver, that it is scarcely possible to be at once a Papist and a man. First, there sits the priest on the throne of God, the keeper of that man's conscience, the jailor of his mind, and the factor of his eternal inheritance—do you expect such a man to stand erect before this dread deity; to dispute the will, however capricious, or resist the commands, however intolerable, of that ghostly father, whose smile is heaven, whose frown is hell? "I have power to strike you dead this minute," exclaims Maria Monk's confessor. Of course, with any but the most hopeless unbeliever, this must have ended the controversy.

Then, reader, place yourself, where that poor Papist must often kneel, at the confessor's feet. There, on pain of incurring mortal sin, you must open to him the very depths of your soul; thoughts which you would rather die than to disclose to any other, must *all* be divulged to him. There is no escaping, for with the help of a thousand suggestive questions furnished by Dens and Bailly, he will, ere you rise, worm himself into your inmost heart, and sound the lowest depths of your bosom. And this scene is so often repeated, that in effect, whatever you are doing, you feel as in the presence of this terrible being; it is as though he were ever dogging your steps, penetrating your most retired haunts, and like some ghost entering your midnight chamber and peeping through the curtains of your couch. Could Satan have devised a more deadly engine by which to obliterate within you every trace of manhood? Is it possible to look in *his* face, who knows all your secrets, and feel yourself a man? If yet any shame has survived this prolonged course of degradation, must you not feel overwhelmed in presence of this personator of the great Searcher of hearts? Now, surely one needs but to remember that this engine of moral slavery is worked every day in every parish of Ireland, in order to understand why the Irish Roman Catholic is so often a spiritless and crouching serf. Can you wonder to hear of the Connaught peasant, who crawled out on the road as the priest rode by and kissed the footprints of his horse? or feel much surprise to hear of O'Connell kneeling down in the mud of Cork streets to receive the priest's benediction? or the English Arundel and Surrey lately doing the same before the priests of Limerick? No, let but this serpent coil itself round a man's heart, and *English* or *Irish*, he is a man no longer. Well, accustomed to crouch before one man, it becomes natural to bow down to all. The willow that one storm has effectually bent, can never afterwards stand erect against any; and the man who humbles himself to his priest, comes almost instinctively to do the same to his landlord and his master: and hence the obsequious servility of the southern Roman Catholic, so singularly contrasting with the northern Protestant's sturdy independence.

But there yet remains to be noticed another element of moral slavery more terrible still. One would have thought that with the afore-mentioned engines of subjugation, Rome might have sat down content; but lest amongst her prostrate millions, there might yet be found one to raise a freeman's head, she has invented her doctrine of "intention," according to which the validity of every ordinance depends on the intentions of the priest who performs it. If from ignorance, neglect, or sheer malevolence, he does not in the ordinance "intend to do what the church does," the ordinance is *ipso facto* utterly null and void, and the victim of his carelessness or wickedness remains still in his sins.

We ask, Can Brahminism or Buddhism present anything like this? On the priest's intention, for instance, it depends whether the flour is a wafer or a god; or whether, in partaking of the eucharist, the worshipper is swallowing the Saviour, and thus securing salvation, or adoring a bit of paste, and thus committing mortal sin! So is it with all the other ordinances—on the priest's intention everything depends, and the worshipper knows this. How absolutely overwhelming is such a man's power, whose mere intention can send a whole parish to purgatory or farther! Why, the Almighty himself must be utterly lost sight of in presence of this impostor-deity;—in his hands, and at his mercy, must the genuine Roman Catholic believe himself to be for time and eternity. Would you mock such a man by talking to *him* of freedom, who lies at his priest's feet in the most abject prostration, who has nothing that he dare call his own, and who believes that heaven is his if he can only please and bribe his master, while hell waits on this spiritual tyrant's word, and follows his ghostly displeasure? Oh! the most galling yoke that ever crushed the African was liberty sweet to this. *His* chains at most can but pierce into his bones, but here are chains which eat through a man's soul; and the deepest atrocity lies in this, that it is his very feelings of devotion, his very concern about his soul, all that is to be admired in him as a poor sinner seeking salvation —it is these which are taken advantage of, the better to enslave and ruin him. Surely it is not difficult to guess the author of such a contrivance; we trust there is but one being in the universe capable of the reach of wickedness it betrays. Say, is it strange that our poor countryman, on whose credulous ignorance such a doctrine is from infancy so industriously palmed, should submit to any abuse which his priest may choose to heap on him; to be flogged and kicked, nay, perhaps to see the last indignity offered to his wife or daughter without daring to complain? "What, sir," exclaimed an Irish laborer, when beaten by his priest till his face was covered with blood, and asked how he could endure it—"What, sir, strike a priest! if I would touch a priest, my arm would wither from the shoulder blade."

Well, surely this at least completes the list of Rome's enslaving schemes—surely this must be the last fold of that fearful net, in whose meshes her victims seem so hopelessly entangled—and surely the skill of Popery's subtle author has nothing worse to add. Alas! our painful task is not yet done—those who have read Michelet's "Priests, Women, and Families," will understand that there remains to be unfolded one other device, the most deeply diabolical of all. We have already hinted at the amazing wisdom and goodness displayed in making man "male and female;" to that single arrangement, with all the relations it creates, is our race indebted for not only its existence, but a very large amount of its virtue and happiness. The felicity of paradise was imperfect without it; and the relation which was thus found necessary to complete the joys of innocence, contributes more than any other, when its laws are duly observed, to mitigate the woes of fallen humanity. The church, therefore, which would frustrate the designs of this great arrangement, instead of laboring to secure its fullest, healthiest results, must be an unutterable curse to mankind. Well, we have seen the fearful effects even of a partial interference with it in the celibacy of the Romish priesthood—the terrible revenge taken by nature, even for this comparatively slight violation of her laws. Then what must be the effect, if, as we now proceed to show, Rome has ever labored not only to rob this divine arrangement of its benign influences, but to invest it instead with malign ones; and not only to frustrate woman's holy destinies as the "guardian angel" of each generation, but to attempt to transform her into its "destroying angel?"

Be it remembered that God has given woman an influence almost incalculable, and a sphere to exert it in all but boundless. By endowing her with the softer sensibilities of our nature, he has made her, in her own sphere, omnipotent for good. Her weakness thus becomes her strength, and her reign one of love; and she moves through society a centre and a source of influences inestimably valuable in a world like ours—softening its asperities, refining its grossness, sweetening its bitterness, and alleviating its woes. And these she exerts *everywhere*—as a child in the nursery, as a sister in the family, as a daughter by her parents' side, in the hallowed affections of a wife, and in the exquisite tenderness of a mother. Oh, it were demon wickedness to mar or blight such a merciful arrangement as this! No wonder the arch-fiend has always aimed to destroy woman first as the surest means of destroying man; you see it in the first temptation, in the history of the flood, and all over the world. Wherever Satan reigns, there woman is debased; she is the Mahommedan's toy, the Hindoo's captive, the African's beast of burden, and the prostrate slave of all. And if you would see the Satanic skill and iniquity of this, you need only to contrast the Christian mother with the Heathen, or the Monicas with the Agrippinas of mankind; the one giving the world an Augustine, the other a Nero, and each the source of a stream of moral influence, of which the one proved a river of life, and the other a desolating flood.

In Popery he has pursued the same policy, but with a profounder subtilty. First, by his various contrivances for discountenancing marriage—such as its entire system of nunneries—he seeks to frustrate the designs of woman's existence;—to rob mankind of her precious influences, and reduce herself to a social nonentity, buried alive in gloomy cloisters, with nothing but the ghost and shadow of womanhood remaining. And thither that hapless creature is consigned; to wage, as best she can, perpetual war with all the feelings and adaptations of her own nature;—by this dark contrivance transformed at once from being the fairest creation of God to be a pitiable anomaly on earth, unable to be an angel, yet not permitted to be a woman, and thus doomed to virtual suicide.

But since celibacy is too great an outrage on our nature for even Rome to commit with much success, her next and grand aim is to take possession of the soul, which she cannot thus blight; and to transform those females whom she cannot thus banish from society, into tools by which the better to effect her deep designs against it.

As the *convent* is her great instrument in the one case, so is the *confessional* in the other ;—and will the reader just attend while we briefly unfold a contrivance as diabolical as ever was hatched in hell, for destroying woman's purity and degrading her soul. The process begins in very infancy; at the tender age of *five*, the joyous-hearted little girl is dragged to the confessional, like a lamb to the slaughter, to have sins suggested of which she never thought before, and questions put from which innocence recoils; and that mere infant must there be cross-questioned as to whether she has yet felt any carnal desires ! !* As years advance, these questions increase in vileness, and that innocent young creature, as often as she approaches her confessor, must be dragged through an examination so disgusting that we cannot pollute our pages even with a sample; it is enough to refer our readers to those depositories of obscenity, Dens, Delahogue, and Bailly, in which there are whole chapters on "immodest thoughts, words, touches, looks, and acts," and all these must be turned into questions, and by the female distinctly answered! There is no escape even for the blushing *virgin*, for a "general confession may not only be unprofitable, but even dangerous and improper,"†

* Dens, vol. vi. p. 204.

† Curr's "Familiar Instructions," p. 123.

and therefore "*it is necessary to explain everything!*"* Neither is *matrimony* the least protection; for these obscene inquisitors obtrude themselves into the marriage chamber, demand the secrets of the nuptial couch, and make the minutest inquiries "*circa actum conjugalem!*" Nay, this infamous system spares not the disconsolate *widow* in her weeds; for it is a mortal sin even "to recollect the joys once sanctioned by her marriage vow, and must therefore be specially confessed."† Only imagine every Roman Catholic maid and matron in Ireland, dragged annually *at the least* through this sink of abomination, at the mere pleasure and after the prurient fancy of some coarse bachelor priest, and all this enacted in the name and beneath the mask of religion! Is it really possible that Roman Catholics can tamely submit to this? Oh, does it not imply a moral degradation absolutely pitiable? How *can* a father permit his lovely daughter to be exposed to such on ordeal?—how *can* a husband endure to have his virtuous wife subjected to such debasement?—above all, how *can* a bashful female, she who would prefer death to a tithe of this dishonor from any other hands, submit to be robbed by an unmarried priest of all that gives dignity to woman, and leave the confessional a degraded thing? We speak not now of its debauching influence, we stop not to ask by what miracle of preserving grace woman can ever

* Christian's Guide to Heaven, pp. 80, 81.

† "Progress of the Confessional." p. 20.

leave such a scene a virtuous being; but we ask, even were all that has ever been said and *admitted* of the confessional's debaucheries a monstrous libel, even were woman always to escape *destruction*, how can she possibly escape *degradation?* If even a *man* of any feeling cannot look his confessor in the face, how can a *woman* attempt to do so? It is simply impossible. Unless such scenes have obliterated her feelings altogether, she must even in her own eyes be a debased and humbled creature; and what a dreadful alternative this, alike fatal to her dignity, either to have her modesty extinguished or continually outraged!

Now, mark the tremendous consequences. She has humbled herself to her priest, and he has by this means acquired over her a boundless authority. She dare not resist it,—she never does; for one glance from that basilisk eye, darted into her soul, is at any time enough to suppress the first risings of revolt. Well, having thus secured *her*, the priest has secured all the influence which God has given her. All is made over to him, to be employed as he directs, and from that hour she is transformed into an evil genius. Descending from her lofty station as the world's benefactress, she becomes the mere menial and decoy of "the church." The wholesome streams of influence which flowed from her, are now drugged and poisoned; her children, her husband, her whole household, she influences as the priest directs her, and thus, by one fell stroke, the best safeguard of society is laid in ruins. Satan has again succeeded in his first great temptation; and the plea of fallen Adam comes to mind—"It was the woman whom thou gavest to be with me!"

THE FRUITS.—It is impossible here to trace out all the effects of this profound conspiracy against the best interests of mankind—we can only trouble the reader with an example or two. Indeed in this, as in our other chapters, our aim is rather to give him the clue to each chamber of this dark labyrinth, and leave him to follow its windings himself.

It is wonderful how similar are the fruits of all false systems;—how like, for example, are the habits of the Pagan and the Papist, and the condition of the Irish hut and the Indian wigwam. One of the most striking and usual effects of true religion is cleanliness, and of false religion is filth. If cleanliness is not "next to godliness," it is at least closely connected with it; for how seldom have you seen a truly pious household who, in their whitewashed walls and well-swept floor, did not bear pleasing testimony to the gospel's elevating power! Now, in Protestant England, the humblest cottager wages an eternal war with dirt. Enter if you will his little kitchen, and every vessel is shining on the shelf; and could you only pass from thence in an instant into many an Irish Roman Catholic's parlor, you would be at no loss to decide in which of the two you would prefer to dine! In fact, Popery is emphatically a filthy religion. The cabins of Irish Roman Catholics are embowered in dirt,—you can't pass near them without the risk of defilement; and as you see their doors fronted by dung-heaps, on which filthy children are wallowing, while their parents are lazily lounging about, you can't help regarding the revolting spectacle as a visible protest to heaven against a system which could so brutalize immortal beings. Yes; and you who charge this on our countrymen *as such*, have you ever been in other Popish lands? M. Roussel, speaking of his tour in Switzerland, says—"I met a carrier who enumerated all the clean cantons and all the dirty ones; the man was unaware that the one list contained all the Protestant cantons, and the other all the Popish ones."* And in the "holy city," where is so instructively exemplified every feature of the "mother of abominations," we have this one also; for Seymour declares, that "every species of filth, and every kind of odor, greet the visitant on his entrance among the streets of this city of the church." "For filth, for odors, for indecency, for all that is offensive to the eye, to the feelings, to the habits of a cleanly and orderly people, the city of Rome surpasses almost any other city in the world."†

* New York Evangelist, 1849.

† Seymour's Pilgrimage to Rome, p. 139.

Another striking point of contrast between Christian and Pagan lands, is the measure of respect which each shows to its dead. In the latter, for instance, you will see dead bodies lying unburied, and half-devoured by birds and beasts of prey. Now, every traveller has observed that a contrast precisely similar exists between Protestant and Popish countries. In our western graveyards, you will not only see bones strewn about on the surface of the ground, but half-decayed ends of coffins sticking out of the graves; and only just contrast these horrid golgothas with the neat-planted country churchyards of Protestant Ulster and Britain! Yet a still more revolting scene is found in the Irish *wake*—that remnant of the funeral games of Panganism, in which not only smoking and drinking, but all kinds of amusement are indulged in; and these too often winding up with the characteristic *finale* of a row, in which the belligerents have sometimes been known to struggle and tumble over the corpse itself! Yet the priest, by reason of his mighty influence, could easily put down such practices, and vastly improve the people's general habits; but when has he ever made the attempt? And if you ask the reason, his answer is, that it would be useless. So, then, he who is omnipotent when a Bible is to be burned, or a Scripture-reader mobbed, is, by his own confession, only impotent for good!

Instance, again, the general degradation which prevails in all "dark places of the earth," with its attributes of sloth and improvidence. Give an Irish peasant a patch of bog on which to build a hut and plant potatoes, and he seems to have reached the climax of his wishes. His brightest visions seem realized in his cabin of mud,—his highest aspirations in his rood of potatoes,—and the motto of his life seems henceforth to be, "Why should we think of to-morrow?" There he vegetates; but not alone. Whatever other precept he sets at naught, no man seems more reverentially to regard the first great command, "Be fruitful and multiply." Perhaps by eighteen he is married; and we have known the "happy pair" to be obliged to borrow the coat and gown in which the nuptials were performed. During the late famine, a man who received daily relief, in Ballina, petitioned for a double supply, on the ground that the committee were so kind and his prospects had thus grown so bright, that he had married a wife, and the extra relief he sought was for her! Everything else is in keeping: time, the most precious commodity to an Englishman, is, by the Irish Roman Catholic, squandered with lavish hand; while to diligence he is so little accustomed, that when working in the fields he must stop to gaze at each passer-by; and, in *his* case, the plea of the unjust steward is reversed, for we have known him to leave his "digging" in the field to "beg" a half-penny from a passing stranger. Indeed, begging seems the national trade, and never was a race more fertile in expedients to awaken liberality and impose on simplicity. They have been known to make ulcers in their legs with bluestone; and you would think those naked children who pursue the coaches along the road had the most unquenchable thirst for learning, for "the half-penny" is always "to buy a book." Yes, though the sixth of Ireland's population is in the poor-house, this has scarce perceptibly diminished the number of strolling beggars. By the highways, you see them posted like sentinels; as you pass through a town, they follow you, invoking the saints' blessings on your departed parents' souls. If you enter a shop, they instantly surround the door; and, even late at night, you'll hear their monotonous call rising in the stillness of the half-deserted streets.

Do you say it is because they are *Irish?* We deny the ungenerous charge. The Irish Protestant we have known to be half starved in his dwelling before he would divulge his wants. No; it is the necessary fruit of a system which, by degrading the whole soul, begets of necessity the spirit of a beggar; which, by laying such stress on the *merit* of almsgiving, holds out a premium to begging; and which, by its various mendicant "orders," invests the trade with not only the garb of respectability, but the sanction of religion. Hence, what Popish country does not swarm with beggars? While you travel for weeks through Protestant America without meeting one, save from Ireland, every traveller tells you how the Popish lands of Europe are filled with them.

Mr. Wylie had no sooner crossed the torrent which divides the Protestant republic of Geneva from the Popish kingdom of Sardinia, than amongst other characteristic marks of desolation, he met troops of beggars, whose "numbers seemed endless. Every other mile, in the day's ride of 50 miles, brought new groups, as filthy, squalid, and diseased, as those which had been passed." * Or, perhaps you may say, 'tis necessity which makes the Irish beg? Alas! the shortest way to get rid of the importunity of some of them, is, as we have known, to offer them employment. And is it not common for Irish laborers to beg their way, not only going to the English harvests, but returning from them, no matter what earnings they may be carrying back; nay, to resort to various schemes to avoid paying their fare in the steamers which bring them home? We have seen the mate sometimes confining them in the hold, sometimes kicking them round the deck, sometimes stripping them almost naked, before they would confess they had a farthing about them; and in one case, the honest sailor, in his indignation, flung the poor wretch's waistcoat overboard, whereupon he raised a howl of lamentation, exclaiming that he was a ruined man; and then the truth came out that he had several pounds sewed up in its folds!

And these are thy trophies, O Rome—the proofs of thy divinity—the fruits of thy celestial sway! Oh, how oft, when witnessing such scenes as these,

* Wylie on the Papacy, p. 482.

has our very soul burned, not only with shame for our country, but indignation at the system which has made her the world's very scorn! And we have felt amazed at the effrontery of those priests who, daily walking amid the ruins they have wrought, can not only lift their heads like other men, but rage and bluster the while against England as the cause of all this mischief, and speak of themselves and their system as the peerless embodiment of transcendent and persecuted worth, and the only hope of Ireland's elevation!! Surely in the light of these astounding facts must the mist which has so long enveloped Ireland be dissipated, and the contempt of which she has been the innocent object, be henceforth levelled against her cruel enslaver. For, if beneath even bodily slavery the finest race on earth degenerate and become in time mere wrecks of humanity, O! what must be the effects of such a moral thraldom lying with its whole weight on our countrymen for ages!—a thraldom which, masked in the guise of Christianity, kills the energies that divine religion quickens—brutalizes the feelings which it refines—debases the nature which it exalts—in a word, as thoroughly curses as ever it blessed—and makes the whole man, to which the gospel would have given the swelling bloom of health, like some spent and palsied frame, the shattered remnant of what it was!

CHAPTER V.

ROME BLASTS MAN'S TEMPORAL STATE.

SUCH, then, is Rome. Like some parasitical plant which embraces and kills the noblest tree, it twines itself with deadly grasp around man's whole nature; or like some poison poured into the veins, it sends its moral death-drugs through his whole soul. And now, having seen how it MUST destroy a people, it only remains to show how, in Ireland's case, it HAS done so. And for simplicity's sake, we shall take up the leading topics of the two first Parts of this work which have not already been disposed of; and briefly applying our *whole line of argument* to Ireland's financial, physical, social, and political state, proceed to the completion of our demonstration.

THE FINANCIAL.—Rome has impoverished Ireland *indirectly* by its *influences*, and *directly* by its *imposts.*

If she keeps her people sitting in darkness while others are enlightened, steeped in vice while others are virtuous, and their whole souls like a bow unstrung while others are nerved with energy and life —then, unless God were to rain gold from heaven, is their poverty as inevitable as eternal laws can make it. Why, Rome's very *holidays* tend in this direction: her calendar contains a fast or feast for every day in the year, and demands the observance of seventy of these, exclusive of Sabbaths; so that nearly a fifth part of every "good Catholic's" lifetime is consumed in the worship of dead men and women! And what must be the effect of such continual interruptions to business on a nation's wealth, and on all those *habits* which are the springs of wealth? or how can the man who idles on Monday and Wednesday, help feeling the *unsettling* effect throughout the rest of the week?

If, then, Rome's very *devotions* tend to poverty, what must be the influence of her vices and crimes? We have proved that it is she that has filled the land with violence; at her door then lie, of course, the disastrous consequences. It is she that is mainly chargeable, not only with our enormous military, constabulary, and jail expenditure—not only with our ruinous outlay on law and lawyers—not only with our crushing poor-rates—not only with the actual expense of our immoral habits themselves, but with all the calamitous effects of these, direct and reflex, on the *trade and progress* of the country. And who can pretend to estimate these? Think of the loss sustained by one disturbed district, or the injury inflicted by a single gang of ruffians, before they come within the grasp of the law at all; and yet to all this *positive* loss you must add the still larger *negative* item. You must enter our *criminals'* cells, and estimate, not only the injury they inflict on society, but the good they would have conferred on it, had they only been virtuous—you must wend your way to our *seaports*, and reckon the loss sustained by the flight of our best people, who, in a better state of society, would have prospered at home—you must then pass through every *town* and *parish*, and calculate the loss incurred by the paralysis of our trade, and the wretchedness of our agriculture;—and, finally, you must visit every *stream* and *harbor*, and reflect how many capitalists our social disorder has driven from our shores, and how many more it has hindered from approaching them; all this, and more, you will be obliged to estimate, before you can form a correct idea of the financial curse of Popery.

We have already seen a little of Rome's *direct* imposts, and in truth but a little; for the amount it wrings from the starving Irish is scarcely credible. Poverty itself brings no exemption;—we once knew a common *char*-woman to fast from her dinner for days in order to procure her "*voluntary* offering;" and in various towns you see magnificent chapels now rising to the skies, but while pleased with their beauty, you perhaps little dream, that like the Egyptian pyramids they have been reared by the sweat of bond slaves, and owe their existence mainly to the hard earnings of the poor.

We have shown how, during the horrors of the famine, Rome fed on the alms of charity, and "gleaned in the rear of starvation." It was during these horrors that the Pope fled to Gaeta; and at the very time when the priests were appealing to Protestant liberality on behalf of their starving millions, they were sending thousands of pounds to his "holiness;" who, in return, sent them his *blessing*, and a few hundreds of their own money to distribute amongst the dying! No wonder, truly, that our poor emigrants breathe freely when they reach the shores of the west, and express themselves as thankful for having escaped the exactions of their priests as those of their landlords. No wonder that, with all their efforts to "bring their friends out," they are never known to bring out their priests! and where an occasional priest does follow and join them, no wonder that the first lesson they take pains to teach him is that he is no longer in Ireland. "Sir," exclaimed an Irish laborer on the banks of the Delaware, to a priest who had insolently refused to take five dollars for some rite—"Sir, do you think it is in Ireland you have me?"

Nay, not only has Rome extracted the morsel from the mouth of hunger, but outraged those feelings of our nature which even barbarians are accustomed to respect. A young pair become attached, and the priest often hastens the marriage for sake of the fee, although he knows they must borrow the money wherewith to pay him. Nay, one of our missionaries has detailed a case in which not only was the match made by the priest, but the bride never saw the bridegroom till she met him on the way to be married! and he adds, that when they met, the poor bride thus addressed her future spouse—"May I make bold to ask what is your name?" But Rome's golden harvest is by the deathbed and the grave; and in those solemn scenes where the most rugged nature has melted,—where the hand of extortion has let go its grasp, and unkindness itself has been known to weep, she alone has remained unmoved; and by working on a dying father's terrors, so often robbed his children, even while weeping over him, that parliament itself has been obliged to protect them by its Charitable Bequests' Bill. Oh, think of a church of God thus feeding like a vulture on the dead as well as the living! Surely the bold highwayman is honorable in comparison to the men who creep into the death-chamber, and, alike unmoved by the groans of the dying and the anguish of the living, do their pilfering work beneath the cloak of religion and the forms of law!

Nor must we blame the Irish priest alone; Rome is everywhere the same spiritual maelstrom sucking down the wealth of nations; and the successor of the fisherman who had neither "silver nor gold," has in all ages been the world's great plunderer. While the whole state revenue of Rome is but 8,000,000 or 9,000,000 of dollars, its church property is worth 400,000,000 of francs, and yields a revenue of 20,000,000 a-year.* Ay, and poor miserable Spain, unable to pay any one else, is this moment paying the priests 50,000,000 of dollars per annum. Now,

* Gavazzi, 13th Oration.

if *bankrupt* nations are thus mulcted even in these days of Rome's impotence, imagine, if you can the state of things when Europe lay in chains at her feet. At one time a large portion of its entire property had been drawn into her capacious jaws; and it was to prevent her from swallowing England up that the law of mortmain was enacted; while those who see the ruins of abbeys, cathedrals, and monasteries which are thickly strewn over Europe, and reflect on their enormous revenues, may form some idea of the pecuniary millstone which once hung on the necks of nations.

THE PHYSICAL.—We have only space for a word or two on the soil and climate of Popish lands. "What!" you exclaim, "does Rome even mar the face of nature?" Yes, dear reader, the ground was cursed for man's *first* apostasy, and why wonder that it should feel the effects of his last and greatest? And as if to show more clearly her scathing influence, it is usually the finest countries which God has permitted Rome to occupy, while the poorest have as commonly been assigned to Protestantism. To the one he has given green Ireland, fair France, and sunny Italy; and to the other barren Scotland and sandy Holland; yet the latter are blessed, and the former so thoroughly blasted, that of Italy, for instance, a late traveller could not help exclaiming,—"The devil has again entered Paradise:" and this, too, while Protestantism found Britain a paltry island, and America a vast wilderness, and has made them the pride of the world! It is the same in Ireland; Rome has possession of not only its best provinces, but its most romantic spots. To her belong Wicklow, Killarney, Rosstrevor, and Lough Gill; and who that has visited these lovely scenes can forget the nuisances which are found in their midst—who can forget the filthy beggars, for instance, who in Killarney torment the tourist at every step like summer flies in some sweet bower; or help adopting the very words of Baptist Noel, when gazing on a similar scene at Killaloe:—

"But in Ireland there is an omnipresent mischief, and when you would let your thoughts repose among the sweet influences of nature, then Popery looks in on you like a spectre; or, if it be half concealed like a snake among the flowers, 'there comes a token like a scorpion's sting,' warning you of its hateful presence. I felt it at Killarney, I felt it at Rosstrevor, and here it is again." Yes, and not only can you trace the trail of this serpent along the ground, but you sniff its odors in the breeze of heaven. Cultivation affects climate, and cleanliness promotes health; and if to Popery we are indebted for undrained bogs and filthy cabins, then it is it we must mainly thank for that damp which is the result of the one, and those diseases which are caused by both. If, then, Popery injures even *our* salubrious clime, what report can we expect from other lands? Instance Italy, "the seat of the beast;" and in the days of the

Cæsars, towns and villages stood where the Pontine Marshes now send up their poisonous vapors, and that *malaria* was but slightly felt which is now the scourge of the land.

But it is in the *race* you see the chief physical effects of Popery. Eden suffered much by the fall, but Adam suffered more; and we appeal to the reader if we have not proved that those blemishes which attach to our countrymen, are chiefly chargeable on Popery. The very body feels its curse—you see the "mark of the beast" not only on the "forehead" but the frame; and no marvel, when you think of the influence of crime and misery on bodily strength and stature. The contrast is remarkable between the Roman Catholic peasant of Kerry, and the Protestant peasant of Antrim; and what is yet more striking, between the Roman Catholic and the Protestant of Kerry itself. The same contrast is seen between the Frenchman and the Englishman; and what demonstrates that this is owing not to anything *natural* to these races, but to some influence exerted *upon* them, is the fact that the stature of the French has diminished, while that of the English has increased. For, according to Raudot in his "Decline of France," the height required for a French infantry soldier in 1789, was but 5 feet 1 inch, and in 1832, a time of peace, it had to be reduced to 4 feet 9 inches and 10 lines; while in England, on the contrary, the *minimum* height 20 years ago was 5 feet 4 inches, and now it has risen to 5 feet 7. If such are the effects of Popery on the body, what must be its influence on the soul? We appeal for answer to all Popish lands. What a contrast is the Brazilian to the American, and the Austrian to the Englishman!—or where was ever a finer race than the ancient Andalusian? and what have the priests now made them?—"they took in hand a nation of heroes, and they have produced a generation of hens."* In a word, no matter how different the race, Protestants have *everywhere* the same great moral features of resemblance; and so have Roman Catholics. And what singularly proves the degrading power of Rome on the Irishman in particular, is that it affects the very bravery which is his national quality. How can a moral slave be a hero? And so marshal him under priests as leaders, with crucifixes as ensigns, and you find him flying before Cromwell, before William, before the soldiers of 1798; but place him in the ranks of the British army, where his priest can no longer *trample* on him, and though he remains a Papist, and is therefore the most troublesome soldier in his regiment, his natural spirit of bravery comes again, for it was not dead but sleeping, drugged by the opiate of Popery—and so he has contributed his full share of those laurels which England wears on her brow!

And thus we demonstrate that if the Irishman is worse than other men, it is Rome which has made him so; and, oh! it is melancholy to see this poor

* Bishop Mechior Cano—quoted by Gavazzi, 8th Oration.

victim of her guilt wandering the world, like some outcast from society, with that reputation blasted which is more precious than life. True religion gives a character, and in these days character is everything; but, alas our poor countryman! his very name is enough to close against him the avenues to success. How often do you read in advertisements for clerks and servants, the humiliating *nota bene*—"No Irishman need apply!" How often when in search of employment in English and Scotch towns, is the door rudely shut in his face the moment his brogue is heard! And how often have we known him on that account to deny his country and try to disguise his fatal shibboleth! Yes, and because the Ulster Protestant *has* a character, and the Munster Roman Catholic has *none*, how often does the latter in other lands attempt in his distress to pass himself off as a native of Ulster! What a fearful odds is against him here, when at the least he requires years of good conduct to *make* the character with which a Scotchman starts the first hour! And what a pitiable condition is this to be reduced to: if he remains at home to be in danger of starving,—if he leaves it in quest of an honest livelihood, to be still exposed to starvation,—and however innocent he may be, to find himself everywhere a shunned and suspected man!

The Social.—On this section we need scarcely dwell. If, as we have shown, Rome violates those eternal principles on which the *existence* of society depends ; surely social *disorder* at least must be the result. It follows inevitably from our whole argument, that the direct tendency of Popery is to lay in the dust the entire social fabric. And it is truly wonderful how distinctly its effects are seen in the general *condition* of its victims. It has smitten the *man*, and you see the results on all that is his—in his filthy dwelling and ill-trained family, his weed-grown fields and broken fences. The master mind of the household is injured, and you see the effect on everything around ; the mainspring of the watch is out of order, and it tells on the motion of every wheel. How truly exemplified have we already found this to be in our countryman's HABITS ; it only now remains to trace it in his PURSUITS.

Remember, then, dear reader, how Christianity quickens, and Popery kills, the energies of man ; how the one is like the sun in spring, waking all nature to life, and the other like the frost in winter, overspreading it with the dreariness of death ; and you have the reason, which some cannot, and others will not see, why there is as great a contrast between Protestant and Popish communities, as between the flowing tide and the stagnant pool. How mournfully illustrated in Ireland's case ! How much has been done by public and private philanthropy to infuse a little life into her sluggish veins ! yet, like some exhausted patient, she continues to sink in spite of every restorative : each proves, at the best, but a temporary stimulant whose effects disappear as soon as it is withdrawn; and when there does seem a slight amendment, you are afraid to trust it, and can never tell whether it may be only like the occasional flicker of a dying lamp. The priest sits as a nightmare on the social energies, and presides the evil genius of the stagnation he creates. And this is so manifest, that could Ireland and Scotland exchange populations, the one would become a garden, and the other return to the wilderness state; and could each have its ancient inhabitants restored, how soon would it resume its ancient character! Is it not the same in all Popish lands? What a social contrast they present to Protestant ones, in spite of their superior natural advantages—instance the two great European *peninsulas*, Spain and Italy! What prodigious commercial facilities are theirs! Yet how long, think you, would *their* inhabitants have dwelt in the woods of America, or on the swamps of Holland, before they would have made them the homes of commerce and wealth? In truth, wherever Popery flourishes, nothing is in vigor but Popery. Had it still reigned over Europe, where would now have been its steamers, its railroads, its telegraphs, its forests of shipping, or its ten thousand inventions, which are the wonder of the world? Nay, with all the surrounding stimulus of that Protestantism which has created these, how much of them have Popish nations *yet*? Look at their miserable towns, with grass on the streets, and the people lounging about as though motion were a burden; or their best seaports, with a few paltry craft, and their finest harbors, almost like that of Tyre, a "place for fishermen to spread their nets;"—everything *still* as though they were asleep, or like some blighted forest which hears not the voice of spring;—and all because they *are*, in reality, lying benumbed and stunned beneath the stroke of this moral torpedo!

Moreover we impeach Popery as the grand *indirect* hindrance of our social progress; as the parent, for instance, of that feudalism whose remains still so much impede it. That curse cannot exist under a pure Christianity; its spirit cannot *but* exist under Paganism and Popery. And so we find that, if brought forth by the former, it was, at least, brought up by the latter; flourished most in Rome's palmiest days; received its deadly wound at the Reformation; and in every country has just decreased as pure Protestantism has increased. And it MUST be so. Popery being the intensest form of spiritual despotism, not only has the strongest affinity for civil and social despotism, but creates that social condition from which they necessarily spring. We have seen that the man who is accustomed to crouch before his spiritual superior, soon comes to crouch before his social superior. Slavery becomes his state: and once divide society into haughty priests and prostrate people, and it will, of consequence, divide itself into barons and serfs, masters and slaves, and produce, through all its ramifications, those various forms of petty tyranny beneath which Ireland, and all other Popish countries, groan. Instance our chief social grievance, landlord tyranny; and is it not, in *all* our provinces, mitigated in proportion to their Protestantism, from Connaught to Ulster? Just because Protestantism, by begetting all those qualities which improve the *man*, renders any extensive oppression impossible; for, if it does not so improve the landlord's own heart that he *will not* oppress, it so elevates the tone of society that he DARE NOT. And this healthy tone is, after all, not only the best preventive of abuses, but, in the long run, the only effectual one; for not only do all useful laws spring from it, but without it they are comparatively worthless. Now, we have demonstrated that Popery either destroys or prevents the existence of such a tone; and so it follows, that the landlord tyranny against which our priests exclaim, would, at the least, be greatly mitigated but for themselves. What landlord would dare attempt in Kent or the Lothians the same acts of cruelty which are committed with impunity in Galway? And the Tenant-Right leaders themselves admit that their chief hindrance is the want of that lofty, virtuous public feeling, which is the best means of overawing the oppressor; which would compel both landlord and legislature to listen to their claims; and which nothing but the blessed Bible has ever yet created.

Here, then, we have a monument of Rome's destroying power mournfully instructive—a country at once a garden and a grave; indented by harbors without a sail, pervaded by rivers whose banks are still; with *above* the finest clime unavailed of, *beneath* the richest mines unwrought, *around* the most fertile soil untilled; and inhabited by a race, which in natural parts have few superiors amongst the sons of men. Well, let the extent of the ruin at least serve to convince us of the malignity of the cause. And when we behold Ireland teeming with natural stores, yet starving; covered with improvement societies, yet a desert; and receiving millions of aid, yet a beggar;—when we see Scotchmen in *our* banks, and Irishmen in *their* prisons; foreign ships doing our trade, and our countrymen not the crews but the cargoes;—when, in short, we look on every jail and poorhouse, soldier and policeman, oh! let it give fresh zeal to our evangelistic efforts, and fervor to our prayers on behalf of a land on which God has so long permitted Rome to do her worst,—as if He thereby designed it to be a SPECIAL WARNING to all nations to beware of her blasting power.

THE POLITICAL.—We charge on Popery mainly Ireland's political evils. First, but for it those grievances which exist amongst us would either have been mitigated or long since removed. There is a moral state which invites misrule, and another which makes it impossible. Demosthenes keenly felt this when he told the Athenians that even were Philip dead, their conduct would raise up another Philip. It has been the experience of all ages, that rulers will enslave if the people will let them; and that the only effectual breastwork against the encroachments of the one, is the elevation of the other. It is only *below* a certain moral level that a nation *can* be trampled on, and the moment it gets *above* this it flings off the oppressor. Hence, Popish lands are the home of despotism, and Protestant lands the sanctuary of freedom. Hence America, Scotland, England, have flung off the tyrant's yoke. If, then, Ireland is in bondage, as some maintain, it must be because she lacks those qualities which would have secured liberty for her just as certainly as for them; and hence those priests who loudly complain of her thraldom, are themselves convicted as indirectly the cause; for had any other nation than England been placed by her side, would not the result have been the same? The *same*, did we say?—Let the present state of Europe answer the question. It was in England's power to oppress Ireland to any extent for aught such a priest-ridden nation could have hindered her; and had England continued Popish, all history is a fable if she would not have oppressed her. Thus it follows, that the political blessings Ireland enjoys, have sprung from *England's Protestantism*, while such political wrongs as she suffers are indirectly owing to *her own Popery*. Nay, in truth, the worst grievances she has ever endured, are *directly* chargeable on Rome. Were not those "disabilities," for instance, of which Roman Catholics have so loudly complained, in great part of their own procuring? Did not Rome convince our fathers, by too many unmistakable proofs, that they must either bind her, or themselves submit to be bound? And when they saw that she never got her hands loose but the first use she made of her liberty was to spring on *themselves*, what else could they do but bind her again?

So much for our political *grievances*. We next assert that Popery robs of their benign influence most of our political *blessings*. Instance its influence on our *laws*. A highly virtuous state of society makes somewhat tolerable the worst laws, while a vicious state renders mischievous the best; the one turns the evil into good, and the other the good into evil. In Scotland, for example, those taxes on servants, dogs, &c., from which we are exempt, have proved blessings, by leading the people to a simpler style of living; while our exemption has proved a curse, by encouraging in us a more expensive one. In Ulster, again, the *poor-law* works so well, that several poorhouses are almost self-supporting; while in Munster several unions are bankrupt, and the very guardian's board rooms are the scenes of party violence. And had the Scotch Presbyterians got those £8,000,000 of relief which we so shamefully mismanaged; judging by their whole character, we are entitled to assert that they would have annihilated pauperism in Scotland.

Alas, it is the same, with almost every other effort of legislation. O'Connell boasted he could "drive a coach and six through any Act of Parliament;" and thus, in direct contradiction to the whole aim of his life, unconsciously proclaimed how little mere legislation can do if it has not a virtuous community on which to operate.

Instance, again, our glorious *Constitution*. Take that very bulwark of liberty, *trial by jury;* and we have demonstrated by various facts that Popery has in numerous cases made it an absolute mockery, and that justice would be infinitely safer in the hands of the judge. Hence the friends of truth and order are rejoicing in the late "Justice's Act," which virtually transfers so much power from the juries to the magistrates. So utterly incompatible is the genius of Popery with that of liberty,—so unsuited does it seem to any other state than one of slavery,—that even this trifling approximation towards despotism has done wonders in quieting those horse-whipping priests, who, turning our very constitution against itself, trampled down the liberty of whole districts because they knew that no Popish jury would convict them.

Take one other bulwark of British liberty, the "elective franchise." Between the landlord and the priest this has also been little better than a mockery; for the people must generally vote for whatever candidate these masters direct. If they disobey the former, they are ejected; if they rebel against the latter, they are "damned." "Whoever," exclaimed Father John O'Sullivan from the altar, on the eve of an election for Kerry—"whoever will vote for that renegade, the Knight of Kerry, I won't prepare him for death, but will let him die like a beast, neither will I baptize his children."* Fancy, then, these people between those two tyrants—the one threatening temporal ruin, and the other eternal! It is all very well when both support the same candidate; and right thankful are the poor creatures to escape by being simply robbed of their rights as freemen. But the landlord, being often a Protestant, is frequently opposed by the priest; and then, imagine if you can the dilemma of the people! Still the Scylla of beggary is nothing to the Charybdis of perdition; the terrors of the confessional far exceed even those of the "crowbar brigade;" and so the priests generally carry it over the landlords, have frequently boasted that they could "return cow-boys to parliament," and have often led their dupes to the hustings when they scarce even know the candidate's name! Thus one of the dearest rights of freemen is by Popery transformed into not only a yoke of bondage, but such an instrument of ruin, that thousands of the people would deem its withdrawal the greatest mercy that England could extend them. Yet these priests are the champions of *popular liberty!*—and one of the standing themes of their platform harangues is

* See Progress of Confessional, p. 66.

the deficiency of the suffrage, and the necessity for its extension ! !

Finally, Rome is the direct cause of our *political agitations.* It has been well said, that it is her nature to produce tyranny when she is in power, and rebellion when she is not; and this single sentence is the key to the political intrigues of the priesthood in every land. How has it been exemplified in Ireland, making her entire history one of disaffection and rebellion! Or who so simple as still to doubt, that the *real* aim of the Irish priesthood, through all their political struggles, has not been equality but ascendency, not liberty for the people but supremacy for themselves? Shall we call it charity or infatuation which refuses to see that the real meaning of Irish agitation is the restlessness of priestly restraint? Can any man believe that the love of popular liberty is the reason why these reverend agitators have kept the country simmering for ages, and sown it thick with the seeds of lawlessness and crime; or doubt that the real yoke which galls them is our FREEDOM, and that had we but the laws of Italy or Spain, which degrade the people and exalt the *priests,* they would be as loyal as their brethren of those realms? Talk of Popery as the friend of liberty! whose every dogma breathes despotism, and whose every act exemplifies it! That any Protestant should ever doubt its intolerance, because its priests have had sometimes the hardihood to deny it, is to us a matter of perfect astonishment. Surely the last two years might be sufficient to open the blindest eyes. Those priests, during the revolutions of 1848, with a subtlety altogether worthy of them, appeared foremost in the republican ranks, and were the noisiest of the crowds who shouted, "liberty, equality, fraternity,"—were *all the while* quietly waiting the turn of the tide; and so are NOW the avowed leaders of that dreadful conspiracy which is formed against the freedom of Europe. Liberty! Are they not making every effort which conscious guilt and terror can suggest to extinguish the spirit of freedom in the world? Is not Pio Nono at this moment the rallying point of all Europe's trembling despots? Has he not heaped paternal benedictions on the perjured tyrant of Naples, and the unprincipled usurper of France? And is not his own despotism so intolerable, that he needs two nations to protect him from the violence of his oppressed children? Liberty! His own poor subjects cannot wring from the "Holy Father" one single drop of liberty's sweet cup. And is not the whole Romish Church publicly rejoicing in a series of the most shocking outrages, ever committed against liberty and humanity, by Louis Napoleon Bonaparte? Did not Cullen himself, in a late letter to the *Univers*, echo the blasphemy now ringing from every continental altar, and ascribe these atrocities to the special interference of Providence? Yet he is the *head* of those Irish priests who have for years been the champions of freedom!—and who *now*, while lavishing their blessings on Europe's basest tyrants, are defaming its most hallowed patriots! Instance Kossuth, that representative and symbol of outraged freedom. When the world was doing honor to the illustrious exile, they not only stood sullenly aloof, but betook them to their usual weapon, slander; when gladness beamed on the brows of thousands, the scowl of vexation lowered upon theirs; and when both shores of the Atlantic resounded with shouts of welcome to the Magyar hero, their conduct clearly testified that they would have shouted more joyfully over his grave. How often have we heard Irish Roman Catholics speak with rapture of American freedom, and long to fly to that land of promise from Britain's Egyptian thraldom; little imagining that America owed this liberty, under God, to those puritans whom they are taught to abhor, and that but for them it might now have been like such lands of Popish colonists as Brazil and Mexico! Yes, the poor creatures little know that the freedom that they enjoy even *here* is owing to Protestantism; that were Ireland's rulers Popish, it would fare no better than other Popish lands; that in Protestant countries ONLY can *Roman Catholics* breathe and speak freely, without dreading a spy in every companion, and an arrest in every corner; and that if over such Popish lands as France, during her short-lived republics, liberty has ever hovered, it has only been, like the bird of Noah, over a wide waste of waters seeking in vain for a spot to rest on!

Thus Popery in various ways blasts man's temporal state. By demoralizing it degrades, by doing both it impoverishes, and by impoverishing it farther degrades and demoralizes. By withholding knowledge it enslaves and beggars, and by these it renders the acquisition of knowledge impracticable; so that here we have a course of action and reaction going on, of cause and effect constantly reproducing each other. And thus, like the snakes of Laocoon, this great red dragon has twined itself round every limb of the body social, in so many deadly coils that disentanglement seems hopeless, and death inevitable. Yet think of the unblushing effrontery with which the Irish priests are this moment lauding it as God's choicest blessing to man. Think of Dr. Cullen, while doing his utmost to complete the degradation of which his predecessors have left so little to be done, having the hardihood to say, that Rome "*has been the instructress and civilizer of all nations of the earth. Every noble and useful institution that we possess has originated with her; and to her are due the preservation of the arts and sciences in the age of darkness, and their revival and diffusion at a later period!!*"* Ay, these are the terms in which "the Primate of all Ireland" addresses Christendom in the nineteenth century! If he had meant the most cutting sarcasm on his religion, he could not have expressed himself better; and this single sentence proves how utterly hopeless are the men

* Address to the Corporation of Drogheda, Aug. 17, 1851.

whose own Chief is so reckless as to make such an outrageous assertion in the very face of the world. When at the late Dublin "Defence" Demonstration, Mr. Moore ventured to hint that a Pope could persecute, this "head of the Irish Church" in holy horror stopped him, assured him that Rome was "the parent of liberty," and *proved* it by refusing him liberty to explain! Oh, if such is our metropolitan primate, what must be our rural priests! If he could thus speak in the face of Christendom, what, think you, will they stop at amongst a peasantry whom by such fearful contrivances they have so well prepared to believe any falsehoods! If he thus ventured to bully a member of Parliament, how must they handle their degraded slaves! And if that member did not dare to open his lips in reply to a statement so outrageous, what must be the prostrate vassalage in which the common people crouch and cower at the feet of their ghostly tyrants!

CHAPTER VI.

ROME BLIGHTS MAN'S ETERNAL PROSPECTS.

We have now reached a part of our subject before which all the rest must fade like the lamp in the light of day. It is the unceasing assurance of One who has the best right to know, that in comparison to *eternity* all which ever engrossed us in time is as the dancing bubble on the stream. He assures us that we stand on a narrow isthmus, with on one side an ocean of bliss, and on the other a lake of fire; and He conjures us by such motives as might wake the rocks and stir the tenants of the grave, to seek the one and flee the other. If, therefore, we find Rome exposing its dupes to that fiery perdition while pretending to save them from it, and in order to do so, borrowing the name of Jesus, and stealing the passwords of heaven, then are all its other atrocities angel innocence to this; and it stands forth to the execration of the universe as the most dreadful plot against the human soul that ever was hatched in the depths of hell.

In proof of this, it were surely enough to refer to our previous argument. Would you say that a system which so utterly blasts the earth, could be possibly fit for the skies?—that a church which makes a hell below, could make a heaven above?—or that those eternal laws which are essential to the safety of the universe, are dispensed with only in its great metropolis? The point, therefore, is *already* proved, unless you suppose that God requires higher qualifications for earth, his footstool, than for heaven, his throne; or that He who cannot endure sin even on this fallen earth, permits it to deluge the most glorious of worlds? But as there is a godless liberalism abroad now-a-days, which calls it bigotry to say that the Romanist is in any great danger—which, beneath the stolen garb of charity, dishonors God, leaves souls to perish, and paralyzes the efforts of those who *would* save them—and which, perhaps, may even say that we have drawn too dark a picture of Rome in this book—we shall now take her even as they would dress her out for view; and, to leave them forever without excuse, prove our fearful charge with all the clearness of demonstration.

They will at least grant that happiness or misery depends mainly on the state of the HEART. They are aware that Haman, a premier, was wretched because a gate-keeper would not bow to him; and Ahab, a king, took to bed because denied a patch of ground; and the world's Conqueror wept because he could not push his conquests to the stars: and they will surely admit that men torn with such passions must *anywhere* be wretched. Yet *all* men have within them the *germs*, at least, of the same passions; and hence, till these are crushed, TRUE happiness is out of the question. Surely they must see this; yet we shall make it still more plain. God himself is infinitely happy only because he is infinitely GOOD. It cannot be because he is in heaven, for he is everywhere; nor because he is Lord of the Universe, for he was happy before it was made: nothing, therefore, remains from which it CAN spring but his own infinite excellence. 'Tis the same with all his creatures. Angels do not surely leave their bliss behind them, when they come down from heaven on errands of love; nor devils their misery, when they come up from hell on their schemes of wickedness. No; their own bosoms are a heaven and a hell respectively. We ourselves also feel this; with all our efforts to find happiness *without*, our truest happiness is found *within*, and consists not so much in *where* as in *what* we are. We see it in the serenity of many a cottager, and the suicide of many a prince; in the dark scowl of villany, and the sweet smile of kindness; and even in the peevish face of the child when naughty, and his beaming countenance when good. If, therefore, you would make us happy in any world, there is but one way—make us GOOD. Substitute in our hearts one set of affections for another, radiant kindness for lowering malignity, transparent truth for sneaking falsehood, noble generosity for despicable selfishness, open frankness for sullen suspicion, in a word, ethereal holiness for foul pollution; and is it not perfectly manifest, that such a mere exchange of affections were to pass from hell to heaven, and that *without* this no external enjoyments *could* materially avail?

Now, to effect this change is the grand object of the gospel. Its whole aim is to PURIFY THE HEART. By doing this, it nips both sin and misery in the bud, and thus necessarily secures happiness on earth, and meetness for heaven. Here is its blessed plan, which, for simplicity of design and perfection of success, is worthy of its glorious Author. Here is neither mystery nor magic, but the most perfect system of adaptation. By the Divine Spirit thus turning a man from sin to holiness, he must become a *good* and therefore a *happy* man.

Look now to false systems of religion, and they *never once* aim at the heart; on the contrary, Satan's grand object seems throughout them all to be to prevent the entrance of one holy feeling. Their whole round of worship is a substitution of the *formal* for the *spiritual.* Everything is designed for the senses, and nothing for the heart; so that their most imposing ceremonials are but pompous mockery, and their devoutest worshipper a whited sepulchre. Yet is not this a perfect picture of Rome? In her system, all is *pardon*—regeneration is unknown—salvation *in* sin, never salvation *from* sin. The very term holiness is bereft of its meaning, and made a mystic sign—so we have holy water, salt, oil, clay, wells, loughs, trees—everything but a holy heart. All is external—penance of the body for sorrow of soul, confession to the priest for contrition before God, corporeal sufferings on earth, and material fires in purgatory. Even the means of grace are made *substitutes* for grace. Those pipes and conduits of the waters of life, whose whole virtue lies in their connection with the Fountain, are substituted for the waters they were meant to convey; so you have devotions whose value is their number, not their fervor—the *fact* of their performance is everything, the *spirit* is nothing at all. We ask, *can* this sanctify? *Does* it do so? We see in God's gracious plan the most beautiful connection between the means and the end; but what connection is there between holy water and a holy life—between bleeding knees and a bleeding heart? The one, religion cannot but make holy, yet it is a "damnable heresy;" the other can only do so by some such magic as the witches of Macbeth would have employed, yet it is the religion of the holy God! Oh, if this system can save, of course so can paganism; for its scheme of salvation is precisely similar. Do you say we are overstating the case? Enter any Irish chapel during mass—mark that priest in his fantastic robes, surrounded by boys in white frocks, often the greatest scamps in the parish—observe his mystic movements, his bows and genuflexions; now turning to the altar, and then to the people; shifting the mass-book to one side, and then to the other—and remember that most of all this is dumb show, and when he does speak, it is to mutter in a language the people neither hear nor understand. And do you say THIS has the least effect on their *hearts?* Then observe their vacant, devotionless looks!

Indeed, if the endless prayers of the Roman Catholic had the *least* sanctifying power, he could not but be the purest of men. Yet observe the scenes of abomination enacted at every holy lough and well. Visit St. Patrick's well on midsummer eve—see those crowds of devotees, with bare feet and tied up heads,—some running in circles, some kneeling in groups, some jumping about like maniacs, most of them covered with dust and sweat, not a few with blood, and all taking incredible pains that neither trowsers nor petticoats shall protect their knees from the sharp stones; while from the whole crowd a horrid din continues to rise to heaven. And you call *this* devotion! Then read the following picture, drawn by an eye-witness:—"Shouting, and howling, and swearing, and carousing, filled up every pause, and threw over the spot the air of hell. I was never more shocked and struck with horror; and perceiving many of them intoxicated with religious fervor and all-potent whiskey, and warming into violence before midnight, at which time the distraction was at its climax, I left this scene of human degradation in a state of mind not easily described." Do you say the priests are not accountable for such scenes? Then read a little farther:—"On this occasion, the Irish Catholic clergy were the mad priests of these bacchanalian orgies—the fomentors of fury, the setters on to strife, the mischievous ministers of the debasement of their people, lending their aid to plunge their credulous congregations in ceremonious horrors."* Thus, under their own priests' *special* direction, their very prayers are made pretexts for sinning. Instead of being a means of removing sin, they are made the purchase-money for greater indulgence in it; and their rounds of devotion are designed to clear scores with the Most High, in order to begin iniquity *de novo!*

* M'Gavin's Protestant, pp. 403, 404.

But even supposing such things were not so, and that the utmost we could charge on this church was mere *formality*, you will please recollect what this means. What would you call professions of penitence which is not felt, and of desires for holiness which are not cherished? What else but a mockery—a lie? And *this* is presented to the Holy One, before whom angels veil their faces—and as Rome's *best service!* So that unless He who denounced the Pharisees for such guilty homage has since changed his mind—unless He who abhors hypocrisy everywhere, accepts it at his altar—unless the august Sovereign of worlds takes pleasure in mummeries with which any mortal would feel insulted—the worship of Rome must be an abomination in his eyes. If it were either pleasing to God or profitable to man, would you not at least see some signs thereof in the priests themselves? You say they "fast oft;" well, to judge by their portly forms, the exercise seems to agree with them. You assert they keep Lent most scrupulously; be it so, they seem to thrive as well on salt fish as the three Hebrew children on pulse and lentiles. You say their prayers are manifold—we deny it not; we see their Breviaries in their hands, even on the tops of the coaches. But are they indeed *God-fearing-men?*—do their souls melt with the *love of Jesus?* Let our previous pages answer. There is only too much reason to fear that many of them are infidels in heart. "Do you know," asked a Kerry priest of a gentleman well known to the author—"Do you know what religion I am of?—you think me a Catholic priest, but in reality I am a Mohammedan. I believe Mohammed was as good a teacher of morals as Christ, and far more successful; when other means failed, he employed the sword, and beyond a doubt it is the best means of propagating morals and religion ! !" Oh ! the judgment-day will reveal the fearful process through which the mind of many an intelligent priest has passed, commencing with superstition, and ending in skepticism. When he emerges from Maynooth, we have little doubt of his fanatical sincerity; but once clear of its gloomy cloisters, it would be strange indeed if some of the light which surrounds him would not in course of time reach his mind. We will admit that he believes much of Rome's worst mummeries, for we know the "strong delusions" under which some are left. We will say he sincerely thinks Rome can reverse the divine aphorism, "To obey is better than sacrifice," and can even make right wrong. We will allow that he is convinced God is at certain times offended with flesh meat, and propitiated by fish, and that the food which is good on Thursday is pernicious on Friday. We will grant that in all this and more, he may be a devout believer. But hark !—he is just telling that trembling mother on whose brow sits distress, that he has prayed her darling child a certain length out of purgatory, but that it will need so many more masses, which in Rome's vocabulary means so much more money, to pray him wholly out. The poor creature believes him—but can he believe *himself?* And will you call us uncharitable for suspecting that man's honesty?—a man whom one such act leaves no choice between the character of a fanatical maniac and that of a foul impostor—whose intellect superstition must have shattered, or else who must *know* he is deceiving that poor woman, and driving a villanous trade on all that is tender and sacred in her soul.

Fellow-Christians, what can you say to all this? Behold our degraded countrymen, with many of whom the best hopes of heaven are *the priest*, and the loftiest views of happiness, *a drunken fit*. *Can* you say such creatures are meet for the angelic throngs? Then unless there *is* a purgatory, where else must they go? View that hoary wretch bending beneath the weight of crimes and years—his hands perhaps stained with blood, and his priest the keeper of the horrid secret. He will soon enter eternity—*as he is*. What place is he fit for?—*heaven?* One starts at the thought. Is it a little oil rubbed on the body of that dying and now unconscious sinner, that can purify his soul? or even if there *were* a purgatory, what more virtue could its sufferings possess than those earthly penances, in spite of which he lived a wretch? And if he were admitted to heaven, what would it serve him? If the whole Church of Rome were translated thither bodily, as she is or ever was in her palmiest days, what could this avail her, unless you suppose that place to be the heaven of the poets of Greece or the prophet of Mecca? But if you grant it is a place of *transcendent holiness*, whose employments, and ENJOYMENTS too, consist in *serving God;* then, what happiness could it bring to a church which regards virtue as a bore—absolution from it a blessing—the Sabbath a weariness—and prayer a penance? Why, *such* a heaven would be utterly insupportable to her *genuine* votaries. Its bloom would be dismal, and its purity hateful to them. The holier its throngs, they would be to them the more revolting; the sweeter its strains, they would grate the more harshly on their ears; and though to minister to their happiness you could drain every cup, and rifle every flower of paradise, you would still find them wandering in misery through its bowers, sighing to escape from its *holy* restraints, and regarding such a deliverance as their highest heaven.

Can the reader ask farther proof that Rome blights man's eternal prospects? What then, he may inquire, is there no salvation in that church? Adored be the living God, we believe there is. By various arrangements, truly wonderful, He makes some rays of heaven to struggle even through its bars and gratings. That *truth* which Satan's cunning has mingled with this system, the better to *seduce* therewith, God's infinite grace often makes the means of saving; and while many receive only the error and perish, some receive along with it enough of the truth to neutralize its deadly power. Yes, many Roman Catholics are saved, but, think you, does Rome deserve the credit?—let her own conduct answer. Is it on her best or her worst men that she has usually conferred her favors?—which class has she thus *proved* to be most after her heart? —has she not almost as uniformly persecuted her good men, as she has canonized her bad? You tell us of Fenelon—we reply, that she banished him. You speak of the Port-Royalists—do you know their sad history? You quote the name of Pascal—his godly sister was hunted to death, and he died a heretic, if papal bulls be true, and would have certainly died a martyr had he not slept in his tomb ere the authorship of his "Letters" had transpired. And you call these her children?—her step-children you mean. Yet it is with their good name she would ofttimes fain perfume her foulness; and it is with their mantle that even "Protestant" pseudo-liberals would sometimes seek to hide her deformity! Why do they not rather quote the men whom she *has* delighted to honor? Why won't they go to her own authentic catalogue of canonized saints—of those who in her judgment best deserved heaven—such butchers, for instance, as Simon de Montfort, who figures in the list as the holy St. Dominic. THESE are the men whom Rome lauds on earth and sends to heaven! Oh! could they enter that blessed place, retaining the character, and free to perpetrate the crimes which *procured* their canonization, they would soon wreck it of every vestige of its loveliness, and convert it into a pandemonium.

And now, in conclusion, when we speak of Popery as a Satanic conspiracy against the human soul, we surely do not mean that its priests are in the plot—they who are likely to be its worst victims—or that they even know the work they are doing, and the master they serve? We are convinced that, in this respect, they "know not what they do," that they as little dream as their flocks of the master-mind which presides over their system, and that, in this sense, at least, "they be blind leaders of the blind." No; the plot is too deep even for Jesuitism to contrive; a greater than Loyola is here; and it is this conspiracy against the soul that proves at once its paternity and iniquity. If it only cursed our countrymen for time, it were bad enough; yet this is the mere underplot of this "master-piece of Satan." It is its fearful distinction, that it traffics in "the souls of men;" that, not content with blasting them in time, it pursues them through eternity; not satisfied with destroying them on earth, it shuts heaven against them, follows them beyond that grave where wickedness usually ceases from troubling, and reserves its most tremendous curse for that other world whither ordinary hatred refuses to pursue!

And now, fellow-Christians, we must not, cannot leave this awful subject, without a word to you. Is it really so that we nightly sleep calm on our pillow, while souls all around us are passing before the throne—their best preparation the unction of a priest, and their fairest plea the merits of the Virgin? Have we lived for years amongst them, and though often told of their danger, folded our arms and shut our eyes, content with that specious plea of indifference disguised in the robes of charity—"God is merciful?" Or, if we have felt some Protestant zeal, has it been kindled by the strange fire of party strife full as much as by the holy flame of jealousy for God and love to souls? We implore you to ponder this chapter on your knees. Others may deny its truth, but you, at least, admit it; indifference on your part, then, is left without excuse. You know the unregenerate soul could not be happy in heaven, cannot be truly happy anywhere;—that, could it roam creation in quest of felicity, it would find the words emblazoned on every star it approached—"There is no peace to the wicked." But, even could it be happy in heaven, you know it were impious to suppose its admittance there. Satan was hurled thence the moment he sinned: and could one sinner enter its gates, his presence would hush, in an instant, its myriad harps, and darken the brows of its radiant throngs. Then, what insensibility holds us back from greater exertion on behalf of Rome's victims? How many of them may, on that awful day, plead our guilt in palliation of their own, and cry, "Refuge failed us; for these *Christians* would not care for our souls!" Then, by the love of Him who SAVED US, and commands us to make known his salvation to others; by our own tremendous responsibility as the keepers of our brethren's souls; and by the inestimable worth and unutterable danger of perishing millions, let us awake from our stupor and fly to their rescue. Imagine, if you can, the obsequies of one lost soul! What, in comparison, is earth's most dreadful catastrophe? The waves of Time's vast ocean, how soon they will close over the world's most fearful shipwreck! and the historian will scarcely mark, by one passing sentence, the spot where it occurred. But, oh, ONE LOST SOUL! Well might the infidel thus rebuke the Christian, and exclaim, "If I believed the half of what you *say* you believe, I would fly through the world with the awful news;—I would force my way with it into every dwelling;—I would make it ring from every steeple, and float on every breeze;—till my tongue would cleave to my jaws, and exhausted nature sink down and expire."

PART IV.

THE CURE.

Thus have we traced the causes of Ireland's wretchedness through their manifold complications; shown how they are like wheels within wheels; and while estimating the share which various subordinate causes have had in creating it, traced it to Popery as the Grand Primary Source. That there are other causes than Popery, we have therefore freely acknowledged; but we have proved that these are either produced or aggravated by it. That there may be others still, which the brevity of this work has forbidden us to notice, we as freely allow: but after making the most liberal discount on the score of all these which can with the least reason be demanded, still Popery stands out in such fearful prominence, that they seem in comparison as the drop of the bucket, or the chaff on the summer thrashing-floor.

And to prevent the remotest possibility of a fallacy in our argument, we have conducted it through the twofold process of induction and deduction—of analysis and synthesis. Like some great river, we have in our Second Part ascended the dark stream of Ireland's woes to its source, and found that to be her Religious state, marking as we passed the principal tributaries. And then, to put the case beyond cavil forever, we have in our Third Part turned and sailed down the turbid stream, and demonstrated not only that Popery is its main channel, but that to *it* these tributaries chiefly owe their existence, course, and power; that, to carry out the figure, it is the enormous valley which *it* has in the course of ages scooped out, which has of necessity reflected them towards it, and increased their force, however distant their rise or different for a time their direction.

And, that Rome might have nothing to complain of, we have traced her through every age and land, and still found her true to her own motto, *Idem semper ubique*;—that her whole course through the moral heavens has been that of some blood-red comet, wild and fearful. And we have drawn our proofs of this, not from her old musty records, those "relics of a barbarous age," as she would fain have us regard them; but from Rome *herself*, and especially as she NOW lives and moves in the full costume of those newest fashions with which she has bedizened her haggard form, in hope to enamor modern Christendom.

Nay, we have done more still. Our manifold facts and arguments we have based on *eternal laws*. We have shown that there are *certain laws*, which, being complied with, man MUST BE HAPPY, and being disregarded, he MUST BE WRETCHED in both worlds; that by nature we violate these, hence all the miseries of earth and hell; that true religion, by *restoring* us to their dominion, blesses, and that false religion, by *disregarding* them, curses in a thousand ways. Now, we have seen that Romanism crosses all those laws, and therefore MUST be a country's curse and poison. Our argument is thus based on eternal laws; therefore to oppose it were as preposterous as to oppose those sciences which rest on the same foundation. And all the anathemas which Rome can hurl against it, prove not its weakness but her own, and resemble at best the impotent attempt of the fabled Titans to storm the heavens and dethrone the God of gods.

And thus every part of Ireland's great puzzle we have solved. The mystery of her state we have laid bare to the light of heaven; and that so distinctly, that the blindest eye can scarce help seeing every chamber of its dark labyrinth, illumined by that single word—POPERY; and the deafest ear can scarce help hearing the doleful sound echoing from every hill and valley, rock and stream,—ROME IS THE GRAND CURSE OF IRELAND.

We now proceed to our last part—the Cure. But as this has been already so clearly foreshadowed, it will need neither elaborate nor lengthened examination. We shall sum up all we shall deem it needful to say under the two heads of the *Medicine* and the

Treatment. And for the sake of greater clearness and conclusiveness, we shall here also pursue the double process of induction and deduction. And as we have seen how clearly the cure has been foreshadowed in the cause, we beg the reader to notice, as he proceeds, how remarkably every part of the argument on the cause is confirmed and illumined by each successive step in the cure; and how, like two reflectors, they thus shed on each other such a flood of light as gives the entire demonstration the radiant clearness of noonday.

CHAPTER I.

THE MEDICINE—THE POPULAR REMEDIES.

Of the numberless *panaceas* prescribed for Ireland, we think it necessary to notice only the following. One class of men, full of her civil grievances, propose legislation; another, chiefly impressed with her ignorance, preach education; a third, looking mainly at her natural richness and actual poverty, cry, develop her industrial resources; a fourth, in view of her moral and religious degradation, declare that the gospel is her only true remedy; while a fifth class, believing that each of these remedies is more or less needed, say, let us have them all. We shall briefly attend to the claims of each.

THE CIVIL.—We have already proved that legislation can do little for us, and that almost the only ground which remains for it to occupy is the *land question*. We need some more sweeping measure for the transfer of land than even the Encumbered Estates' Bill; a thorough reform of those ruinous Chancery laws by which so many proprietors have doubtless been beggared; and, above all, a new and equitable adjustment of the relation of landlord and tenant. No one can doubt that the want of such an adjustment has been fraught with evil, and it has, in a secondary sense, been the cause of many of our agrarian crimes. It has done much to train our peasantry to insubordination, and beget that chronic discontent which now glooms on the brows of thousands of them. It has caused many of our bloodiest murders. It has furnished priests and demagogues with their best text against the "Sassenach;" proved a screen for Rome to hide her own desolations behind; and thus served to break the force of the demonstration that *she* is Ireland's grand curse. It is desolating the only fair, because the only Protestant, province in Ireland; provoking even *its* peaceful inhabitants to outrage; and thus destroying that moral tone which its *gospel* ministers have so carefully cultivated: and how much more serious those outrages would now be but for these gospel ministers, on whom some are disposed to father them all, is pretty evident from the fact that they are almost exclusively the work of Ribbonmen.

And what has this ruinous delay of a measure so obviously just, gained for the landlord himself? Whereas he might now have been beloved and prosperous, at least in Ulster, amidst a grateful and flourishing tenantry, he has done much to ruin both himself and them. And those concessions which he might once have easily made, and which *then* would have saved all parties, he can now scarcely make without beggaring himself. A fearful position! but how is it to be avoided? We are passing through a social revolution; and the landlord who has done so much to cause it, must just take his share of its trials. It can save *neither* party, but must eventually ruin *both* to continue to stave off this question. It is idle to decry the tenant-right agitation, or denounce its advocates as incendiaries and communists. Were they all that is charged on them—and some of them are far from faultless—this would not affect the question an iota; for it is not with "Reverend Agitators," but great laws, you have to contend. To Protection the country *cannot* return. Therefore to Free Trade principles *every* interest MUST be adjusted. To apply them to produce and not to land, to some things and not to others, is the only course which *cannot* be long persevered in. There is no help for it then; the landlord must, like all other mortals, bow to great laws; and, as we have said, the longer the delay, the reckoning will be the more terrible.

But beyond a few such measures as the above, *civil* remedies are perfectly useless, and many of them in our present state positively injurious. There is a *nonage* in nations as well as individuals, during which to invest them with political immunities were like giving the child all the rights of a man; and a *corruption*, too, which perverts into a curse the best civil blessings, and during the continuance of which, to confer them on a people is just to increase their powers of mischief. And is not this the state of multitudes in Ireland? Instance the basis of all society—Truth. "As to finding out the truth," says Mr. Inglis, "by the mere evidence of witnesses, it is generally impossible. To save a relation from punishment, or to punish one who has injured a relation, an Irish witness will swear anything." And lest this should be deemed the language of Protestant "bigotry," hearken to their own champion, Dr. Doyle:—"The witnesses as often labor to conceal, as to manifest the truth;—one class of them anxious to defeat the law, the other only intent on procuring conviction; both regardless of the obligation of an oath, and perfectly indifferent about contributing to the ends of justice."* Yet this is the man who, in the very same letters from which this sentence is extracted, declares, that "when it pleased God to have an island of saints upon earth, He prepared Ireland from afar for this high destiny. The Irish are,

* Letters of J. K. L. (Dr. Doyle), p. 22.

morally speaking, not only religious like other nations, but entirely devoted to religion!"*

Does not this demonstrate, as we have already shown, that in the minds of both *priest* and people, piety and crime, prayer and perjury, are perfect compatibles, and that Rome's religion is a system of magic, and never aims to improve the heart? How often have we ourselves seen justice paralyzed on the bench, guilt escaping, innocence martyred, and the entire trial made a mere farce by perjured villany! Nay, how often is the priest himself the guiltiest; and, to quote the confession of counsel regarding his reverend client, who had been detected in the very act, how often is he a "common perjurer," and obliged "to leave the court a degraded man!"† Talk of political immunities to such beings!—in whom are destroyed those moral obligations on which all the value of such rights depends. And would THIS be your cure for Ireland's evils? You *could* not inflict a greater curse on a corrupt nation than to give them a code adapted only for a virtuous one; for this were just to hold out a premium to their profligacy, and increase their powers of mischief. Political rights, to be blessings at all, must be in hands which won't abuse them; and however their *sound* may catch the thoughtless crowd, and suit the designing demagogue, slavery is better than outraged freedom. France might ere now have

* Letters of J. K. L. (Dr. Doyle), p. 58.

† Report, Sligo Assizes, March 13, 1837.

taught us this much. Twice has she tried a republic; and by the votes of three fourths of the nation, she has not only confessed that she is unfit for freedom, but that military despotism is to her a blessing in comparison. Nations can only be governed by *moral* or *physical* power. And if men's consciences will not prevent them from robbing or murdering, what else can you do but chain and fetter them? And when, as in our wretched land, Rome has so debauched the moral *sense* as to leave moral *influence* nothing to lay hold on, it is the most mischievous folly that ever was heard of to propose as her cure an increase of those immunities which her corruption has already so fearfully abused. Hence despotism always *does*, and always MUST, prevail in Popish lands. There, there is no moral principle for moral power to operate on; and were our most ardent champions of freedom made rulers there, they would soon find their visions of liberty dispelled; and that in a corrupt community there is not a foot of standing-ground between despotism and anarchy, between the chains of Loyola and the arms of Robespierre. And is it not amazing that men have not long since learned this? Seventy-six years ago, Protestant America became a free nation, and has ever since enjoyed unexampled prosperity; while, within the same period, Popish France has twice passed through the various phases of freedom, anarchy, and iron despotism. Two goodly vessels! The one,—her chart, the Bible; her ballast, virtue; her compass, true to the pole-star of heaven,—has been ploughing her glorious way over Time's mighty waters, freighted with blessings to all mankind. The other, without compass, or ballast, or chart, with mutiny on board and storms around, has been driven about amongst shoals and breakers, a spectacle and terror to the world! Would that the exclamation of her dying statesman rung in our own rulers' ears—"France *cannot* do without a religion!"

But why argue the question thus? Have we not proved that, by the devices of Popery, the immunities which Protestant simplicity would extend to the Papist, in hope to break his chains, are transformed into means of binding them more firmly around him?—that to "extend the suffrage," for instance, to the *people*, is just to increase the power of the *priests?*—and that while there are a thousand Father Walshes to threaten all with "everlasting punishment" who will not vote for the candidates of their choice, our champions of "equal rights" are only forging new chains for our countrymen, and playing into the hands of the worst tyrants the world ever saw!* Talk of *civil* rights beneath a system whose *head* thus sneers at man's chief *birth*-right!—"From this polluted fountain of indifference flows that absurd and erroneous doctrine, or rather raving, in favor and defence of liberty of conscience;"† and which raves, too, against that "ever-to-be-detested

* Report of Select Committee on Bribery and Intimidation.

† Encyclical Letter of Gregory XVI., 1832.

liberty of the press," and would, if it dare, give the world's best literature the doom of the Alexandrian Library! A *free* Papist! Have you, then, forgotten the confessional? Other tyrants take cognizance of your words and actions; but Popery penetrates your bosom. Others have policemen at your door; but it keeps a priest in your heart. The Pope, with his myriad confessors dispersed over the globe, is both omnipresent and omniscient, and millions of bosoms lie open to his gaze. Talk of political rights beneath such an ubiquitous EYE! which watches every government; and wherever it can, makes kings mere puppets, and premiers the wires to work them by;—which looks in at every door, and so completely murders family, and even conjugal confidence, that no man can breathe freely by his own hearth, or confide his secrets to the wife of his bosom;—and beneath whose dreadful glare the father sees the brow of his innocent child growing darker each time she has been to the confessional! We protest, then, against the folly of looking to Parliament for what it *cannot* do; of applying *civil* remedies to a *moral* disorder; of increasing the *liberty* of the people, while their priests only turn it to an engine of *slavery;* of curing our disturbances by enlarging the powers of our surpliced disturbers; or of causing the olive-tree to flourish by strengthening the arms that would pluck it up by the roots!

THE EDUCATIONAL.—On this subject there prevail

in Ireland, as elsewhere, very conflicting opinions,—one party opposing all education from which religion is severed, and another resisting all with which it is united—the National Board being the symbol of the latter, and hostility to it the characteristic of the former. In both parties we have something to approve, but more to condemn. We object to the violent ultraism of the former. Forgetting that the Board, if an evil, has at least displaced a greater evil, the "hedge-school;"—that if a "curse," it is chiefly of their own procuring—for had *their* system wrought well, it had never existed; there is a certain class who seem to regard it as the Gnostics viewed matter, and denounce it as fiercely as though *it*, not Popery, were the grand apostasy, and Marlborough Street, not Rome, were the seat of the Beast! Well, the impression somehow prevails, that this enmity does not wholly spring from heavenly motives, but is as much prompted by the spirit of Diotrephes as that of Jesus. We ourselves cannot forget how pertinaciously these men continue to assert, in the face of all fact, that in Protestant schools connected with the Board the use of the Bible is more restricted than in those of their own Church Education Society.

To the national system we know there is much to object; but while men like Mr. Trench patronize its schools, we cannot regard it as the root of all evil; and when men like Dr. M'Neile eulogize its efficiency, we cannot but regard it as the source of some good. Thousands of Roman Catholics, who but for it would now be sunk in hopeless darkness, are rejoicing in a substantial education. And why should these brethren seek to destroy a system which, though not all they could wish, confers such important benefits? If our countrymen won't have *all* the knowledge we desire, shall we therefore give them *none?* If they won't use the Bible at *first sight*, shall we prevent them from ever being *able* to use it? If they won't instantly emerge from Roman bondage, shall we therefore put it out of their power *ever* to emerge? On the plea of not violating *our* consciences, shall we thus act a part which requires the immolation of *theirs*, and, in the name of Protestantism, seek their conversion by such Popish compulsion? And since *we* cannot conscientiously aid the Board in enlightening a country whose darkness is a disgrace to Christendom, must we not only hinder those who *can*, but impugn their motives and denounce their conduct?

Besides, what is meant by this cry of "godless knowledge?" The sum of all knowledge is God and his works—is it this they call godless?—and under the plea of *piety*, are they guilty of profanity? "*All* his works praise" and reflect Him; and if we do not see Him in every star and stream, the fault is not in the book but the student. On *all* are marked the footprints of the Creator; and if learned men have been infidels, it is not because, but in spite of their pursuits. We protest, then, against this narrow-minded attempt to set the God of grace against the God of nature. It has been the fruitful source of the infidelity which is complained of: shunning secular learning as an object of suspicion, we have left her in the hands of wicked men, and if they have sometimes perverted her testimony to their own bad ends, the fault has been ours for leaving her with them. Then we say—Flood Ireland with secular knowledge; better this than none. All kinds of light are sisters, prismatic rays from the great Sun of truth, and, though differing in their hues, yet constituent parts of the same celestial element. Rome hates all kinds of knowledge; and this alone might teach those *Protestants* that all kinds are useful. She knows well that secular and religious light are as closely allied as civil and religious liberty, and that *all* these conspire to *elevate* and *bless;* and it is deplorable that what Rome sees so clearly, Protestant imbecility cannot see, or Protestant bigotry will not. They say they dread infidelity! Should they not, therefore, dread Popery more than the Board—for what is infidelity but "an excrescence on the back of the Beast?" What produced the entire school of Voltaire but this grand insult to the human understanding? And why dread Infidelity *more* than Popery? Is not the former often the inquirer's first resting-place on his journey from Rome to Jerusalem? Infidels *think*—but Papists can only *believe;* which state, suppose you, is the more hopeful one? And whether is Infidel France or Popish Spain this instant more accessible to the gospel missionary? But where is the monster brood of infidels which it was predicted this Board should bring forth? Are not all wise men now beginning to admit that it is going to be a grand engine for the overthrow of Irish Popery?—and the very best proof is Rome's anxiety to get rid of it. It has penetrated into her inmost camp, where the gospel missionary *could* not have followed. It has dived into her deepest dungeons; and, as it brings out her victims to the light, should not we stand at the door with the gospel to receive them? It is teaching them to read—let us be ready, when it has done so, to give them a Bible. It is springing the mine—let us stand prepared, when all is ready, to lay the train and put to the match. It is thus being overruled as a pioneer of the gospel, by Him who makes even the most imperfect plans of sinful men to subserve his glorious designs; and let not us, the ministers of that gospel, wrangle and split hairs, refusing to avail ourselves of the good it may do, because not done in the mode we would approve: so shall we best prevent the infidelity we dread, and most effectually promote the Christianity we desire.

But still more are we opposed to the sentiments of the opposite party, who would preach mere secular knowledge as Ireland's gospel. It is a strange and ominous sign of these times, that from so many of our seminaries where all other good books are admitted, the best of books alone is excluded; and that in the circle of what is termed "*useful* knowledge," *religious* knowledge is never embraced. In the name of that Christianity which is man's best friend for *both* worlds, we solemnly protest against this. And is it *thus* you would propose to heal the complicated maladies of Ireland? Have not learning and philosophy been already tried in various lands and in all ages, and what have they done to purify the social mass? Their utmost achievement has been to throw an external decency—or *splendor*, if you will—over the corruption, like the phosphorescence of decay; but what have they ever done to arrest the putrefaction itself? Look, ye idolaters of mere education, to Greece and Rome, and was it not when their learning had attained the loftiest point that their virtue had fallen the lowest? Corruption was sapping Rome amid the glories of the Augustan age; and troops of philosophers filled the academy, while the degraded Athenians were selling their country to Philip. Or look, if you will, to modern France—France, which in knowledge stands *next* to England, and lacks nothing but virtue to steady and direct it. But, wanting this ballast, it is the abundance of her sails which is ever threatening to swamp her. Was it not her *philosophers* who brought on the first revolution; and what was the "Reign of Terror," but the monster progeny of this unnatural wedlock of learning and wickedness?

We ask you then to enlighten our country, but we ask you still more to make her virtuous—to give her that knowledge which is power, but to give her also a conscience to guide it withal—to endow her with a "giant's strength" if you can, but also with such principles that she will not "use it like a giant." Is it by mere *education* you can do this? You propose to elevate Ireland—what, then, is the task before you? To give honesty to thieves, and truth to liars, and diligence to idlers, and energy to all—to banish perjury from our courts, robbery from our dwellings, and murder from our highways—to extinguish the fires of discontent, lay the demon of rebellion and set up the reign of peace—and thus to empty our jails and poorhouses, disband our soldiers and police, and bring back to our shores the tides of prosperity! And are you serious in proposing to do this by an alphabet and spelling-books? Can you thus think to transform the schoolmaster's rod into an enchanter's wand? No; we want knowledge, it is true, but we want *virtue more;* and till we get this, even your boasted knowledge can confer but half its benefits. Without this, you may enlarge your jails, they will continue to fill them; and multiply your police, they will elude or defy them; and increase your tribunals, they will outswear or outface them; and enact new laws, they will break or evade them. Their chief disease is in the *heart.* It is vain to confine your treatment to the *head.* Hence it is not literature but "righteousness which will exalt our nation,"—not the Pierian spring, but the "fountain of living waters," that can remove those corruptions which cause its decay.

But even suppose our whole reasoning false, and that *schools* could do more than their fondest admirers ever fancied in their dreams, *can* you educate Ireland so long as Rome reigns over it? Will a church whose empire is darkness thus give you peaceable possession of one of her best-guarded provinces—a church whose history is light read backwards—which, wherever it has the power, either arrests all knowledge or perverts it to her own worst purposes; and which has been lately teaching the most obtuse amongst ourselves, that the real fault of our colleges is not their "godlessness," but their existence, and that all her struggles for liberty to teach in her *own* way, mean liberty not to teach at all? It is the veriest folly, then, to talk even of *educating* the Irish Papist, unless you can destroy Irish Popery; of illumining Ireland unless you dissipate the Lethean fog with which *it* has enveloped her; or of enlightening her people while immured in the vast cavern of Popery,—with sentinel priests so blocking up its mouth as to hinder either the escape of a prisoner or the entrance of a ray?

THE INDUSTRIAL.—Industrial training is fast becoming the favorite remedy. The rush of our empirics has of late been from the parliament to the plough; and even from the school-book to the sewed muslin manufacture. Addressing our people thus, they say,—You are the cause of your own miseries, your existence is artificial, and your lives are a fiction—your tradesmen's sons are *gentlemen*, and your farmers' daughters *ladies*;—there must be an end to this: your young gentlemen must doff the sporting jacket, and don the farmer's frieze, and turn aside from their hounds to follow the plough; your young ladies must lay down their embroidery and take up the keys, and transfer themselves with all speed from the parlor to the kitchen. In short, you must alter your entire mode of life—you must go down into the bowels of the earth, and bring up its minerals—spread yourselves over your bogs, and form peat companies—go out upon the seas, and catch the cod and herrings—build ships, and circumnavigate the globe;—in a word, turn Ireland into a workshop as we have turned Britain, and *then* your country's millennium shall have dawned! Here is their proposal; and to show that they are no visionaries, they would have schools in every parish for agriculture, industry, and trades of all kinds; aided, of course, by adequate grants, and superintended by competent managers.

An exquisite dream this!—we have dreamed it ourselves. Yet we do not mean that it is all a dream. Doubtless by enormous cost, prodigious trouble, and ceaseless care, much could in this way be done for Ireland; and we therefore rejoice in every such movement. We are thankful to those who would dress one ulcer of our diseased country, even though they leave untouched the Malady which has caused it. But, alas! such external applications can give little relief. And while you are healing one eruption, the rankling disease within is throwing out others around it. We are so far agreed, that if you would reclaim Ireland, you must first reclaim the Irish; that if you would develop the country's resources, you must develop the people's energies;—and that any scheme which aims not at this, inverts the order of things, and begins at the wrong end. But you make no provision in your plan for what we have proved to be Ireland's *chief* want. You have given her the head and the hands, it is true, but you have not given her the *heart* and *conscience*. Her people want honesty, energy, steadiness, perseverance. Is it by lessons on embroidery and farming you propose to implant these principles? Yet WITHOUT them, of what ultimate avail is anything you can do? You may build factories—perhaps your own workmen will burn them; and establish trades—your own journeymen may *combine* against you; and make what improvements you may—it is too likely your clerks will deceive you, your customers rob you, your servants take advantage of you whenever they can: and after years of the most anxious toil, you will too probably find that your best plans have been frustrated, and your money put into a "bag with holes," and be compelled to retire in disgust from the scene! You think this too gloomy a prediction? Alas! it is not prophecy at all—it is well-known *history*. What else has been the fate of most of the philanthropic schemes of which Ireland has already been the scene? Who does not know that in our *present* state, the best men come here only to peril their fortunes, and their most generous efforts are often turned into evils? Those who give are forgotten—those who lend are *not always* repaid—those who trust are imposed on—and those who confide their capital to Irish hands, often find it squandered in rash speculation or fraudulent jobs. And why?—because Popery and prosperity are elements as incompatible as fire and water. For apart altogether from the *direct* intermeddling of the priest, whose favor you cannot *expect* but at the price of truckling subserviency, and whose endless annoyances you cannot *prevent*, so long as the people you operate on are his slaves, and know of no other criminality but that of displeasing him—apart, we say, from this altogether, you will find yourselves in the midst of a *deluge of depravity*, contending against the most hopeless odds; and even when you think you have found some standing ground, it will most probably turn out to be a shaking bog or a trembling quicksand.

We say, then, to our industrial economists, *your* scheme, too, is radically defective. You may *teach* the people industry, will they *practise* it? You may invoke its spirit, will it come at your call? You may bring railways to every town, and canals through every parish, and reclaim our bogs, and deepen our rivers, and drain our whole country to its mountain tops, will this implant those great moral principles on which the value and permanence of all such improvements depend? You have given the machinery, it is true, but where is the moving power? And you have your choice either to continue working it yourselves, or see it stop and go to ruin as soon as you withdraw. And at the very utmost you can only by such means make Ireland like one of your large Asylums, with its grounds beautifully laid out, and its inmates working here and there; but all superintended by other hands, and supported by general charity. No; Ireland wants something that mere industry cannot supply, ay, and without which it cannot *exist*. We are thankful for your well-meant exertions, but they can only palliate, they cannot cure. And oh! how often have we looked with sorrowful interest on those schemes of mere worldly benevolence which are now going forward here and there through our country, and mourned to think that, for want of that MORAL element which alone can give them permanence, they must sooner or later come to naught! And we have been reminded the while of the child's frail embankments on the sandy shore, which are doomed to vanish before the flowing tide!

THE SCRIPTURAL.—It is truly mournful to be obliged to prove that *God's* remedy for Ireland is the best:—in this *nineteenth century*, the brightest era of the gospel's triumphs—and in this *United Kingdom*, the richest storehouse of its trophies—to have to go over the argument anew, as if Paul were only setting out on his first journey. Nor can we imagine a more humiliating fact, than that Britain owns not a few statesmen, and *philanthropists*, too, who, while they call themselves Christians, seem to think a people's religion has as little to do with their prosperity as the color of their hair; nay, who speak of the gospel as though it were some superior kind of superstition, fitted for weak but not for manly minds, or at best some mystic thing designed for the dying rather than for the living, and suited to the cloister, but unfitted for the world; and who even smile at the "bigot" who would assert that God knows best what "exalts a nation," and retail with baptized lips those sneers at the "foolishness of preaching," which used to be confined to heathen cynics!

At a late meeting of poor-law guardians in Connaught, a Roman Catholic member of the board boldly declared his belief—of course, amid cries of "order" from the priests and their minions—that the Bible was the secret of Ulster's prosperity, and that nothing else would elevate the other provinces. What an affecting circumstance! Was the poor man led to make this remark by some such instinct as guides other creatures to select the aliment which suits them best; or merely by the feeling which prompts the blind man wishfully to turn his dark eyeballs to the sun when he hears all nature around him rejoicing in his morning beams?

We have already demonstrated that to nothing else than the Bible can Ulster owe its vast superiority. The subjoined tables show that nearly five sixths of all Ireland's Bible and Sunday-school instruction are confined to that single province.* According, therefore, to those priestly blasphemers who pronounce the Bible the "gospel of the devil,"† Connaught should be a paradise and Ulster a pandemonium; and what must be the effrontery, to say nothing of the wickedness, of the men who, though perfectly aware that the *reverse* is nearer the truth, rave on against this volume as they have never raved against "The Age of Reason?" We are told, it is true, with an air of triumph, that many Protestants are as bad as Roman Catholics. We admit the fact,

* SUNDAY-SCHOOL SOCIETY FOR IRELAND, 1851.

Provinces.	Number of schools.	Number of scholars.	Number of gratuitous teachers.
Ulster,	1931	164635	14151
Leinster,	457	32314	3006
Munster,	400	17160	1774
Connaught,	216	12403	822

HIBERNIAN BIBLE SOCIETY, 1851.
Bibles, Testaments, and Portions.

	Sales.	Grants.	Total.
Ulster,	1424	15408	16832
Leinster,	224	2911	3135
Munster,	160	930	1090
Connaught,	186	3667	3853

† Encyclical Letter of Leo XII., 1824.

but are they *Bible-loving* Protestants? This is the point, for Rome's quarrel is with the Bible, and "THE BIBLE IS THE RELIGION OF PROTESTANTS." If these godless Protestants are Bible *readers*, and our godly ones Bible *haters*, then will we admit the force of the objection; for the grand point in dispute is, Does the free circulation of the Scriptures do good or harm? But if, as is *perfectly notorious*, our godless Protestants are as innocent of the crime of Bible reading as any priest could wish them; if their religion is that mere formalism which is *essential Popery* beneath whatever name; if the virtue of every person is just as his love to the Bible; and finally, if that parish is always the most virtuous which has been longest blessed with a Bible-loving ministry, and that always the least so which has been longest cursed with Bible-neglecting hirelings;—then is this objection the *strongest corroboration of our whole argument.* For it proves that such godlessness is owing, not to the Bible, but to the *want* of it, and therefore not to the presence but to the absence of TRUE Protestantism. And it effectually confirms our position, that where Popery is most intense there is the deepest degradation, and where Protestantism is most pure there is the highest elevation; and, therefore, that when Papists are bad, it is *because* of their system, and when Protestants are bad, it is in *spite* of *theirs.* We will now add, that the godless Protestantism which is complained of is owing much to the corrupting atmosphere of Popery, and the "virtuous Popery" which is gloried in, to the antiseptic power of Protestantism; for is it not notorious that our worst Protestants are generally found in the most Popish districts, and our best Roman Catholics in the most Protestant? What different things are the Roman Catholics, ay, and the Protestants, too, of Ulster and of Connaught respectively! For in the one province grows a moral upas-tree, and even Protestants suffer by its deadly emanations; in the other grows the tree of life, and even Roman Catholics, who will not taste *its* fruit, are the better for dwelling beneath its shade. Here is the solution, and there can be no other. You have in our country two atmospheres, a pestilent and a pure one, generated by the Breviary and the Bible respectively, and commingled in different proportions in our various provinces. The *pestilent* predominates as you go south and west, and the *pure* as you come north; and the moral health of *all* denominations is affected in exact proportion to the quantity they breathe of each.

Yet ignorant depravity asks to this hour, What has the Bible to do with Ireland's elevation? How can any man read it, and doubt that the only thing necessary to make the whole earth a paradise is just to follow its instructions? How could men, for example, obey the golden rule, and "do to others as they would have others do to them;" or the two great commandments, and "love God supremely, and their neighbors as themselves," without bringing back the innocence of Eden? Will any man hazard his character for sanity by venturing to deny this? Why, our most florid conceptions of the change which would follow the universal reign of such principles, are meagreness itself. Is it not perfectly obvious, that beneath their sway every demon of vice and crime must fly back to the pit whence he came; and that in the atmosphere they would create, man would attain his loftiest moral stature, his stunted mind its largest growth, his shrivelled heart its divinest expansion, and therefore his earthly habitation its highest pitch of improvement? Yet the Bible has nothing to do with a nation's greatness!! Had it ever once *failed* to elevate, or had mere worldly expedients ever *succeeded* without it, then might there be some excuse for this stolid skepticism. But what have the best schemes of *mere* philosophy, philanthropy, or political economy ever yet done to stay the crimes or tears of mankind? Why, human wickedness has laughed to scorn, and human woe has only been mocked by such paltry expedients. While men have been wrangling about their *measures*, whose only good provisions, if any such they contained, were borrowed or pilfered from the Bible, that book has in reality been maintaining the chief struggle with the world's corruptions, and diffusing those principles which, just as they prevail, supersede the necessity of laws, and without which mere statutes could no more control the agents of crime, than fetters and chains would bind the demoniac!

We make our proud appeal to facts. A few illiterate fishermen go forth from the banks of Jordan on an errand so seemingly wild, that men knew not whether most to pity their "insanity," or punish their "presumption." Yet somehow, by their story of "one Jesus," the most colossal fabrics of idolatry were strewn in fragments, the thrones of monarchs trembled, and the world was revolutionized!

A solitary monk once disentombed a Bible from the sepulchre to which Rome had so long consigned it; and, as at the resurrection of its divine Author, its "keepers became as dead men;" the "Triple Tyrant" trembled on the banks of the distant Tiber; his mighty fabric of superstition was cracked and riven as though struck by the bolts which shattered Babel; and Europe looked out as from a new creation! Or look, ye moral reformers, to that uproarious village, remarkable for nothing but its vice and misery! You have exhausted your nostrums on it, and how much have you done? Stand aside, then, and make way for that unlettered itinerant, whom some call an enthusiast, and others a fanatic,—a man who knows no language but his own, nor scheme of reform but that of salvation, in whom the love of Christ and souls supplies the learning of Greece and Rome, and England too! Observe how *he* goes to work, for it is worth your notice. His sole weapon, a Bible; his chief agency, schools and prayer-meetings; his church, a barn; his auditors, rude villagers; perhaps his only orders, "the love of Christ constraineth me;" and his manner, possibly such as to shock the slave of frigid canonical decorum. Yet that man in time transforms that village!—the tavern is exchanged for the house of God, the bacchanal song for the evening hymn; and should you pass through its quiet streets, as the summer evening sunbeams linger on the neighboring hills, you could scarce help exclaiming, What enchanter has been here? Do you still hesitate to believe that the Bible did all this, and give most of the glory to your civilized institutions? Then behold that band of missionaries ploughing their trackless way to some distant cannibal island, and see how in time one and another of those wild savages, whom nothing else could tame, undergoes the most complete transformation! But why need we proceed? What has any land ever been but a field of blood and crime till the Bible has dispelled the sulphurous clouds with which hell had shrouded it, roused its people from the Lethean slumbers in which Satan had bound them, cleared its moral soil of a thousand poisonous weeds, and sowed instead the seeds of numberless improvements? And hence, where but in Bible lands will you find arts flourishing in fullest bloom, science shedding its purest rays, or benevolence dispensing its divinest blessings? Or what else has made Britain the queen of nations, and the theatre of wonders, with her thousand trees of life and liberty waving in the breeze and spreading to the sun? Yes, compared with the Bible as a mere *civilizer*, how contemptible the best schemes of statesmanship! for they can only repress the crimes which it eradicates, and punish the atrocities it wholly prevents. And whát proves its *marvellous* power is, that even where it does not convert, it at least moralizes and restrains; where it does not give life to the dead mass, it at least retards its putrefaction; where it does not clothe the moral waste with verdure, it at least warms its atmosphere, and lessens its dreariness;—insomuch that each sanctuary it rears has ever proved like the light-house on the ocean's verge, which not only gives light to its own attendants, but sends its struggling rays far out over the gloomy wave!

Such is the FACT; and here we might rest and leave our *Christian* philosophers to sneer on in their pitiable blindness at God's glorious plan "for the healing of the nations." But we shall now meet them on their own ground, and demonstrate the matchless wisdom and power of the gospel as an engine of social elevation; and prove that before it all other remedies for Ireland, or any other land, must hide their diminished heads in despicable insignificance, and fade as the stars before the rising sun; and that in reality it were as rational to commence a new search for the philosopher's stone, or the elixir of life, as to expect any other cure for our country's maladies.

CHAPTER II.

THE MEDICINE—THE GRAND SPECIFIC.

DOUBTLESS one cause of the unbelief above referred to is, that men do not see the *reasons* of the Cross, or never think it *has* reasons; but deem it some sort of magical thing which saves because God has *appointed* it to save, but in which there is no more connection between the disease and the remedy, than between the Rod and the Red Sea. What amazing ignorance! to suppose that God, whose matchless *contrivances* and *adaptations* pervade everything else, excludes them here, where they are most perfect! Dear reader, it is impossible, in a few brief pages, to give full drawings of a plan so glorious—to conduct you through all the chambers of a structure so magnificent. We can only introduce you to the porch of this glorious temple, give you a mere glimpse of the interior, and then leave you to pursue your discoveries for yourself. Be good enough, then, to refer to our first principles, in page 109; and as we have found how Popery sets them all at defiance, let us now see how perfectly the gospel embodies and develops them. We have found that love to God and our neighbor is the sum of the decalogue, and therefore of all virtue. We shall now briefly prove that *every form of personal and social happiness springs from this twofold com-*

mand, just as branches issue from their stem,—that on this simple and glorious pedestal, the moral universe stands, and that it CAN rest upon no other.

THE PHILOSOPHY.—I. Love to God and each other is the *sure* source, and the *only* one of endlessly increasing virtue and happiness amongst ALL rational creatures. There are but two kinds of government under which God *could* have placed the universe—the reign of fear and the reign of love, and it is only the *latter* which can secure these results.

1. Love alone can secure *virtue*—and it does so most perfectly. What without it may be done from a cold sense of duty, and is therefore some day but too likely to be neglected, we are in no danger of overlooking, so long as love strongly impels us. Could I wrong a beloved brother, or disobey a parent dear as my own soul? Therefore, if God would have every *duty* to himself and to our neighbor observed, he has only to inspire *love* to himself and our neighbor,—*and it is done.*

2. Love alone can secure *happiness*—and it does so most perfectly. What even in this cold world is our source of purest enjoyment? Is it the acquisition of earth's richest spoils, or the bliss of loving and being loved—our " house full of silver and gold," or full of domestic affection—our hearts throbbing to the voice even of flattering fame, or the far sweeter tones of one too fond and faithful to flatter? So freely does the heart resign itself to the potent spell

of this delightful affection, that not only have poets sung, and even sages felt its charms, but the deepest depravity seems scarce able wholly to dispel them; and men have smiled over their infant's cradle, and wept over their mother's grave, long after they have ceased to weep or smile over any other spot on earth. Therefore, if God would make his universe *happy*, He has only to fill it with *love,—and it is done.*

3. Love alone provides for the *endless increase* of virtue and happiness, and it does so most perfectly. Mark, first, the necessary effect of love to God. That blessed Being centres in himself infinitely more goodness than is distributed to all his creatures. It is therefore most obvious, that the more they know and experience his goodness, the more they must *love* Him, and the more must their *virtue* and *happiness increase*, of course. Observe, next, the effect of love to each other; it would naturally exhibit itself in a thousand acts of *mutual* kindness—these, *reciprocated*, would call forth renewed acts of affection, until it would become a conflict with all which could do the other most good. Now, you have only to imagine myriads of creatures the subjects of such constant and increasing love, and employed in all those schemes of amelioration, which, as their endlessly growing knowledge would *enable*, so their endlessly growing love would *prompt* them to devise; and you have at once set agoing a train of influences which in their manifold forms and combinations MUST produce an amount of bliss and advancement

which baffles all conception. Such, then, is the glorious platform on which God has reared his universe. And such was man's condition before the fall. His soul the seat of angelic love, was the seat also of angelic virtue and happiness, and contained *the germ of angelic improvement.*

II. Love to God and each other is *peculiarly* necessary to the virtue and happiness of the HUMAN race. We have *hearts*—and to be happy, must love some object. We have *minds*—and that object must be capable of engaging them. We are *spirits*, and *immortal*—that object must therefore be immortal and spiritual. Our minds and hearts are formed for *endless growth*—that object must be capable of satisfying these endlessly increasing demands upon it. While it must be able to supply all our *wants*, as well as suit all our capacities. We are weak—it must be able to impart strength; and changing—it must never change; in short, it must be an object independent of all vicissitudes, and adapted to all times, places, and circumstances. Finally, as we are many, dwelling together, and required to love each other, it must be such an object that each can have enough without diminishing the supplies of the rest, else you introduce a fatal element of discord amongst us: and if, instead of thus endangering, you would ensure our mutual concord, it must be such an object, that in giving of it enriches even the giver himself. Now, all these requisites are found in GOD ALONE. He is a spirit—

immortal, immutable, almighty, all-wise, containing in himself such boundless excellence as must enrapture the mind and rivet the heart, no matter how inconceivably expanded they may become. And our possessions of love to Him—that truest wealth, instead of diminishing, increase the stores of others. We have only to tell them of His goodness in order to increase their love, and by a blessed reaction to increase our own!

III. The violation of this law of love must CONSEQUENTLY entail on the human race *endlessly increasing sin and misery.* Alas! man has made the fearful experiment, and what have been the results? Formed to find happiness only in God, we have, by transferring our affections to earthly objects, crossed the laws of our being at a thousand points; and the *necessary* consequence has been INDIVIDUAL misery and SOCIAL disorder. Being spirits, no amount of earthly things can satisfy us. With minds and hearts craving after endless expansion, these cravings are disappointed, and we are thrown back upon ourselves. And setting our affections on objects, which even, if otherwise satisfying, change and decay, we ensure our wretchedness beyond the possibility of escape. Our laurels wither on our brow—our friends die in our embrace—our sweetest pleasures pall the soonest—our costliest treasures are often the first to perish; and as a fit conclusion to a conflict so unequal with the laws of God and of our own being, at length comes death to strip us of whatever may have yet escaped the wreck of changing life. Then the inordinate love of such objects ensures *social* disorder; for the more wealth and power one enjoys, the less remains for others. There could scarce be a dozen of Napoleons, nor a hundred Rothschilds on earth; and even if there could, the dozen would enslave, and the hundred would beggar the world. Now, does not this shed a sunbeam of light on the cause of every nation's miseries? It is just the inordinate love of such objects as riches, honors, and pleasures, with the violence and wrong it produces, which has drenched the world with tears and blood. And you have only to recollect that this is the exact condition of our wretched country, to explain in an instant its crimes and miseries.

IV. It follows *unavoidably* from the foregoing propositions, that THE ONLY POSSIBLE WAY *effectually* to restore virtue and happiness to any country, is therein to restore love to its ancient sway. Now, this is simply *the object of the glorious gospel.* We have demonstrated that the law of love *must* secure individual and social virtue, happiness, and prosperity; and that its violation *must* entail equally extensive crime, misery, and desolation. It follows, therefore, that until *it* is restored to the hearts of men, these evils MUST continue; and all the efforts of statesmen and philanthropists can *without* this,

> But "skin and film the ulcerous part,
> While rank corruption, mining all within,
> Infects unseen."

Now, it is this restoration which the gospel effects, and HENCE ITS MATCHLESS POWER AS A REMEDY FOR NATIONAL MALADIES. But in order to this restoration, two things are indispensable.

1. God's laws being infinitely perfect, their violation must be an infinite *crime*, and therefore demanding an infinite *punishment*. Of course, for God to let such crime pass unpunished, were not only to invite rebellion and overturn his throne, but to forfeit all claim to the character of justice and truth. Not even an earthly sovereign could permit his laws to be trampled on without bringing contempt on himself and anarchy on the country; and for God to do so, were to destroy his character, and with it the *confidence*, and therefore the *love*, and hence the *virtue* and *happiness* of his entire creation. So that the pardon of the rebellious part of his dominions (perhaps a very small part), could only be effected by destroying the whole and blasting his own perfections. But how could a sinner bear such a punishment? It is clearly impossible. God must provide some one who can bear it, or we are UNDONE.* Indeed, so utterly unable are we to make any reparation for our sins, that if God could accept one hour's obedience as atonement for a whole life's disobedience, we have it not to give—not only because our supreme love to God being due every hour upon its own account, one hour's intermission of it can

* Acts iv. 12; Rom. iii. 23-28; Gal. iii. 10-14.

never be overtaken, but because no mere sinner loves God at all even *for a single moment.**

2. Suppose such an atonement made, then our hearts must by some divine agency be restored to the dominion of that law of love in which virtue and happiness alone are found. *Without* this, even AN ATONEMENT would be VAIN. While our hearts are placed on earthly things, mere *pardon* could not make us either virtuous or happy. But let heavenly affections only displace the earthly—let the heart, from being torn with restless passions, become the serene seat of ethereal purity and angelic love, and you SOW ONCE MORE the seeds of endlessly increasing *individual* and *social* virtue, happiness, and improvement.

Now, is it not self-evident, that did the above principle of love universally prevail, the earth would return to its Eden innocence, and therefore resume its Eden loveliness?—and that the degree in which it does prevail in any country, must *indicate* the degree of that country's happiness and prosperity? It MUST be so, if we can trust our reason. It IS so, if we can trust our experience. For thousands can testify that this love to God and man is no mere dream of enthusiasm; and millions who think so still must own, that to *such* enthusiasm the world owes its best blessings. To be plain—this is CHRISTIANITY if the Bible is true, and *must* be if God is perfect. That blessed religion tells us, that love is

* Rom. viii. 7; James iv. 4.

the grand law of the moral universe, whose obedience secures perfect virtue and happiness; that man has violated this law, and hence the crimes and miseries which desolate his abode; and that the grand object of the gospel is to restore in his heart the dominion of this law as the ONLY way to restore virtue and happiness. That in order to this, the blessed Saviour died to atone *for* his sins,* and the Divine Spirit is sent to turn him *from* his sins;† and that through the work of *both*, and that alone, we are delivered from sin's *punishment* and *power*,‡ if we only *repent* and *believe* on Jesus;§ and that by this divine agency that *great inward change* commences, which, just as it goes on, restores more perfectly the sway of that law of love, whose observance or breach insures all good or evil.

Such, then, is a very meagre sketch of this matchless plan, and O that we had space left to show the equal wisdom of the mode of its application!—to show that in all respects there is as perfect an adaptation between the cross of Jesus and the heart of man, as between the light of heaven and the eye it enters. But we have only time to state the fact. Like some medicine which is so compounded as to act on every organ at once, He who has made the heart of man has made his blessed gospel to touch every chord of it, wake an echo through every cham-

* Rom. iii. 24; iv. 25. † John iii. 5; 1 Thess. v. 23.
‡ Eph. ii. 8, 9; Titus iii. 5, 6.
§ Mark i. 15; Acts iii. 19; xxii. 31.

ber of it, grasp every power and rouse every feeling of it;—and this so universally, that Chalmers in Scotland, and Walker in England, and the Moravians in Greenland, all declare that whereas other schemes of amelioration they tried but in vain, they no sooner preached salvation to the sinner through Jesus' blood, than *this* waked emotions which had slept till then, and one and another was melted and changed. And this has been the experience of *all* Christian men—that the gospel is the true and only catholicon; that as the magnet attracts every particle of iron, however different its shape, or size, or place of concealment, so is there a something in Jesus which, when he is lifted up, draws all men unto him; and that as the breeze of heaven wakes the melody of a thousand Eolian harps, how different soever their form and tone, whose music sleeps until swept by it, so the story of Christ's amazing love wakes, in breasts of the most diverse characters, responses which nothing else could stir!

And thus appears clear as heaven's sunshine the secret of the gospel's amazing power on the nations. Love is just to the moral universe what Attraction is to the material; and were that great law suspended which preserves the planets in their orbits, it were not more absurd to propose to remedy the consequent disorder without restoring *its* dominion, than to talk of re-establishing true happiness on earth without restoring the love which alone can produce it. Now, is it not surprising that in days when such homage is done to *physical* science there should be such forgetfulness of *moral* science; that men who can eloquently describe how the mote in the sunbeam is governed in its wanderings by unchanging *laws*, seem as if they thought the immortal spirit subject to no laws whatever; and that while in obedience to the *former* men plough the ocean, rear the engine, and make the elements their ministering servants, they act as though the *latter* could be disregarded with perfect impunity! Propose to endow the Ptolemaic system of astronomy, because 80,000,000 of our heathen fellow-subjects believe it; and the idea would be pronounced insane, and the man who would entertain it fit only for a bedlam, for thus attempting to turn back the world on its onward march. But a *Ptolemaic* system of religion prevails amongst us, yet *it* is smiled on and pensioned; its disasters begin to be felt, and, by way of cure, the smiles are multiplied and the pension is increased; tens of thousands are voted to a college to teach it, and then hundreds of thousands for a force to keep down the evils it creates; and thus the ruin goes on, till the country's dissolution draws nigh, and statesmen are at their wit's end; and *all* because, despite every warning, they *will* continue to set at defiance eternal laws, as fixed and immutable as those which guide the stars in their courses. Nay, some of them will tell you that a country's religion is its merest accident, and not worth a statesman's thoughts, unless when it becomes necessary to humor the people's *prejudices!* And hence the ignorant cant to which we are so often doomed to listen, which pronounces it true liberality to regard all religions alike, and weak-minded bigotry to recommend heaven's own statute-book as Ireland's remedy! Bigotry, forsooth! to say that those laws by which the universe is governed should form the basis of earthly legislation! And enlightenment, forsooth! to scout those eternal principles with which even the supreme Governor could not dispense without turning his fair dominions into chaos!

THE FRUITS.—Such is the *philosophy* of the glorious gospel, and we can now only take a mere glimpse of its *fruits.* And, for the sake of more perfect conclusiveness, we shall follow the order observed while tracing the baleful influence of Popery,—and show the benign effects of the gospel in awakening the *mind*, purifying the *conscience*, warming the *heart*, elevating the *whole nature*, and so blessing for *time*, and fitting for *eternity.*

1. *The gospel awakens the mind.*—If superstition, its *un*healthy state, paralyzes it, true religion, its healthy state, must proportionally invigorate it. Besides, the *Christian's* mind is constantly exercised on themes inconceivably grand, and above all others calculated to promote its growth and vitality. Hence his usually intelligent countenance, so remarkably contrasting with the superstitious devotee's contracted brow. Who can daily study a

book which contains all that most concerns the Creator and creation, and is the very synopsis of the laws and principles of the universe, without finding in it the most nourishing food and powerful stimulus to the mind? Talk of your philosophy in comparison! Your men of science dabble in the streamlets of knowledge,—this leads you to the great Fountainhead. Now, only contrast the mere effect on the immortal mind during a long lifetime of such ambrosial food, with that of the senseless trash of Popish legends; and if even the insect takes the hue of the leaf it feeds on, what must be the influence of such mental diet on the Protestant and the Papist respectively? Just what you see in Ireland. If the mind of the Clare peasant had been nourished on the Bible, would he have fled in terror at the priest's threat to turn him "into a goose or a turkey-cock?" and were *it* universally read amongst us, where would be our holy wells, and the thousand other schemes of priestcraft to filch the cash from the pocket of credulity? The effect would be just the reverse of what we have found that of Popery to be. The Papist's mind *mesmerized*, and the Protestant's *stimulated* at the altar on the Sabbath, each feels the effect throughout the week. The one *paralyzed* and the other *quickened*, in reference to their *eternal* concerns, you see the respective influences on all their *temporal*. In the one case, the whole process cramps and deadens; in the other, it quickens and expands.

And this at once explains how art, and science, and every improvement are as common in gospel lands as they are rare in Popish. Nor must we forget the enormous contributions which the Bible has *directly* given to learning and philosophy. For how many of the worshippers of science have adorned their idol with laurels stolen from it; how many of our poets have gathered their richest gems in its mines; how many of our infidels have taken their only good thoughts from its pages; and thus resembled the pirate who would rob the ship of her treasures, and then try to scuttle and sink her! And hence it was that the immortal Newton could step from the study of the stars to that of his Bible, and feel no change except from high to higher pursuits.

2. *The gospel purifies the conscience.*—Yes; and it *alone* can do so. If vice could have ever been charmed out of its propensities by the magic spell of eloquence, or crime arrested by the lightning of genius, or the sinner induced by witching persuasion to go and sin no more, it would surely have been by the enchanting powers of the illustrious Chalmers. Yet, as we have found, even he could not *moralize* until he had first *evangelized*. And is there any miracle in this? How can that man wrong his neighbor who *ever* sees the eye of God above him, and a yawning hell beneath him; who knows that every sin deserves eternal wrath, and is impelled to every duty by all the sanctions which can be drawn from time and eternity? Is it not perfectly obvious,

that beneath the sway of *such* a religion no treachery could wear the mask of friendship, nor heartless stoicism personate humanity, nor midnight assassin lurk behind the hedge, nor villain escape under forms of law? Is it not manifest, that beneath its breath party influence must expire, that before its glance corruption must flee appalled, that at its voice neglected worth would emerge from the shade, and merit become the only road to honor, and that under its sway "nothing would be found to hurt or destroy?" Oh! did such a religion only sit by the monarch on his throne, and the merchant at his desk, and become the presiding genius of every family, the companion of every closet, and the inmate of every heart, how soon would the earth look out from her mantle of woe, with her pristine smile of paradisaic joy! In view of a system so divine, the prophet's most glowing pictures of the millennium are stripped of their poetry and transformed into sober prose. If it only prevailed in Ireland, where would be her crime and criminals? Yet men, who have tried all other remedies upon her, and only to have their failure recorded in the already copious records of their blundering and shame, will scarce listen gravely when we suggest this divine specific for her maladies, but will pension and smile on that *antagonist* system which has ruined her!

3. *The gospel gives a heart;* and here is its chief glory. Before its benign smiles, chains and fetters, racks and thumbscrews vanish. It has penetrated

the criminal's cell, relaxed his chains and washed his stripes; it has reared its asylums, and filled them with the poor and the maimed, the halt and the blind; it has rolled the tides of eloquence on behalf of distress, until the heart of stoicism has melted, the hand of avarice has relaxed, luxury has dealt its bread to the hungry, and vanity cast its jewels to the poor. See that good Samaritan pouring oil into the stranger's wounds, that amiable Dorcas clothing some beggar-boy, that angel of mercy in human form standing by the dying bed! See that retreat for the destitute, that infirmary for the dying, that refuge for the fallen, that hospital for orphan childhood, that almshouse for infirm old age, and far above all, that divine array of institutions for causing the waters of life to circulate over the world! Say ye these are the fruits of civilization? Deny ye the glory to the despised Nazarene? Then look to your favorite Greece and Rome! Do our bards surpass their poets, our builders their architects, our sculptors their Phidiases, our orators their Ciceros? They have left behind them monuments of pride and cruelty in abundance; where are their monuments of mercy and love? Pass through Imperial Rome at the zenith of her power; or survey at this instant her ruins of proud magnificence, glowing in the splendors of an Italian sunset. You gaze on that amphitheatre of monumental wonders—the Capitol—the Pantheon—the Portico—the Forum—the Arch of Titus—the Coliseum, where men were butchered for amusement. And is there amongst them all not one monument of mercy?—no hospital for the sick—no asylum for the helpless—no school for the poor? No, NOT ONE! And it would be difficult to find in their purest classic writers a word answering to our idea of *infirmary;* they never possessed the institution, and did not want the name!

4. *The gospel elevates the whole nature.*—Indeed, Christianity cannot but make great and noble characters. Infusing the loftiest principles of virtue, and enforcing these by motives drawn from the *skies*, it inspires the Christian with that heroism which others too often simulate, and gives the substance while they have but the shadow. With him, Divine principle takes the place of the hectic stimulants of earthly honor and applause. Being "God's offspring," he is of course "a partaker of the Divine nature," and as such is incapable of grovelling meanness. The man who communes with the skies, can *he* lick the dust in crouching servility?—or the man who fears his God, is *he* likely to tremble before a worm of the dust? No: such a religion *must* impart the loftiest dignity to the whole character. Hence it has numbered thousands of men, and *women* too, in the ranks of dauntless martyrdom; and given birth to a heroism far more sublime than was ever felt by mere worldly bravery;—instance Paul before Agrippa, or the wife of Welsh before James! And thus is at once explained the fact, that Protestant nations are as great and free as Popish ones are

mean and degraded. The one is subjected to a process which indefinitely elevates, and the other to a process which as indefinitely degrades; and hence the prodigious superiority in the tone of the former. There, woman is found in her true place, by the *side* of man; there, man indignantly spurns every chain which cruelty would forge, or cupidity fasten; and there alone is realized that liberty which Paganism knows only in its poetry, and Popery only in its dreams. In truth, without the gospel *real* elevation is impossible. Would you ever think of looking to other than to Bible lands for all that gives true moral dignity to man? No; while beneath its divine sway serfdom and barbarism are simple impossibilities, without it you have *virtual* degradation even amid the splendor of arts, like ancient Greece, and arms like ancient Rome, and both like imperial France.

5. *The gospel blesses man for time:*—and how simple the means by which it does so; and how well worth your study, ye statesmen and philosophers! It approaches the thief and the robber, and how does it act? Does it *philosophize* on the rights of property, &c., and by these conjure him to reform? If it did, then we own ye might *indeed* sneer. No; taking far loftier ground, it pours out the denunciations of the Almighty, and pictures the horrors of the damned, until he turns pale and stands aghast: and then telling him of a Saviour who has purchased mercy even for him, and assuring him of pardon if he will repent and believe on Him, and Divine aid to

enable him to do so if he will sincerely seek it, it conjures him to turn to God, and walk in his ways; and in thousands of cases succeeds. Now, must not such a religion perfectly annihilate the worst causes of social misery? How can that people be restless, who are thus taught "to be content;" or disloyal, who "fear God and honor the king;" or dishonest, who "render unto all their due;" or idle, who dread the sin of being "slothful in business;" or turbulent, who "follow peace with all men?" What child does not see that a parish of real Christians must be one of loyal subjects, industrious people, united families, honest masters, and faithful servants? Here is the whole secret. You begin at the wrong end when you address yourselves first to men's temporal interests:—we teach them to "seek *first* the kingdom of God and his righteousness," and this necessarily involving every subordinate object, "all other things are" of consequence "added." Securing their duty to *God*, we secure, *of course* their duty to *man;* and by this simple means of prevailing on them to seek their eternal salvation, we bind them *à fortiori* to observe all those virtues which enhance their temporal state.

Here, then, ye statesmen, is the source of true national greatness. If you would bring back the golden age, it is not by turning everything into gold, but by the nobler alchemy of the heart. If you would improve a people's social condition, improve their religious tone; and the effect of this will go out in directions of which you never thought. As the morning sun enables the shepherd to guide his flocks to pasture, but is by the same beams waking a thousand forms of life around him, so would the Sun of Righteousness enable you to guide this great nation, and at the same time shed on it a thousand blessings of which you never dreamed. Here too, ye patriots, is the true parent of *liberty.* The Saviour was one of the people; and it were impossible to half obey his precepts without banishing all despotism from the earth. Here is the true friend of *equal rights;* forbidding alike the tyranny of the sovereign and the treason of the subject. Here is the inspirer of that genuine *patriotism* to which so many only pretend, and the parent of that peace of which your "peace societies" idly dream. Attempting to take out of the hands of the Prince of peace his own proper work, these utopian visionaries lately assembled in the Crystal Palace as their temple of concord; but their schemes of peace proved as fragile as the building they met in. There "all nations" shook hands, it is true; but thence they departed, and rumors of wars immediately sprung up! Alas! they knew not the true talisman of peace, which alone can make men "beat their swords into ploughshares, and their spears into pruning-hooks." Here too is the grand source of individual wealth. True, many believers have *little;* they would have less but for believing. For no man can be a Christian without possessing those qualities, and earning that character, which *tend* to advancement. And to see this, you need only contrast the career of the followers of Paine, or Pio Nono, with that of the disciples of Jesus. And while the gospel thus leads to wealth, it not less wonderfully sustains in poverty. It is emphatically *the poor man's religion*;—and, oh! what a counterpoise he feels in its promises to all the ills that flesh is heir to! Taught to walk by faith in his heavenly father, he can maintain a placid brow amid the gathering storms of life; for he sees his Parent's love in the dark skies of adversity, as well as in the bright beams of prosperity, and hears it in the loud howlings of life's storms, alike with the gentle breathing of its zephyrs. Oh, the treble wrong of Popery! first to reduce our countrymen to misery; next to rob them of a religion so consoling; and then to inflict instead a superstition so baleful! Yet Newman says that religion has nothing to do with a nation's greatness!! Another proof that *his* religion, *according to his own confession*, lacks that "righteousness" which does and *must* "exalt it." The Sun of Righteousness cannot but bless for both worlds;—for as the light of the natural sun, his type, not only reveals the azure depths from which it came, but spreads a mantle of beauty over the earth it falls on; so does He not only reveal our relations to God, but spreads over all the mutual relations of man that moral verdure, without which society would be a waste.*

* Williams.

6. *But the gospel mainly respects a better world.*— True, it is like the majestic river, which, while urging its course to the main, clothes with verdure the countries it flows through;—but this is only its *secondary* object. True, this angel sent to bring God's people home, smooths and cheers the path they travel on; but its grand commission respects the *performance*, not the *comfort* of the journey. And it were an insult, not an honor, to view it as a mere system of police, and forget its glory as a scheme of salvation; and as absurd too as to suppose that Christ its author, because he restored the sick, came to heal men's bodies, and not to save their souls. Its grand concern is with eternity. And as our whole line of argument has already demonstrated that it, and *it alone*, can fit for heaven, additional proof is perfectly useless. Since then it is needless to address the *judgment* further on the subject, we eagerly seize the opportunity thus afforded of making our solemn appeal to the *heart*. Then, dear reader, whoever you are, bear with one remark. The subject of this work is almost too general to impress the individual conscience. Speaking of an entire nation, one is apt to get lost in the crowd; but our national connection, how brief it is! Soon must we retire from the scene, and leave our country in other hands; then how prodigious our folly, if, while concerned about *its* salvation, we should be found to have neglected our own! How is it with YOU? If heaven at all differs from earth, you would

gain nothing by being removed thither without undergoing such a change as would fit you for that difference. Hence as it is a place of HOLINESS, "*you must be born again*," and undergo the meetening process of *progressive sanctification.* Is your *grace* then *ripening* into *glory*, your path shining MORE AND MORE? It is thus you may read your destiny in your *character and life;* and this is the only infallible test. Then, by the worth of your souls we implore you to apply it. Indifference here is the worst kind of insanity. Indifference!—in a case in which enthusiasm is sobriety, and exaggeration is impossible!—the wildest fanaticism were rational in comparison, and the gloomiest skepticism not half so perilous.

Such is a mere outline of the fruits of the gospel of Christ! No wonder, indeed, that angels sung his first advent, and the earth herself will become vocal at his second. Yet "these are but a part of his ways;" and in drawing this brief sketch, we have felt like one who surveys the placid ocean from the masthead, and can but descry a few miles around, while a boundless expanse of waters stretches away undiscovered beyond. Yet this is the system of which some exclaim, "What has religion to do with national greatness?" and men who will sit at the feet of Smith or Blackstone, to learn the secret of a nation's government, will scorn to sit at the feet of Jesus! If his minister presents his great statute-book at the senate house, he is told that its sphere is the nursery or the sick chamber. If he brings it to the college, he is derisively asked, What has religion to do with learning? And if he would introduce it to the school-house, he is informed that it is too holy a book to put into the hands of children! Are the men fit to rule this great empire who do not yet know *what has made it great*; or to govern Ireland, who will not learn the lesson its northern province would teach them? Ye godless statesmen, go to Ulster, the only part of Ireland which saves your credit; and say, is it the ministers of the Crown, or those of the Cross, who deserve this credit? While the turbulent priest has been sowing the fair south thick with disorder, visit that northern congregation. Mark their intelligence, their decorum, their quietness so profound, that the thought of disturbance has never crossed them in their dreams. Where are your police, your soldiers, your magistrates? They are not there; for they are not wanted. Then, who has done all this? A *single gospel minister*. That man's voice it is which has hushed that parish to stillness. That man's hand it is which has sown it so thick with industry, that no beggar is seen there; with light, that superstition is unknown there; and with peace, that were an agitator to come there, the only breach of the peace at all likely to ensue would be one committed on himself; and his secret is—THE GLORIOUS GOSPEL. Or, if you are yet so obtuse as not to learn this lesson from Ulster, then cross the channel, and say, what has subdued the rugged Scot, once as wild as his mountains, and spread peace and gladness over all his borders? What else but the everlasting gospel? And if you will not receive this at our humble lips, surely you will hearken to Scotland's own deathless orator—Chalmers—when he tells you that, but for this, "the ferocity of their ancestors would have come down, unsoftened and unsubdued, to the existing generation. The darkening spirit of hostility would still have lowered upon us from the north; and these plains, now so peaceful and so happy, would have lain open to the fury of merciless invaders. Oh, ye soft and sentimental travellers, who wander so securely over this romantic land, you are right to choose the season when the angry elements of nature are asleep! But what is it that has charmed to their long repose the more dreadful elements of human passion and human injustice? What is it that has quelled the boisterous spirit of her natives?—and while her torrents roar as fiercely, and her mountain brows look as grim as ever, what is that which has thrown so softening an influence over the minds and manners of her living population?" "What would they have been at this moment, had schools, and Bibles, and ministers been kept back from them?"

CHAPTER III.

TREATMENT—INFORMATION.

We have thus got distinctly before us the CURSE and the CURE—the poison and the medicine. And the question remains, What are the best means of removing the one and dispensing the other? Our first obvious duty is to inform the public as to what *is* the curse and the cure. Rome has long flourished on Protestant ignorance. In these happy realms, we see but the skirts of her foul garments; hence that good old horror of Popery which our godly fathers felt, has grown unpopular; and there has sprung up a class of Protestants who, while revelling in the blessings those fathers wrung from her with their blood, denounce them as narrow-minded bigots;—men whose own creed is their condemnation—who betray the principles they profess to uphold—who are the inquiring Romanist's worst stumbling-block, and furnish Rome with her best argument—who even presume to read us lectures on Christian *charity*—and whom we are chiefly to thank for the vast growth of Popish power amongst us, and that suicidal pro-Popery legislation, under which the kingdom begins to reel. Some *good* men, too, have followed their example; and forgetting that Rome is a "beast," they have thought, in their ignorance, to coax and conciliate her, and discountenance, as *improper*, those terms which God himself applies to her. "The Man of Sin" is, in their parlance, the sovereign pontiff, and the "Mystery of Iniquity," the Catholic Church; "Popery," is Catholicism, and the "priests," the Catholic clergy! By this course, they have thought to conciliate Rome, as if Satan could be vanquished by smiles and compliments! and to convert her people, as if the best way to alarm their souls was to half conceal their danger! Alas, such are neither the men nor the means God usually honors! We stop not to ask on what grounds our country's great Destroyer is entitled to such courtesy; we would only say, that those who would encounter the Popish "Antichrist," can still less afford to "wear soft raiment" than either Elijah or the Baptist. We ourselves once thought that blandness was better than boldness; but experience has taught us God's infinite wisdom in giving so much sternness to his best reformers, and amply explained why Luther and Knox were so much more successful than Cranmer and Melancthon. Now, we must get done with this misplaced suavity, and in order thereto, strip off the drapery in which Protestant pseudo-liberalism has decked out Rome, and uncover her nakedness to universal gaze. We must take means that the whole nation shall make their *perfect acquaintance* with her; and then they will instantly see that the robber is entitled to as much courtesy as Rome, and that gentleness to her is cruelty to her victims.

This information should be practical and scientific as well as theological. Perhaps we have made the whole question of Popery too much an ecclesiastical one; and this may be the reason why many feel no interest in it, and deem it, for the most part, a sectarian squabble of little social importance. Now, we must deal more with the *practical* of Rome; show that it concerns the politician as well as the theologian; the citizen of this world as well as the expectant of the next; and convict it as man's great foe, not merely from revelation, but from *science* and *fact*. It has a prodigious advantage of us while we treat it on merely religious grounds; for that is a province so repulsive to some, and so mysterious to others, that they will not follow us into it. We must, then, for their sakes, come down from the mount; and, as the great apostle met the philosophic Greek on Mars Hill, as well as the superstitious Jew in the temple, and with arguments admirably adapted to each, so must we show *practical* men the *facts*, and *scientific* men the *philosophy*, as well as *religious* men the *theology*, of this question. Had Popery thus long ago been treated; had its falseness been demonstrated by an appeal to fact and philosophy, as well as to Scripture; had it been shown to be a violation of the *great laws of the universe*, as much as the incantations of witchcraft, what could have hindered it from sharing the same fate? At least surely we would not now hear the cry of practical infidelity, What has religion to do with science?

—nor that of sickly pietism, What has science to do with religion?—nor would we have appeals against Popery characterized as the effusions of bigotry; nor a college endowed for teaching transubstantiation, any more than schools for propagating the Hindoo notion that the earth rests on an elephant's back, or the Peruvian belief that eclipses are attempts of a dragon to devour the sun.

Moreover, Popery is not enough felt to be Satan's GRAND CONTRIVANCE TO COUNTERWORK THE GOSPEL. We have not been at sufficient pains to trace the career of this great agent of evil, and show that as he had ruder snares for earlier ages, he has more elaborate devices for modern ones;—that as all truth is ONE, so in reality is all error; and that as God has gradually developed the *truth* to suit the gradual developments of our race, from the patriarchal to the Christian age, so has Satan as gradually developed the *error*, from the rudest forms of early idolatry to Popery his masterpiece;—that as in the various systems of light, you have the same great features of salvation by grace *through* a divine Saviour, and *by* a divine Spirit, reproduced with *increasing* clearness till we reach Christianity, the MYSTERY OF GODLINESS, so in the various systems of darkness we have the same counterfeit features of salvation by works through priests and mummeries, till we reach Popery, the MYSTERY OF INIQUITY;—and that as the *gospel* is the last and most perfect development of the one, so is *Popery* of the other. Yet it is thus we ought to handle Popery, and prove that it is the elaborate result of ages of Satan's experience in the art of ruining souls; and that in order to its consummate perfection, that evil one has laid all his other systems under contribution, and not only rifled Judaism, but culled from Gnosticism and plagiarized Paganism. Here, for instance, you have Pharisaism contributing its outward purifications and "traditions of the elders." Here you have celibacy, self-inflictions, and monastic austerities, borrowed from the Gnostic, who thought matter the source of evil, and the flesh the seat of sin. And here, above all, you have Paganism baptized in the name of Jesus; with Peter for Jupiter—Mary, the Papist's queen of heaven, for Juno, the Pagan's—and saints and angels for gods and demi-gods. Ay, and so shameless has been the plagiarism, that purgatory is accurately described in Virgil's Æneid; the present statue of Peter at Rome is the identical statue of Jupiter Capitolinus; even the Pope's chair is said to have been pilfered from the Mussulman; and Romulus and Remus are worshipped as two holy bishops, under the names of Romulo and Remigio!* *Such* is the ground we should take—exposing the *Satanic philosophy* of Popery, and showing that it is an *eclectic* system of evil, contrived with fearful skill to thwart every law of God and of our nature, and to poison the springs of salvation; and all under the most ingenious guise of Christianity. In a

* Seymour's Pilgrimage to Rome.

word, it should be our labor to show that Popery was born at the fall, and came of age when the triple crown was mounted; and that as light was God's first creation, but was diffused through the firmament till centered in the sun on the fourth day, so in reality Popery was Satan's first offspring, whose diffused spirit you can distinctly trace through all false systems, but which only attained a fixed and visible centre when enthroned on the seven hills.

It is also of immense importance that Rome's tactics *in these kingdoms* should be thoroughly understood. They are embraced in two words, *cunning* and *blustering*—admirably adapted to the infirmities of the English character. The Englishman, honest himself, is disposed to think all others so, and to forget that it is the greatest deceivers who smile most sweetly, aud the greatest cowards who bluster most vociferously; and so he who rules the main, and gives laws to the nations, has been alternately cajoled and frightened by a few priests. And to what terrible account they have turned this great error! Just as England has yielded, they have encroached; and she has never stood firm but they have at once knocked under. The more sops she has thrown to these Irish Cerberuses they have only growled the louder, and she has never chastised them but they have cowered into their dens. In 1641, the tampering of Charles brought on a rebellion; Cromwell came, and in six months made the country that honest men could live in it for half-a-century after. In the latter end of last century, the volcano began once more to smoke and rumble. Pitt, to quiet it, founded a college, and promised emancipation. The rebellion of 1798 was the gratitude he received; and *coercion* again quelled the storm which false *conciliation* had occasioned. A brief interval only elapsed, when the priests returned to their old trade of hatching rebellion; concession was again tried; and when, in 1829, emancipation was granted, they *pledged* themselves that they would henceforth be quiet. Did they keep their pledge a day? No; agitation only increased; and our rulers, to quiet it, increased the Maynooth grant, proposed to endow the priest, ay, and *approached the den of the beast* to beg he would keep "his Irish cubs," as they have been termed, in order;—so that even a Connaught peasant was heard to exclaim, "They would pension the devil, sir, if he would promise to keep the priests quiet." Well, this *petting* ended as before, in another rebellion; troops once more came, and peace was restored. Last of all, Wiseman arrived—England arose—and the Pope trembled; but her splendid Protestant demonstrations ended in a ridiculous Aggression Bill; and *instantly* the "Catholic Defence Association" was formed, which proposes to change even the "Protestant succession." Now, we must get done with this absurd and ruinous policy, and restore the true difference between the righteous and the wicked. What claim have these men to this excessive dandling? Is it their *usefulness?* Yes;

and Ireland is its monument! whose every town is polluted by their intrigues, and pestered by their outrages. Is it their *loyalty?* Yes; and our rebellions are the proofs! And shall we continue extending them privileges which we see uniformly turned against the givers, and only employed to effect our own overthrow? Is not hatred of England the feeling they are constantly instilling into their credulous people's minds?—and with such fearful success, that thousands of emigrants are yearly leaving us with scalding curses on their lips against her, and even from their new transatlantic home the western breeze wafts many a deep malediction; insomuch that were another American war to break out, England's deadliest foes would be those of her own household, and their very children would rush as to a sacred duty to revenge their fathers' "wrongs." Indeed, Irish priests take no pains to disguise their malignant hate, or conceal their joy at England's most trifling embarrassments;—who can forget their delight, for example, when the first reverses of the Punjaub were announced? Yes; and this hatred no kindness has been able to mitigate. If ever one transient glow of gratitude could have been kindled in their breasts, it would have surely been by England's kindness during the famine; when, from the Queen to the cottager, from the church to the theatre, all ranks and classes poured in their munificent offerings. Well, scarce had that famine abated, when the convulsions of Europe occurred; the priests could not conceal their *ecstasy* at the prospect of England's being involved in a continental war; and in hope of this they fomented the rebellion of 1848! Thus, while Britain's meat was in their mouths did they attempt to stab to the heart the benefactress which had saved them alive, and give too just ground for the remark, "That Rome was like the hyena, which hunger could not tame, nor kindness conciliate!"

Finally, it needs to be proclaimed with trumpet-tongue that the priests have for years been playing a deep game for the reconquest of "perfidious Albion;" for there are thousands of our people whose eyes no amount of evidence on this point has yet been able to open. Forgetting that Rome is "all a lie," and therefore more dangerous in her smiles than her fury—forgetting that unerring Scripture has assigned her the twofold character of beast and serpent, and that when she dare not be the one, she is sure to be the other—forgetting that while in Naples she is strewing her noisome lair with dead and dying captives, in England the language of meekness drops from her lips soft as the dews of Hermon,—forgetting all this, multitudes still listen unsuspecting to her brazen protestations of innocence and truth. And skilfully has she traded on this incomprehensible stupidity! If we say she is *mild* because she dare not be *fierce*, in tones of injured innocence she complains of our bigotry; and adjusting the mask of virgin loveliness over her haggard face, and the robe of angel purity over her hideous form, she walks through Westminster, looking up to heaven with eyes of meek resignation! AND MANY BELIEVE HER! Scarlet, they say, may once have been her dress, but now it is virgin white! Infatuated men! Will no amount of treachery open your eyes?—and will you really adduce in proof of her dove-like innocence, that simulated smile which most clearly proves her the child of him whose

> "——— Gentle dumb expression, turned at length
> The eye of Eve—"?

Will you not at least believe *herself*—for she makes no secret that England is the dazzling prize she struggles for? Were you not told by Father Ignatius, of "praying societies" for her conversion, and of the 300 days' indulgence lately granted to all who would say a "Hail, Mary," for this object? Were you not told by Gavazzi of "Jesuit servant societies," for enabling these pests of mankind to creep into Protestant families in the guise of domestics? Is not the bull "*In cœno Domini*" read from every chapel each holy Thursday, thus proving to all who are not willing dupes, that Rome has never abandoned her demands on England's fealty? And if she claims to ride over us now when she *cannot*, will she not do so the first moment she *can?* And think you the man who for this object keeps his fanatics praying, and his Jesuits prowling over the land, would not hurl our Queen from her throne if he could, and put a Mary or a James in her room? Then let all Englishmen know assuredly, that Rome's deadly eye is on "their faith and their firesides;" and that wherever they meet her clouds of priests, whether heading a mob, horsewhip in hand, or at vice-regal levees in silken hose; whether putting down a school in Connaught, or *getting up* one in Edinburgh; all—ALL are patiently performing their several parts in this gigantic conspiracy against Protestant England. The serpent's great design is on that Eden of Protestantism, and he has for years been stealing steadily towards it; and whether he has been *now* taking a circuitous route to beguile the simple, or *again* hiding amongst the flowers to elude the suspicious, or, *as in the late aggression*, making a visible SPRING—be assured of this one thing, that ON HE COMES. And even granting that Rome has for ONCE made a blunder, and having missed her spring, may now slink into the thicket and wait a better opportunity—even granting that she has found the breach not yet practicable, and may suspend the *assault*, in order the more noiselessly to expedite the *mine*—what doom do we deserve if we ever forget the lesson she has taught us? SHE will profit by her blunder—and if WE do not, the stolid infatuation of Samson, while fondling with another harlot, was sagacious vigilance in comparison; and, resembling him in his folly we will assuredly be like him in his fate!

CHAPTER IV.

TREATMENT—LEGISLATION.

SOME have a prejudice against legislative interference with Rome, as though it were an encroachment of the temporal power on the spiritual. They forget that Rome is a power, both *temporal* and spiritual—that the Pope is God's viceroy as well as his vicar, and wears a crown as well as a cross; that "all power is Christ's in heaven and on earth," and must therefore be *his*, as Christ's *representative;* and that those principles which they guard with such praiseworthy jealousy are therefore inapplicable to Rome. Of course, she denies this also; and in Britain, notwithstanding Wiseman's *office* and acts, claims to be merely *spiritual*. But has she not ever proved the most intolerable temporal tyrant that ever trampled down the nations? Is not the Pope "*dominus totius orbis*"—and not content to be a king *among* kings, has he not ever claimed to be king *of* kings? How many monarchs has he dethroned, and kingdoms absolved from their oaths of allegiance? How often has he made sovereigns hold his stirrup, and their prostrate necks the steps from which he mounted it? And if such things occur not now, think you is want of *power* or of *will* the reason? Yet, in the face of her history, her decrees, and all her acts this moment, many have somehow been cajoled into the notion, that we ought to deal with Rome as a mere *spiritual* power. So boots and thumbscrews are spiritual weapons!—stakes and fagots spiritual arguments!—and the annual declaration above noticed, that our Queen is a heretic usurper, who must lose her crown if not her head on the first opportunity, a spiritual announcement! In truth, it is this very masking of the temporal beneath the spiritual power, on the ground of which she would claim *indulgence*, that forfeits all her claims to it; just as the skulking robber deserves less mercy than the open manly one. It is therefore no wonder that many good men are at this moment asking, Is it a right use of *liberty* to extend it to a system which denies it to all others: or of *toleration*, to grant it to a church which tolerates none who dare think for themselves? But we would not be intolerant even to Rome, though we thus speak. We would have the world see that there is in Europe *one* glorious country which can afford to tolerate even *her;* and the legislation we would now propose in no wise interferes with the sacred principles of religious liberty. We would only demand, that beneath the name of freedom we shall not have *favoritism*, nor continue to *endow* what at most we should only endure. And therefore two measures, *at least*, we claim at the hands of the legislature:—that Rome's "religious" prisons shall not be the *only ones* on our soil exempt from public inspection; and that if she will be allowed to diffuse her poison through the realm, she shall at least support its chief manufactory herself.

The Convent.—"Retreats of piety"—how sweet the sound! None knows better than Rome "how much is in a name"—Rome, that mistress of the arts of nomenclature; which calls her most villanous order "the Society of *Jesus*," and her most infernal tribunal "the *holy* office!" She is like other serpents, generally most dangerous in her gayest fascinations; throws the most imposing drapery round her most iniquitous scenes, and baptizes her foulest deeds with the fairest titles. And oh! how exemplified in the convent! We have traced the young female thither, and found her leaving her happiness at the gate, and commencing a struggle with the laws of her being compared to which crucifixion were mercy. We have seen that unless the laws of nature are a delusion, that young creature must there stifle all the fond throbbings of a woman's soul, commit suicide without the relief of dying, and bury herself alive without finding that rest which the grave usually brings to the weary. And this is Rome's best oblation to heaven!—her most transcendental type of piety!—to pluck the young heart out of the gentle bosom, and attempt to replace it with a lump of marble—to inflict upon its victim the feeling of wretchedness, from which she can only escape by getting rid of *all* feeling! We now add, that it is the nature of this gloomy prison-house to decoy those young females whose hearts are least capable of such petrifaction. It is the artless girl of pious tendencies—the child of romance and sentiment—whose glowing young fancy throws a halo round everything, who is most easily ensnared by visions of conventual bliss. And thus this dreadful old sorceress not only drags the young female from life, just when its vernal flowers are all bursting around her; but selects for the sacrifice the most precious victim, and makes her very excellence and piety the means of her decoy! Ah! fancy that girl's feelings when the spell at length breaks—when she awakes, and behold it was a dream—when the *mirage* melts away, and she finds a dreary desert where she looked for living waters! Perhaps some simple Protestant replies, "But I have been to convents, and the nuns who showed us through them said they were all so happy." And was there nothing suspicious in the great pains they took to convince you of their felicity? Then what mean those high walls and iron gratings? And why does a church so sagacious needlessly provoke suspicion, by giving such *paradises* the air of prisons? Ah! think you there is no occasion? Then read the honest narrative of one, who in England seemed favorable to Popery, but went to Rome and was effectually cured. The scenes Mr. Seymour describes as being at this moment enacted in Italian nunneries are absolutely heart-rending. One friend, in particular, who knew several nuns, and was well acquainted with "the secrets of their prison-house," assured him that "the broken-hearted looks, the shades of deep and indelible sorrow, the lines of settled and unalterable sadness, the expression of resentment or despair that characterized many of these young creatures, used to affect his heart, sadden all his best feelings, and trouble his very dreams. He could not think or speak of the subject without such feelings, but that the tears would come into his eyes, saying, that it was inconceivable the number of nuns that went to an early grave under this system." He assured him that numbers of them, when the religious hectic which brought them thither had subsided, and they awoke to all the dreary realities of their state, "soon pined and saddened, and, sinking into despair, DIED OF MADNESS;" that this was "the melancholy destiny of the greater portion, and that nothing on earth could induce him, with the knowledge he possessed, to allow one of his daughters to take the veil, for that the majority of nuns at Rome *died of madness before they were five-and-twenty years of age!!*"*

Now think of hundreds in our own land annually offered on this dreadful altar, flowers that might have shed beauty and fragrance on their entire circle, ruthlessly plucked in their first vernal buddings, and consigned to those cells to droop and perish! In Ireland alone there are A HUNDRED AND THIRTEEN

* Seymour's Pilgrimage to Rome, p. 182. For a distressing account of the order of nuns called the *Sepulte vive*, or "the buried alive," see p. 188.

CONVENTS !* Throughout the entire United Kingdom they are rising on every hand; and if Rome had her will, these living sepulchres would cover the empire. And for aught we can tell, those which already exist may be scenes of fearful vice and ruffian violence. Maria Monk has revealed the abominations of the Montreal convent, and the Rev. Mr. Slocum has proved the full truth of her disclosures. The French soldiery found sixty-two young women corrupted and ruined in the apartments of the Inquisitors of Spain; and both French and English discovered manifold proofs of guilt on the premises of Peninsular convents. When Mr. Seymour was at Rome, an abbess rushed forth in a frenzy from one of the nunneries of that city, and sought relief from remorse beneath the waves of the Tiber. And what proof can you have that those crimes which are rife in other convents have no existence in ours—that *their* walls witness no villany, and hear no cries of outraged innocence? If we suspect them wrongfully, the fault is their own; for if all is *right*, why is not all *open*? It is vice, not virtue, that hates the light, and suffers from exposure; and piety, above all things, detests concealment, and avoids even the "appearance of evil." "O, but religion must not be interfered with!" RELIGION! that heavenly angel in whose outraged name Rome does her darkest deeds, beneath whose skirt she always hides her guiltiest acts, burying them the deep-

* Catholic Directory, 1852.

er in its folds the more truculent they are! Religion! which never yet concealed anything, because it has nothing to conceal! Religion! which is used as the *decoy* to these prisoners, is forsooth made the plea for preventing their *escape* and concealing the *crimes* of which they may be the victims! Say, shall that be taken as a valid plea, which is in truth the darkest feature of the case; and shall Rome be permitted to transform religion into a jailer of female innocence, and station her at every convent-door, to prevent the entrance of justice, or the escape of woe? Then, fellow-Christians! approach the feet of your Queen, and pray that no convent shall be permitted in her dominions without being open to inspection. And if Rome shall be allowed to prowl through your families, kidnap your daughters, and bear them off to her fastnesses, there to be robbed of liberty, property, and perhaps virtue too—to be tortured, it may be, under the sweet name of "sister," and possibly ruined under the hallowed title of "saint"—to endure actual misery beneath the mockery of pretended bliss, and be compelled to smile while anguish is eating their hearts;—at least insist that these dens shall be examined, and those who are injured protected, and those who have "come to themselves" allowed to go free. Shall Britain, which hunts the man-stealer through every sea—whose fair soil no slave can touch, but his chains burst from around him—which breaks open the private dwelling to deliver the victim of wrong, punished the advocate

Sloane for abusing his little maid-servant—and will not permit one act of "cruelty" even to the lower creation; shall Britain show favor only to this moral monster, and refuse relief to the helpless young females who shriek from its dens? Shall Britain, whose humanity sought for Stoddart amid the sands of the East, and still seeks for Franklin amongst the icebergs of the North;—Britain, the asylum of the earth's remotest exiles, permit her worst foe, on pretences "false as hell," so far to abuse her hospitality, and impose on her credulity, as to decoy and incarcerate her own fair daughters, on her own fair soil, without a chance of escape—and for no other crime than their artless innocence and religious enthusiasm?

THE COLLEGE.—After all we have said of Irish priests, the OFFSPRING, we need not surely say much of Maynooth, the PARENT; nor enter its gloomy walls to discover its genuine character. Every effect has its adequate cause; and to judge correctly of a fountain, it is enough to examine its streams. We care very little what interested witnesses may testify, or official visitors see; while our reason remains we must judge of the tree by its FRUITS, and if, on *visiting days*, all looks lovely and charming within Maynooth College, it is only another proof, not of Rome's innocence, but her serpent cunning.

And why should we look for any thing else? Could we expect a seminary for heralds of darkness to be radiant with light, or a school for patrons of pollution to be redolent of purity? Would the father of this system take such pains to mould the *people* to his will, and be careless only about those by *whom* he chiefly moulds them? Would he who is so watchful of his prisoners, be neglectful only of his turnkeys? No; as sure as Rome is Satan's masterpiece, it is in the training of her *priesthood* you would naturally look for his deepest strokes of policy, and expect to see the art of blasting souls practised in its highest branches. Let us see how far these expectations are realized in the present case. Imagine the great adversary devising such a college as would best suit his dreadful purpose; and his aim would clearly be to contrive such an one as would most thoroughly subjugate the minds of the priests, and, *at the same time*, best fit them for subjugating those of the people. It is clear that to accomplish this difficult task he would give the former enough instruction to raise them *just so far* above the latter as to enable them thoroughly to enslave them, but *no farther*—enough to make them fiery zealots, but not enough to liberalize their minds; in a word, such an education as would qualify them for *mischief*, but not such as would fit them for usefulness. Now, you have only to bear this single fact in mind, in order to have the most perfect key to the entire history, instructions, and character of Maynooth College.

First look to its history. Rome long sighed for such a college in Ireland, for France being a much more enlightened country, *its* colleges were necessarily TOO GOOD for her purposes in Ireland; hence those Irish priests who had been brought up in France returned home *far too liberal and enlightened for her objects!* A *domestic* college, therefore, became indispensable; and one enjoying the smiles of Government was most desirable. Now, mark her consummate policy. In 1793, Drs. Troy and O'Reilly assured Mr. Pitt that if their priests continued to be educated in France, they would all return revolutionists; but if he endowed a college for them at home, such a college would prevent their exposure to the political corruption of foreign governments, and such an endowment would ensure their loyalty to their own! Such was their argument at *the very time* when they were members of a secret society which was hatching the rebellion of 1798!! Pitt seized the idea, *vainly* thinking that whatever contributed to make the priests independent of their flocks would weaken by so much their moral influence among them! It was thus a plot and a counterplot; but priest-craft proved an overmatch for state-craft. Forgetting that Rome's influence was *not* moral, but superstitious; that her slaves were chained to her, not by respect for her character, but dread of her ghostly power; and that the way to emancipate them was, not to endow *her*, but to enlighten *them*;—forgetting this, if he ever knew it, the *premier* was outwitted by the *priest*, and that ill-omened child of God-dishonoring expediency was born in 1795. It is now, therefore, 57 years old; and if its days have not been "few," they have verily been "evil." Never was that retributive decree more terribly fulfilled—"Be sure your sin will find you out." With this college was to commence the reign of Peace in Ireland; the Olive-tree was to bloom on every hill, and that worse brood of serpents than any St. Patrick expelled was to be charmed into perfect innocence by the incantations of the Treasury. Maynooth, in short, was to be a spring of healing waters amongst us; but instead of this, it has proved "a cauldron of seething horrors, around which are squatted the old hags of treason, disaffection, and agrarian outrage; and this has been the chorus of their song—

"Double, double, toil and trouble." *

Look next to its course of instruction, and you will find Satan pursuing with singular exactness the same plan of debasement with the priest that we have seen him pursue with the people, only, of course, on a more refined and subtle scale; and that the entire system of Maynooth training is manifestly contrived to cramp the *mind*, destroy the *conscience*, shrivel the *heart*, degrade the *whole nature*, and hence to send forth just such an ignorant, depraved, turbulent, and vulgar priesthood as now infest the land.

If you look to its *mental* training, to judge by its *programme*, it would seem most respectable; but we

* Rev. Mr. Goold, at Edinburgh Anti-Maynooth Meeting.

need only apply the infallible test of actual *attainment* to find its *real* character. For example, its professor of natural philosophy confessed before the committee of inquiry, that he was not certain if more than two thirds of his students could at the end of the session demonstrate the 47th proposition of the first book of Euclid!—that he thought the majority of them *could* tell the cause of an eclipse ! ! —and that he himself "did not know the subject-matter of Euclid's sixth book ! ! !"* Should this not satisfy you, kind reader, you need only examine our priests themselves, and you will find them, of all professional men, the most ignorant as a class. Nothing can be more extraordinary than many of their effusions, both *oral* and *written*. The following specimen is, we assure you, little in comparison to what we might adduce. It is a reply to a note sent by a Protestant missionary to a Popish priest —whom the author had not long ago to summon for flogging one of his scholars—inviting him to attend a controversial lecture:—"The Rev. Mr. Harrington presents his compliments to Rev. D. Foley, and begs to return his circular. The Rev. Mr. Harrington objects to the lecture for two reasons: *first, he has not time to do so*, for twelve o'clock is the hour appointed for him by the holy Roman Catholic Church to celebrate the holy sacrifice of the mass, and preach a *moral* discourse to his *Christian* hear-

* Evidence of Rev. Nicholas Callen, D.D., Irish Education Report, viii., App. pp. 146–148.

ers, *secondly*, Rev. Mr. Harrington, finding from the *orthography* in the circular that the lecture *cannot* be *orthodox*, lacks inclination to be present at any lecture coming from that quarter.—Castletown, January 27th, 1849 ! !"*

Look next to Maynooth's *moral* training. Its principal class-books are those depositories of vileness—Delahogue and Bailly. The former, for instance, telling us under what circumstances *stealing is no sin;* and the latter teaching that the church has full power to absolve from oaths "*when the honor of God, the good of the church, or the good of society requires it,*" and that "*the superiors of the church are to be the judges in all cases!*"† Indeed, if you look into the Eighth Report of the Education Commission of Inquiry, you will find the witnesses obliged to acknowledge, despite all the shuffling they could resort to, that in Maynooth *everything is fully taught* which is dishonoring to God, subversive of morality, and ruinous to society, in the Popish system; and how *could* it be otherwise in a Popish college? Yes; and while, according to one of the professors, there were a few years ago only TEN Bibles among 400 students, each is required to purchase Bailly and Delahogue, and every week to give 9 hours to them in class, and 48 hours in prepara-

* Missionary Tour through South and West of Ireland. By Rev. D. Foley.

† Delahogue Tract. de Praecept. Decalogi, pp. 232–236; Bailly's Moral Theology, vol. ii. p. 140.

tion. They are, therefore, the constant companions of the student, and over their foul images he is compelled for hours to pore, at that age when his passions are strongest. No wonder an *emancipated* student declared, that "such an effect had they on his mind, as nearly to drive him into a species of delirium! and that in order to save himself from the effects of his own feelings, he has gone down on a cold winter's morning into the chapel of the institution, and there remained till nearly chilled to death reading them on his knees, and praying the while that he might be kept from the evil emotions they suggested to his mind."* Is it strange that when the *mental* and the *moral* of the Irish priest are so blasted, the ANIMAL of his nature should have such complete ascendency?

Observe, again, the influence of Maynooth on his *heart.* He must now learn to become an isolated being, to whom domestic joys are a sinful thought; and that vow of celibacy is here taken which nips in the bud the best feelings of his nature, and sends its blight through his whole soul. Everything is contrived to dry up the springs of affection to God and man. Witness those morose austerities; witness that Breviary, of which he must daily read 30 to 40 pages, and whose endless repetition *must* create formality, and hypocrisy, if not utter disgust at devotion. Witness the *silence* which is strictly enforced, sometimes for weeks together; and, during most of

* Ireland in 1846, p. 34.

the year, for 21½ hours out of the 24.* Witness the suspicious surveillance which never allows fewer than *three* students together, that the third may be a spy on the other two; and to evade which, one student often stands inside a door, and the other outside, in order to whisper through the pannels!

Observe, finally, the system of *subjugation* here pursued. Implicit obedience is the first commandment. The grand maxim of the college is, that each student must "think as his superior thinks." And to this great centre-point, *breaking down the mind to the will of others*, all is made to converge. Only think of such a system pursued for seven years of that youthful period when the mind is most plastic, with but the annual interruption of six weeks' vacation! And so *constant* is its influence, that the students are seldom allowed outside the gates, save for a walk on Wednesdays, and even then they are watched by tutors lest the fearful process should be suspended for an hour.

Now, if so much of this evil system is thus revealed to public gaze, despite the profound secrecy which Rome *in all things* observes, what might you expect to find if admitted to the inmost *penetralia* of Maynooth? And considering this fact in the light of the above details, can any sane man doubt that the *same* plan by which Rome destroys the *people*, is here pursued with more malignant subtlety; until, by the time the victim is made a *priest*, he has ceas-

* Tract on Maynooth by Eugene Francis O'Beirne.

ed to be a *man*, and by this spiritual Medusa is turned into *stone?* You think this picture colored? It *must* be the reverse. Unless Maynooth is a very den of corruption, will you inform us how its priests are usually so bad? or where they learn their wickedness? How else can you explain that they so generally *go in* raw youths, and *come out* social firebrands? We care not what annual reports of Maynooth may say: THEY are its reports—its "living epistles;" and if you would know *assuredly* what its TEACHINGS are, you need only look to their PRACTICE. Behold their very countenances!—what specimens commonly of the "human face divine!" And if you pronounce the scowl that sits on a villain's brow to be just the mirror of his bosom—the collective daguerreotype of the thousand dark thoughts of his soul—say, is this "index of the mind" to be read backwards in the priest's case only? Is *he* the only exception to the laws of physiognomy? And think you was the artless face of the *boy* transformed into the "DOWN LOOK" of the *priest* by nothing but seven years' converse with his God?—or that deep scowl from which infant innocence would instinctively flee, acquired by naught but scenes of heavenly rapture? And what shall we call it?—credulity? fatuity? or that sheer depravity which has so strong an affinity for whatever is depraved? which to this hour defends or palliates the monstrous sin of the world's most Protestant nation endowing *such* a college? And *this*, when ignorance of Rome's iniquitous designs can no longer be pleaded,—when, from its recent agitations, the cesspool of Popery is now sending up its stench over Europe,—when, by our late premier's own confession, the ranks of darkness, led on by Rome, are now preparing to close in around Protestant England! This, too, when not only have the blessings Maynooth was to yield us not been realized, but we have had instead unmitigated curse,—when, in place of rearing doves, as was promised us, it has only been hatching cockatrices,—and when even the cowardly plea of fear of the priests can no longer be urged, since they are fast growing utterly powerless, and will in a few years have completely lost their sting!

Nor is Maynooth merely *aided* by the nation—it enjoys an amount of favor which is denied our very best universities. There you see an extensive pile of building, enclosed in a park of 100 acres, with gardens, walks, and play-grounds; containing numberless apartments for professors and students, besides dining-hall, chapel, and library of 10,000 volumes; with a staff consisting of a president, vice-president, bursar, two deans, librarian, Dunboyne prefect, and ten professors; not to mention a train of servants, including a butcher, baker, and brewer—and ALL maintained at the public cost! And there you find 500 students, generally of the lowest class; their cabin costume exchanged for a black suit, with long black gaiters; and themselves, from having in their humble homes "cultivated letters on a little oatmeal," now amply supplied with smoking joints and potations of ale, and receiving besides £20 *a-year of pocket-money!!* Why, if the strength and glory of the British empire were bound up in those 500—if they were destined to be her shield and stay, instead of her tormentors, they could not be the objects of more bountiful regard. And while these *embryo pests* of society are thus dandled on the lap of royal favor, how many of its *future ornaments* are left to ply the trowel or the shuttle one half of the year in order to support themselves at college the remainder! Can the history of folly present anything like this? The world's most Protestant nation supporting *Popery;* and the very worst kind of it, *Irish* Popery; and in the very worst form, A COLLEGE—not the hornets, but the nest to hatch them in! This nation, continuing the grant despite *the utter failure* of all the ends for which it was given; *increasing* it, too, as the mischief increases; and, in 1845, *permanently endowing it* with £30,000 a-year! Ay, and now *hesitating to withdraw* this endowment, despite the clearest proof that by its continuance they are only fattening the tiger which thirsts for their blood! In a word, the most free and enlightened nation in Europe fostering the worst form of darkness and despotism; the great patroness of all good, nursing Satan's masterpiece of evil; and the most sagacious of nations *continuing* to rear the viper just *after* it has disclosed its deadly designs by making a DART AT HER BOSOM!!

And what are the pleas we hear urged for this? "*Popery is the prevailing religion in Ireland.*" Yes, and so is Hinduism in India! "*But we ought to show some kindness to our Roman Catholic brethren.*" What! by cherishing the delusion which, according to your own creed, is soul-destroying! "*But they are poor, and need a college.*" They who have thirteen colleges in Ireland, including Carlow and Clongowes, need *another!*—and they who can raise any sums for mischief, and have now factiously commenced a Popish university, *cannot support it!* "*O, but they contribute their share of the revenue, and it is just they should get a share like others.*" Have we not shown that Protestantism *gains*, and Popery *costs* the nation far more than the amount of all our endowments together? And because the former *gets back* a fraction of what it gains the country, the latter, forsooth, must be endowed for impoverishing it! "*But, then, the nation is pledged to this grant.*" And suppose it were so, if we pledge ourselves to what dishonors God and destroys the country, verily the sooner we break our pledge the better; for such a pledge we had NO POWER to make, and the sin is in the *keeping*, not the breaking of it. But the allegation is utterly false. Till 1845, this grant was *annual*—abundant proof that before that date there could have been no pledge; *since then*, it rests on a mere Act of Parliament, and a thousand better acts have been repealed! And, as is well known, that act—hurried through the legislature, our readers will guess why—was passed, as Sir R. Peel *admitted*, in the face of a reclaiming nation, only 17,000 individuals having petitioned for it, while 1,284,000 petitioned against it; so that if ever there was an act which the very justice they talk of required to be repealed, it is this offspring of our VIOLATED CONSTITUTION! But what is that cry which comes from a very different quarter? "*By withdrawing this grant*," say some of our *Protestants*, "*you'll endanger all endowments.*" Well, and suppose it were so, have you really, in the dazzle of your endowment, lost sight of the honor of your God? But we assert it is just the reverse. The greatest danger to an endowment that is *right* in principle, is to place alongside of it one that is *wrong*. And so, has not the Maynooth grant given the Voluntary his best argument? Only let all endowments be *righteous*, and the strongest plea against them would cease; but it is this *indiscriminate* support of truth and error that has furnished the strongest handle to the adversary. Therefore, let Protestants beware! "The path of *duty* is the path of safety;" and should any such motives of God-dishonoring selfishness weaken their opposition to this grant, their wisdom may prove their folly, and their sin provoke the Most High to send the evil it was designed to prevent.

Then let us arise and DEMAND the repeal of this suicidal act, regardless of the canting cry which Rome may raise of "intolerance" and "persecution."

Intolerance, forsooth! So, then, not to help is to hinder, not to pension is to persecute! You detect a man foully abusing your hospitality, and, while eating your bread, forming a design against your life; and instead of sending him to prison, you merely tell him he must no longer sit at your table—and that is persecution!! This, too, from Rome—who, while demanding toleration from all men, denies it to all men,—will not tolerate a Protestant chapel within the gates of her capital,—lately refused a Protestant stranger a grave to bury his wife in,—and is even now banishing those of her subjects who would dare read the Bible to the pestilent swamps of Maremma! Ay, and some of our *Protestants* are found to echo the cry, and prove their fitness for the office of "guardians of toleration," by the strangest partialities for its deadliest foe! If we sent Wiseman back to the Flaminian Gate, and required that till a Protestant chapel were allowed in Rome, not a Popish one should stand in London; and that till the Bible were free in Italy, the Breviary should be banished from England;—if, in short, we demanded measure for measure, would Rome even *then* have any right to complain? We must, then, plainly teach her—and all her *Protestant* abettors, too—that she has good cause to be thankful we now ask so little; and that should our rulers continue to trifle with the feelings of a Christian nation, it is not with this humble measure of defence they will be satisfied. No; as sure as delayed justice increases a people's demands, will they require more sweeping legislation. Men are beginning already to ask whether it is *right* to tolerate a system which will tolerate none but itself; or *safe* to endure a thing which will endure nothing else. And should the question come to be, not whether Popery should be supported, but whether it should be suffered, the responsibility of raising it will rest with the men who shall now resist the nation's moderate demands.

And should rulers continue to disregard the nation's voice, then, fellow-Christians, will another duty devolve on you, which, we believe, you have long most grievously neglected. You have, in times past, allowed Satan to choose the rulers of these *Christian* lands, and thus entailed incalculable mischief on the Redeemer's cause. Had you always done your duty, and chosen God-fearing men to represent you, what might now have been the country's state? How many a glorious cause have you *won* over the land and *lost* in the Legislature! Was not this the case with this very Maynooth endowment? Yes, here has been one fruitful source of all our calamities. As if we were not bound to serve God in the *State* as well as in the Church, in our capacity of *citizens* as well as of saints, we have let the government of this Christian country fall into the hands of men whose highest rule of conduct is unprincipled expediency, and who, for their own despicable ends, continue to provoke Heaven's judgments by giving her power to the beast. Then, fellow-Christians, arise, and no longer commit the *sin* of allowing such men to rule over us, nor the *folly* of taking such trouble about meetings and petitions, to have *both* disregarded by your own representatives. But take a lesson from *Rome's* election struggles; and take warning by the Catholic Defence Association, who seem fully resolved to fill the next Parliament with their tools, at whatever cost to the country of blood and violence.

CHAPTER V.

THE TREATMENT—EVANGELIZATION.

HERE is the GRAND HOPE of Ireland! It is little after all which Parliament or even the public can do. They can, at the best, but facilitate somewhat the flow of the tides of salvation in our land, as the wind sometimes increases the tides of our harbors; but in *both* cases the grand influence must come from ABOVE. Popery, like its father the devil, can only be foiled by "the sword of the Spirit," and destroyed by the "breath of God's mouth, and the brightness of his coming." But, as has been truly said, Ireland has never yet had its *Reformation*. If history can be relied on, never was country more neglected by clergymen and laymen. Many a parish is still strewn with the wrecks of ministerial unfaithfulness; and when "God maketh inquisition for blood," dread will be the reckoning of many a hireling pastor and godless Protestant! Oh! how many a minister has given too much ground for the charge of caring only for the fleece! How many a layman has been more sinful, with less excuse than Rome's worst votaries! And how often have *both* exhibited religion, not in its own lovely aspect, but the grim features of bigotry, or the marble coldness of death! True, the priests have poisoned our countrymen, but we have starved them—they have "shamefully handled" them, but we have "passed them by on the other side." Yet you wonder the Irish still remain unevangelized! But, blessed be God, a better day has dawned, and now almost every denomination has begun to do something for Ireland.

THE INSTRUMENTS.—For the reader's information, we shall notice the principal organizations. 1*st*, *The Independent Body*, composed of the members of the Congregational Union and the Irish Evangelical Society, and consisting of 24 ministers and missionaries, actively employed in various parts of the country. 2*d*, *Lady Huntingdon's Connection*, employing a number of Scripture readers, under the direction of ministers of various denominations. 3*d*, *The Ladies' Hibernian Female School Society*, which annually expends about £2000 in the religious and general instruction of female children. 4*th*, *The Irish Society*, for instructing the native

Irish through the medium of their own tongue, established in the year 1826, supported by members of the Church of England, and at present employing 59 readers and 719 teachers. 5*th*, *The Scripture Readers' Society*, established in 1822, and at present employing 84 readers, and expending upwards of £2000 a year. 6*th*, *The Irish Island Society*, connected with the Established Church, which employs about 25 readers and teachers on the islands and coasts, and has brought the gospel within reach of about 13,000 souls. 7*th*, *The Sunday School Society for Ireland*, which, since its establishment in 1809, has disseminated 954,122 copies of the Scriptures, with 114,286 portions, and 1,400,935 Scripture reading-books, &c. This admirable society numbers at present about 3000 schools and 226,000 scholars. 8*th*, *The Hibernian Bible Society*, which, from its commencement in 1806, has issued 1,913,857 Bibles, Testaments, and portions. 9*th*, *The Religious Tract Society for Ireland*, which, since 1819, has issued near 10,000 books and tracts, and established 1,162 depositories and lending libraries. 10*th*, *The Primitive Wesleyan Connection*, which has at present near 50 circuit preachers, and 40 missionary agents in Ireland. 11*th*, *The Hibernian Wesleyan Society*, containing 158 preachers, 25 missionaries, and 62 schoolmasters. With the labors of both these societies, we are intimately acquainted; and find it impossible to speak of them in terms of sufficient praise. We have traced them through almost every part of the country, and found them penetrating its wildest regions, and holding up the lamp of truth in its darkest corners, regardless alike of persecution and privation. 12*th*, *The Irish Baptist Society*, containing at present about 24 ministers and missionaries, who are actively laboring in various parts of the country. 13*th*, *The Church Education Society for Ireland*, which, in 1851, had 1882 schools, and 108,450 scholars on the roll, with an average attendance of 64,647. 14*th*, *The Home Mission of the Irish Presbyterian Church.* This church at present consists of 5 synods, 36 presbyteries, 522 ministers, 483 congregations and mission stations, and about 750,000 souls. Within the last 16 years, it has planted about 160 new churches in destitute localities; established a number of mission stations and out-stations in the south and west; supported from 300 to 400 Irish and English mission schools, in which upwards of 20,000 Roman Catholics have been taught to read the Scriptures; and circulated large numbers of Bibles and tracts in Popish districts. There are, besides, 25 Reformed Presbyterian ministers in Ireland, and 15 or 20 distinguished by the name of Seceders.

Of course, it is impossible to give full details of the operations of so many societies. We must confine ourselves to those of the two chief Protestant Churches of Ireland, and let these serve as samples of the labors of the remainder. One of the principal agencies of the Established Church is *the Irish*

Society. Before the famine of 1846, there were supposed to be 3,000,000 of Irish-speaking Roman Catholics in the country. And this society, availing itself of their proverbial attachment to their own simple and beautiful language, has extended its operations through many parts of the country, and been blessed with much success. The wonderful power of the Irish tongue on the Irish heart, and hence the influence of this agency, may be judged of by the following anecdote. Some years ago, when one of its most active members was preaching in the courthouse of Athlone, four priests stationed themselves at the door, and commenced taking down the names of those Roman Catholics who entered. This kept the people back for a little. But having collected in force, they made a rush to the door, and the priests were not only borne down, but carried before them into the building! The candles had just been lighted, and one of the priests coolly resumed the task of noting the names of the people. This being observed by one of them, he called out —"Mr. Gregg, can you preach in the dark as well as in the light?" "I can," was the reply. In a moment every candle was puffed out, and the people were enabled, in spite of the priest, to hear the glad tidings of salvation. We can only now find space for one instance of this society's success. Amongst the leading persecutors of its teachers at Kingscourt, some years ago, was Mr. Nolan, the young coadjutor of the parish priest. His inflammatory harangues having mainly led to the murder of one or two agents, he was obliged to remove to a neighboring village; and there he commenced to study the Scriptures, the better to fit himself for the defence of Rome. The goodness of God arrested the persecutor; he soon read himself out of the errors of Popery, and that furious bigot became one of the most devoted servants of God.

Two of the most interesting colonies in Ireland are *Dingle*, in the county Kerry, and the *island of Achill*, in the county Mayo; both connected with the Established Church. In the year 1831, the Rev. George Gubbins was appointed curate of Dingle. At this time there was in the district neither church nor school-house; and this excellent man lived in a cabin at one shilling per week, and had stated services in the private dwellings around. In about a year after, the district was visited and fearfully ravaged by the cholera. There being no physician to apply to, Mr. Gubbins became physician-general to the poor; and his kindness during a crisis so awful won the people's affections, and prepared the way for the harvest which soon followed. In 1833, the Rev. Charles Gayer arrived in the district; the following year several of the inhabitants, including two Popish priests, renounced the Romish faith; upwards of 150 families have since followed their example. Some time ago, the colony consisted of 800 converts; and notwithstanding the brutal persecution to which its present excellent missionary,

Mr. Lewis, has been subjected, and the extensive emigration of the people of that district, it now consists of 1200. Amongst the many cheering instances of the Divine blessing on the labors of these missionaries, we may mention that of Mr. Moriarty, the present curate of Ventry, who was once a bigoted Romanist, and went on one occasion into a congregation *on purpose to disturb them in their devotions;* and who, while waiting for the moment when he should commence his interruptions, received such impressions from the truth he heard, as ultimately led to his conversion.

Achill is the largest island on the coast of Ireland. It stands on the extreme west of Mayo, is washed by the billows of the Atlantic, and consists of mountain and bog, interspersed with small patches of cultivated land. Being visited with famine in 1831, the Rev. Edward Nangle took charge of a cargo of potatoes sent to its relief. Having found the people willing to listen to the truth, he conceived the design of founding amongst them a colony on the Moravian plan; and, with the full countenance of the principal proprietor of the island, and the cordial aid of numerous Christian friends, he soon after founded "the Colony of Achill." A wild tract of moor has now been reclaimed, and a number of cottages have been erected upon it for the colonists; a neat church and school-house stand in the interesting little village; several families and individuals have renounced the errors of Popery; the young generation are growing up a different class of beings from what their progenitors were; the sides of the once barren mountain are now adorned with cultivated fields and gardens; most of the island has lately been purchased by the friends of the colony, at a cost of £17,000; and thus the gospel will in future have "free course and be glorified" in a spot which for ages has slumbered in the midnight of Popery!

The Home Mission of the Irish Presbyterian Church has two departments of operation—the one is entirely devoted to the evangelization of Roman Catholics; while the other aims to supply the spiritual wants of the Protestant population generally, and the Presbyterian especially. The mission to Roman Catholics is again divided into two branches, one to the *English-speaking* and the other to the *Irish-speaking* Romanist. The *Birr mission* is an example of the former. It was commenced in 1840; and owed its existence to the singular circumstance of a congregation of Roman Catholics having, with their pastor, spontaneously sought connection with the Irish Presbyterian Church.

The Rev. Messrs. Crotty, the priests of Birr or Parsonstown, King's County, had long entertained doubts of the soundness of their system; and their final renunciation of it was brought about by the following circumstances:—The "holy oil" with which extreme unction is performed, must always come through the hands of the bishop. But the Messrs. Crotty having had some dispute with their diocesan, in order to avoid the necessity of applying to him for oil, began to study the Scriptures in quest of some other channel through which to obtain it! There they found that *bishop* and *presbyter* were terms to signify the same office. This discovery led them to search the divine volume with redoubled eagerness; and the result may be easily guessed. They soon got rid of "holy oil" altogether—the "holy water" shortly followed—the "candles" by and by disappeared—the confessional came next to be closed—and the "mass" itself was finally abolished. Thus did these two cousins grope their way, step by step, out of the delusions of Popery, with the lamp of truth their only guide, until its last enclosure was passed. But being unable to lead their people out of error as fast as they themselves felt bound to travel, every new reform caused a new secession; until, from a large congregation with which they set out from Rome, they could only muster about a hundred followers when they arrived at the end of their toilsome journey. In 1839, William Crotty, with the congregation, joined the Presbyterian Church; and in the following year, Dr. Carlisle of Dublin, undertook the superintendence of the "*Birr Mission.*" It now consists of a congregation of converts, with an average Sabbath attendance of about 70 individuals, flourishing Sabbath schools of about 127 children, with 136 scholars in the daily schools. About 500 Roman Catholic families are visited by the readers; and so promising is this field of labor, that Dr. Wallace, a young Scotch physician, has for some time been laboring as medical missionary in the neighborhood.

The principal agencies of our mission to the Irish-speaking Roman Catholics, are the *Irish missionary*, the *Irish Scripture reader*, and the *Irish school.* The latter consists, not of children assembled in a school-house during certain fixed hours, but of persons of all ages and both sexes, assembled to learn the Irish Scriptures in each other's houses, generally after the toils of the day. And you might see these little groups of mountain peasants during the long winter nights around their blazing bogwood fires, reading in "their own tongue the wonderful works of God!" A better proof of the blessed fruits of these schools it is impossible to furnish, than what is found in the following anecdote. About 14 years ago, there dwelt a young zealous Romanist on the mountains of Tyrone. Being a youth of talent, he held frequent discussions with the Irish teachers of the district; and that he might be thoroughly furnished for the controversy, he commenced to study the Scriptures. The more he studied, the more he doubted; and such were his mental struggles, that he would spend hours at a time on the solitary mountains behind his father's house, in such agony of thought and prayer, that the cold sweat would break on his temples. At length he resolved to go to Stewartstown to hear the Rev. Robert Allen preach. His text on that occasion was, "And the

Spirit and the bride say come," &c., and little did he dream the results that were to follow that sermon. He drew the bow at a venture—the Most High directed the arrow—and the young man left the church a Protestant, and we trust a Christian. He was taken up by a few Christian ladies, educated, and at length ordained. And that young peasant is now the Rev. Michael Brannigan, one of the most honored instruments in the great missionary movement at present going on in the province of Connaught, and of which we now proceed to give a brief account.

Until the period of the late famine, our church's mission to Irish Romanists was, like all its sister institutions, progressing steadily but slowly, and experiencing the peculiar difficulties of this field of labor. But while that fearful calamity was sweeping thousands to the grave, a most remarkable change began to take place in the minds and conduct of many of the people; mainly owing, under God, to the softening influence of affliction on their hearts, and the kindness shown them by Protestants during their trials. Not only were our missionaries admitted to the cabins of those who before would have shut their doors against them, but so anxious for instruction had they apparently become, that wherever a new school or preaching station was opened, it was crowded by young and old. The result has been, that, for the last six years, the mission has flourished so wonderfully, that, in the district of Mayo alone, embracing an extent of 50 square miles, many thousands of young and old have been gladly receiving the Word; and, by the united testimony of all our missionaries, the glorious work seems to be capable of an almost indefinite extension. While almost all our mission districts have been favored as the scenes of more or less awakening, three have attracted peculiar attention. The first and largest is in Mayo and Sligo, the second in Roscommon, and the third in Kerry, in the province of Munster. And nothing can be more interesting to the friends of Ireland than a brief sketch of the plan of operation adopted in these districts. The old missionary system pursued in Ireland has long been felt to be beset with difficulties. It has been found that the minds of the adult population are so stereotyped in ignorance and vice, that little can be done to expand or elevate them; that, besides, they are usually so poor as to need relief, and that this often tempts them to hypocrisy, and exposes us to the charge of bribery; that the priests, by hindering our converts from getting employment, have often forced them to apostatize or to emigrate, and thus have sometimes scattered to the winds our fairest missionary fruits; and, moreover, that the people are usually so degraded as not to see the advantages of a mere literary education, and so bigoted as to be hostile to a Scriptural one. It was therefore conceived, that our chief attention should be turned to the *young*, while yet their minds were soft and plastic; especially *young females*, on whom, as the future mothers of the race, its destinies, under God, so much depended; and that if to the literary and Scriptural element, were added such *industrial training* as would enable them to *earn their own bread*, we could multiply our schools to any extent amongst that starving people, and not only defy the persecutions of the priest, but obviate the necessity for gratuitous relief, *with all its evil consequences;* and, finally, that we could thus eradicate the worst habits of the Irish, as *idleness*, *begging*, *&c.*, and implant instead the principles of *independence*, *self-reliance*, and *self-support*.

Accordingly, in the above districts, nearly 100 *Scriptural and industrial schools* have, within the last six years, been established. About one half of these belong to the "Belfast Ladies' Committee," whose president is Dr. Edgar; and the remainder are supported by congregations and individuals of various denominations throughout the United Kingdom, and superintended by the Rev. Robert Allen, Rev. T. Armstrong, Ballina, Rev. William Chestnut, Tralee, and 12 other missionaries of the Irish Presbyterian Church. They contain about 5,000 scholars in all, some of whom are boys engaged in farming operations, &c.; but the great majority are girls, employed in knitting, netting, crochet, sewed muslin, &c. And it is the unanimous testimony of numerous friends from England and Scotland, who have visited them, that they are *just such an agency* as suits the present condition of the Irish; meeting at once their temporal and spiritual wants, and UNITING the advantages of the *educational*, *industrial* and *Spiritual* schemes, which we have noticed in a previous chapter. Indeed, the transformation they have already wrought on these creatures is almost incredible; and all that seems necessary to renovate the whole country in 20 years, is to bring its rising generation under their benign influence. Those children who, some time ago, were in rags, with their faces often swollen from hunger, and their entire condition little better than that of savages, are now earning near £5,000 a-year! Some of them receive 4*s.* and 5*s.* a-week; many are the sole support of their parents and brothers; and Dr. Edgar's last report of the Belfast Ladies' schools in Connaught, entitled, "Woman's Work and Woman's Worth," abounds with instances of the beneficial results of the system. In one of the Kerry schools, superintended by the author, three little girls are at present earning more than their father and two brothers, though these are in constant employment; and the cleanliness, diligence, and general improvement of the scholars, is truly gratifying to behold. But if the reader would see the full effects of this admirable system, let him pay a visit to Ballinglen, county Mayo, under the able superintendence of Mr. Allen and Mr. Brannigan. On one side of the romantic glen he will see a large model farm, supported by kind friends in Scotland, on which boys, who were lately running wild through the mountains, are now receiving the best Scriptural, literary, and agricultural education; on the other side stands a female industrial school, in which girls who, some time ago, were in a state of wretchedness scarce conceivable, are producing the most elegant specimens of embroidery, &c.; in the centre stands a neat new church, weekly filled by a congregation, who, six years since, were degraded Papists, and had never seen a Bible; the entire district, which was then a scene of utter misery, has undergone the most marvellous transformation; and we are rejoiced to add, that means are now being taken to purchase the whole glen and found therein an extensive Model Industrial Institute for the province.*

The Requisites.—Such, then, is Ireland's evangelistic machinery—sufficient, you would say, for even her conversion. Then what can be the cause that perhaps in no country has the work of grace until recently got on more slowly? We have already given the principal cause. We have had the machinery, but have been deficient in the moving power. And we are firmly persuaded that all that is at present necessary to pentecostal success is simply pentecostal devotedness. The order of heaven

* There is a deeply interesting and successful mission in county Galway, conducted by Rev. Mr. Dallas, and other ministers of the Established Church; but as its plan differs in nothing from the other missions prosecuted by that church, our brief space hinders us from giving a detailed account of its operations.

is, "I will bless thee, and make thee a blessing." It is only those that have freely received, who *can* freely give; and God has usually honored men according, not to their gifts, but their graces. But, if ever there was a work which pre-eminently required the Spirit of Christ on the part both of churches and ministers, it is ours. Perhaps there is not beneath the sun a field of labor in which one is more forcibly taught the utter impotence of human effort, and the special need of divine aid. 'Tis here we are made to feel the whole force of the sublime but humbling sentiment, "Not by might, nor by power, but by my Spirit, saith the Lord," and persuaded we are that every requisite necessary to secure triumphant success even in it is MORE DEEP-TONED APOSTOLIC PIETY. What we chiefly want is that unquenchable spirit of love to Jesus and to souls which glowed in the breast of a Paul and a John. This would give us *men;* and constrain our ablest ministers, instead of aspiring to the highest places in the church, to envy the missionary his hard lot, and say, "Here am I, send me." This would give us *means* —then would our people, instead of giving a little from much, give much from a little—then would those drains of selfishness be cut off, but for which the rich could give vast sums, and the poorest could give something—ay, then would be heard from our treasurers the words which once gladdened Moses' ear, "The people give much more than enough for the service of the work." This, too, would inspire our churches with *that spirit of instant prayer* for our missions, which would conduce more to success than all the wealth liberality could bestow. And oh! how painfully have we missionaries often felt the need of this amid the wild bogs of Connaught and the dreary solitudes of Kerry, shut out from the counsel and intercourse of our brethren in Christ, and obliged to face, single-handed, a thousand difficulties!

How much more successful we might have been, had we always been sustained by the wrestling prayers of the whole church! And how many an appeal, which only fell on our countrymen's hearts cold and evanescent as snow in the sea, might have kindled in their breasts the spark of heavenly love! Fellow-Christians! if Paul needed the church's prayers, how much more do we! No field of labor more forcibly reminds one of our Lord's striking words, "This kind cometh forth by nothing but by prayer and fasting;" and now the abundance of our toils and success, instead of tempting you to intermit this great duty, more urgently demands its observance; for the greater sacrifice laid on the altar, the stronger the fire which is required to consume it. This, too, would inspire that *faith* so indispensable in a work in which our best schemes have so often failed, and our brightest hopes been blasted—that divine faith which, amid all our disappointments, enables us to endure as seeing Him who is invisible, and recollect that His word cannot return void; which, even when doomed to mourn the apostasy of some over whom we had long travailed, enables us to remember, that though Israel be not gathered, still He will be glorified, and thus the *grand* object secured; and which, as the ark of our hopes floats restless and uneasy over the moral deluge which now submerges our country, assures us that the waters will in due time subside. Yes, and by faith would we not effect as brilliant achievements as ever ancient saints performed! It is this glorious grace, which, when other principles of benevolence are faint and languid, or half-quenched by vexing disappointments, still keeps the heart fixed on Jesus as the author and the end of all we do, and enables us to pursue the same evenly course of humble devotedness, whether we experience success or failure, thanks or ingratitude. Let minor motives rise or fall as they may, beneath the power of this heavenly faith, our *grand* one remains the same; and we move on in the path of duty to our Master, like the planets which continue their course round the sun, and scarce feel the disturbance of the thousand stars that surround them. This, moreover, would inspire us with that *wisdom* so peculiarly needed in a field so arduous. The mismanaged Protestantism of bygone days has left our missionaries a vast inheritance of difficulties. And we have not only to contend with the consequent prejudices of the Papist against the Sassenach, so artfully embittered by an envenomed priesthood, but the proverbial difficulties which always attend the *reoccupation* of an old field that has been spoiled in the cultivation, and the evangelization of a race when the best time for enlightening them has passed away, and the tides of opportunity are at least half-run—a race, moreover, whose singular mental conformation requires so much careful study and skilful treatment.

Thus might we proceed, at almost any length, and show that every requisite we need is embraced in, or flows from a *revival of religion.* But our space will only permit us to notice one other grace, which in no country is more required, yet perhaps in none is less practised than in Ireland; and that is, DIVINE CHARITY. It is a distressing fact, that our missionaries sometimes meet more hindrance from their own brother ministers, than from the Popish priests; and that there are some amongst us who have not even the Puseyite's plea, but hold the same evangelic views, and profess the same love to Jesus and to souls, who yet act as if they would rather let millions perish than be saved by other hands than their own. We are willing, in part, to excuse them, on the ground of early prejudice. Some of our dear brethren grow up in the belief that *theirs* is *the church*, and all others are schismatics; that they are *the clergy*, and all others are intruders; and that it were as reasonable to trespass on their farms as their parishes. Their own sections of the church bounds the horizon of their thoughts and affections. To hear them at their public meetings, you would think there was neither church nor missions in the world but their own; and while loudly disclaiming the charge of Puseyism, they either positively consign the honored churches of Knox, of Owen, and of Wesley, to God's "uncovenanted mercy," or speak of them as, at best, mere excrescences on the "tree of life!" These men have long been a grievous affliction to Ireland. Their conduct has operated as a perpetual blister to their brethren of other churches; proved the grand hindrance to every catholic movement amongst us; given priests and Papists reason to laugh amongst themselves; and done the Saviour's cause immeasurable mischief. And never can we expect the Divine blessing on our common Protestantism till this Protestant Popery is put away from amongst us; till we get wholly rid of a class of men who smell so strongly of the Romish priest, and whose very look often reminds one of the monastic cell—men who substitute crotchets for conscience, bigotry for piety, and ecclesiastical hauteur for the humble spirit of Jesus. We speak thus freely, because we love their church; we have ever been her warm friend; and we have, in this volume, proved our regard. We know how severely we will be censured for not giving "the abuses of the Irish Establishment" a place amongst the causes of our country's present darkness. For the sake of brotherly concord, we are willing to bear the blame, and cheerfully make this sacrifice on the great altar of *Protestant harmony.* For we feel that now, when the forces of darkness are combined, and the forces of light are elsewhere combining—when everywhere there is so much danger, and in Ireland so much hope—our great motto ought to be, "*Quis separabit;*" and that the man who, be his plea what it may, would continue the strife which has too long disgraced Irish Protestants, is, whatever his profession, the enemy of the cross of Christ. We speak thus plainly, for the sake of our common faith; for of none has Satan made more use against it than such men, who will not see the difference between co-operation and compromise—who read our Lord's prayer backwards, "That they all may be one"—who "rebuke" and shun all who "follow not with them"—and who, while boasting of theirs as the Catholic Church, act as if bigoted exclusiveness were its truest mark.

And now, fellow-Christians, a word ere we close. Are you aware of the dangers that menace you? The sudden revolutions of 1848 made some think the millennium had dawned unawares; but we would recommend the portentous change which has since occurred, as a useful study to those who, regardless of all history, are accustomed to despise the efforts of Rome. Her priests *may* be as stupid as they think them to be; but is this the character of their Great Adviser? How often have those acts of Rome, which Protestant simplicity has viewed as "blunders," turned out to be *mere feints!* and it much depends, indeed, on Protestants themselves whether the late aggression may not prove one of these.

The man who knows the prodigious progress Rome has made for the last fifty years, and the stupendous efforts she is now putting forth, and yet would despise any move she makes in her deep and dreadful game, must be given over to strange infatuation. Have we not seen her seizing the chief seats of learning in England, and from thence deluging the land with disguised Popery? Has not her staff of Popish priests in that country increased, during the last 60 years, from scarce 50 till now there are EIGHT HUNDRED AND FORTY-EIGHT, with their full complement of schools, colleges, convents, and chapels?* Has not the Popish population of Great Britain, in the same time, grown in proportion? Has not Popish influence for years virtually controlled the legislature, and ruled the empire? Have we not seen Popery, during the last three years, rolling back, by its own single arm, the tides of progress over broad Europe; shrouding the bright sun of the nineteenth century with a deep eclipse; and causing her creatures of night to creep forth in the gloom, as though it were really the midnight of the twelfth? And is it amid such warnings of *Providence*, enforced as they are by those of *prophecy*, that any Christian can sit careless and secure?

* Catholic Directory, 1852.

Is it when a drama of awful grandeur is being enacted around us, when the elements of society are in a fermentation perhaps unparalleled, and when, on a due infusion of the gospel into the seething mass, it must mainly depend whether the issue will be putrefaction or purification,—is it at *such* a time, fellow-Christians, that any of us shall be found sleeping, whose special duty it is to preside over the process, and direct its course?

Christians of Great Britain! you owe our countryman much for your past neglect, and something, too, for his past services. Side by side with his British comrade has he pressed forward in the ranks of death, with that daring courage which is peculiarly his own. And when you have employed him in work less honorable, has he served you with less fidelity? Are not those canals and railways which are the monuments of your greatness, memorials, too, of his humble toil? Then will you aid in sending him that gospel which has so exalted you, and the lack of which has kept him so degraded? Extend our franchise till every babe has a vote; drain our country to its mountain tops; increase your grants till we live on your bounty,—and all must be vain while the poisonous vapors of error and vice are steaming up over the whole land, and blasting every seed of improvement you sow. And think you that *you* have but little interest in the issue? See how Irish Popery is pervading your senate, drenching your country, flooding your colonies, and threatening terrible retribution for your past neglect. How few of your large towns have not now an "Irish quarter?" Are not Irish Papists covering your fair land like locusts? and these, too, the very worst class, who can neither cross the ocean nor exist at home. Are they not at this moment the chief drains on your taxes, contributors to your crimes, and corrupters of your moral atmosphere? You have tried every means to get rid of the nuisance, but in vain. In Liverpool you established a *quarantine*, in hope to keep them back; but found that as reasonably did Canute command the waves to retire. From London you sent them home in droves, to return in greater force by the very next tide. Then finding it hopeless to *get quit* of them, you have next tried to *enlighten them*, and been driven by the stern requirements of *self-preservation* to establish *Irish Town Missions* in various cities; but you have found it utterly impossible to overtake by any such agency the swarms that are fast gathering around you.

Yet vast as their influx now is, it threatens daily to increase; so long as Ireland continues to sink, will they continue to fly from her—and Britain is their nearest asylum. Do you not see *new* hordes daily encamping amid your civilization, like Bedouins amongst the columns of Palmyra, or Goths amid the gardens of Italy? And do you not by this time perceive that either you must do something to save Ireland, or she will do much to destroy you? Once it was a question of mere benevolence

—it has now assumed a much graver form. If the pauper statistics of Manchester be a fair sample of those of your other large towns, then is the one half of your paupers Irish; and while, since 1846, English pauperism has, in that town, increased but 7 per cent., Irish pauperism has, in the same time, grown above 300 per cent!! Yet, what is the mere financial curse to those more deadly *moral* ones which these wretched beings are inflicting upon you! Therefore, we repeat, you *must for your own sakes* take up this question as you have never yet done. It is sheer folly to cry, "We are sick of Ireland;" —if you take not our advice, you will assuredly have cause to be still more sick of her. There stands this great moral marsh by your side; and you have your choice to help us to drain its putrid waters, or take the consequences in the pestilence and death which must follow its poisonous exhalations. British fellow-Christians! we implore you, shake off that security which, amid all those perils, *permits* your rulers to foster Popery; ay, and shelter those Jesuits whom even Popish countries have expelled. Else the star of Britain's glory, which rose with the Reformation, may have reached its zenith, and be destined ere long to go down. May God avert the day! But should Britain continue to favor the "whore," we are persuaded it is not remote; for never yet did country partake of "her crimes" without also receiving of "her plagues." And truly mournful it would be if the future historian should have to trace to Irish Popery the decline and fall of the greatest empire on which the sun ever shone is the circuit of his glorious way—if he should have to tell how Britain permitted the viper to grow unmolested by her side, and even coming to think its nature changed, began to fondle and caress the dangerous creature, till soon as it found itself strong enough, then true to its venomous instincts, it turned and stung to death the too unsuspecting bosom which had nourished it into vigor by its warmth!

Nor is it the inhabitants of Great Britain only who are interested in Ireland's fate—it concerns a large portion of the civilized world—for what has it long been but a nest and nursery of Popery sending forth its annual swarms of wretched beings to infest the remotest regions of the globe? Along the rivers of America, by the lakes of Canada, on the plains of Australia, you meet them in droves. It is said that 20 years ago there was, in the latter country, but one solitary priest; and that now, with Van Diemen's Land, it contains 200 priests, 18 bishops, and 1 archbishop! But especially is America concerned in this matter. Our deliverance is emphatically *her danger*. To us there is little to dread from the present *Popish* "exodus," but the risk of its cessation; but what is to us a ground of hope, is to *her* one of deep solicitude.

Emigration, which is withering the arm of Popery in Ireland, is strengthening that of Popery in America; and the priests are consoling themselves with the belief that what is lost to them *here*, is *more* than gained *there*—that here their flocks are beggars, but they will there become wealthy citizens—and, above all, that the free institutions of that country will enlarge their powers of mischief. Americans, beware! You are yet *confident*, but you know not Popery as well as we do, and God grant you never may! How can you overlook the alarming fact, that the hordes of Irish Papists who are landing daily amongst you, must needs corrupt your moral atmosphere, and that from the nature of your constitution, your country's *only* bulwark is the virtue of its people? Then learn in time from Ireland's RUIN what is AMERICA'S GRAND DANGER! Do you not know that Rome has her deadly eye on your young colossal republic? That, next to England, *you* have the largest place in the thoughts and councils of her Propaganda? And, above all, that she cannot endure a republican government? Has she not in France contrived to make the name of a republic a terror to the friends of order, and in *every* Popish land a satire and burlesque on the name? Yet think of the audacity of Hughes, who chooses the hour of Rome's most dreadful crusade against Europe's freedom, to tell you that she is the parent of liberty and the nurse of republicanism!! O! liberty shrinks at the touch of this monster, and bursts enraged from its embrace as from a ruthless violator. Then, Americans, beware! The serpent which has so long sought to nestle in the mane of the British lion, in hope to sting it to death, is stealthily creeping towards your Eagle's eyrie; and she that lately closed your chapel in Rome, now clamors the loudest amongst you for the rights of citizenship—*the better to enable her to rob you of them all!* Long may your banner float side by side with England's flag! Long may both nations continue together their glorious onward march, dispensing blessings to all mankind,—rivals only in the race of honor and benevolence, and divided by nothing but the ocean that rolls between! But this, be assured, can only be so long as both shall hold fast those Reformation principles which are the source of all their greatness, and be prepared to defend, if need be, with their blood that divine legacy left to the one by her martyred "worthies," and to the other by her "pilgrim fathers."

Protestant countrymen! had we done half our duty, our country had long since been evangelized; and instead of reaping the bitter fruits of our sin in a polluted atmosphere, a ruinous taxation, and miseries manifold, we would now have been blessed in our country's blessedness. But we have lived to witness a gracious revival, and can now point to thousands of as lovely samples of grace in Ireland as may ever be seen on this side glory; who possess the faith without the fame of martyrs, and will stand very near the throne above, and take rank amongst the highest aristocracy of heaven. To such we now appeal. Beloved friends! never did the sun of hope beam on us more brightly than now. What wonders has God of late wrought amongst us! How have his recent judgments broken priestly power, disarmed Romish prejudice, hushed the agitator's voice, and turned upon us the eyes of Christendom!

The dense clouds of Popery are rising off our land, and the beams of heaven begin to gild her mountains. Our heroic missionaries are bearding the beast in his stronghold; that gospel, which elevates the most degraded, is beginning to take away the Irish Celt's reproach among men, and waking his mind from the sleep of ages; and those noble germs of Irish character whose growth Popery has for centuries hindered, like seeds in the mummy's cold hand, how wonderfully they are now springing to life so soon as touched by the quickening rays of the Sun of Righteousness! Nor is this all. God has pleased, by means of the famine, to commence a social revolution amongst us, which promises to effect the country's renovation. Irish Popery has ever relied on its *numbers*—and, to increase these, has encouraged early marriages, and availed itself of the potato's productiveness. But how vain its craftiest devices, when God chooses to mar them! He smites the potato, and its *strength* becomes its *weakness*—its people, who had multiplied like summer insects, vanish like them too—its supplies are cut off—its priests are starving—its chapels are being emptied—and its arm is withered! And it is a matter of easy enough calculation that, if things go on for some years, as, to all appearance, they now *must* do, Popery in Ireland is inevitably doomed. It would seem as if God had resolved to clear out the country in order to replenish it anew. The land is rapidly passing into British hands. With the emigration of the Irish, there has commenced an immigration of the Scotch and English; and numbers are only waiting the adjustment of the land question in order to come and settle amongst us. Thus God is renovating the country by the double process of driving Popery beyond the ocean, and bringing Protestantism from across the channel. We grieve to see our countrymen leaving us; but who that wishes them well for either world, would bid them stay? By remaining, they starve—perhaps eternally perish—and certainly perpetuate the miseries of their race. By going, they better both themselves and their country; for they go from bondage to liberty—from hunger to plenty—from horsewhipping priests to where they may read the Bible, and no priest dare frown. Therefore, we say to them—"Go, in the name of the Lord! If you conduct yourselves well, we shall some day hear of you—and how changed you will be! Quickened to life by surrounding Protestantism you will be seen felling the forests, cutting canals, building railways, rising to comfort, and, best of all, perhaps walking with God. Then go, AND THE LORD BE WITH YOU!" Yes, to Ireland there ariseth light in the darkness. Providence Himself is at work—breaking up our present wretched social framework to construct out of the ruins a fairer fabric. We cannot arrest the process, nor should we if we could. It is just the self-righting laws of the universe at work—God's wisdom and goodness rectifying man's guilt and folly. And it requires, we are persuaded, no seer's eye to behold through the vista of coming years, when this revolution is past, Ireland looking out as from a new creation, like the young vegetation on the moors, that is quickened by the very fires which late have swept over them!

Roman Catholic countrymen! we have been plain with your worst enemy, the best proof of our love to *you*. You cannot suspect us of any sordid end—for it is too late to enter a field which the most artful demagogue has had to quit in despair. Oh! we come not to *strip* but to *relieve* the dying; and surely the messenger of peace may approach unsuspected when even the spoiler is seen to retire. *Can* you think those priests your true friends, who so uniformly turn your ignorance to their own advantage, and have never benighted where they have not enslaved? And, will you trust your souls to men with whom you would seldom trust your substance?—and refuse even to *inquire* till it is too late to *amend?* Then, by that brilliant mind too long enslaved, and that generous heart too long imposed on, exert the birthright God has given you, and judge for yourselves, as you must answer for yourselves. Nor think your priest alone will be accountable if you continue to follow him blindfolded to ruin, any more than would your guide alone be the sufferer if you allowed him to lead you over some fatal cliff. And you, their blind guides!—you must soon meet them at that judgment-seat, where your very best apology shall be,—"We did it ignorantly in unbelief." If we admit your honesty, it must be by denying your intelligence—fearful alternative this, between ignorance and imposture! O, behold the fruits of your dreadful diligence in the wreck of the finest people the great Creator ever formed! And think you, shall that mockery of justice, which so often sullies our earthly tribunals, that punishes them, and pensions you, tarnish the purity of the Great White Throne? No, he who robs men of the key of knowledge, shall *there* at least be held accountable for all the consequences; that ignorance which will be their palliation, shall constitute the main count in your indictment; and whatever punishment may on this ground be deducted from their sentences, must necessarily be added to yours. And are you prepared for a reckoning so awful? If not, even for you there is hope—and this is the crowning proof of God's boundless love. The grace which arrested Saul of Tarsus, was designed as encouragement in cases so desperate; and that miracle of grace may again be performed, which made "a great company of the priests obedient to the faith."

THE END.

BONAR'S (Rev. Horatius) Night of Weeping.................. 30
—— Morning of Joy, a sequel to the above.................. 40
—— Story of Grace.................................. 30
—— Truth and Error. 18mo.............................. 40
—— Man, his Religion and his World...................... 40
BONAR'S (Rev. Andrew) Commentary on Leviticus. 8vo.... 1 50
BONNET'S Family of Bethany. 18mo...................... 40
—— Meditations on the Lord's Prayer. 18mo............... 40
BOOTH S Reign of Grace. 12mo.......................... 75
BORROW'S Bible and Gipsies of Spain. 8vo, cloth.......... 1 00
BOSTON'S Four-fold State. 18mo......................... 50
—— Crook in the Lot. 18mo.............................. 30
BRETT (Rev. W. H.)—The Indian Tribes of Guiana. Illustrated. 16mo..
BROKEN BUD; or, the Reminiscences of a Bereaved Mother. With steel Frontispiece. 16mo.......................... 75
BROWN'S (Rev. John, D.D.) Exposition of First Peter. 8vo.. 2 50
—— On the Sayings and Discourses of Christ. 3 vols. 8vo.....
BROWN'S Explication of the Assembly's Catechism. 12mo... 60
BROWN (Rev. David) on the Second Advent. 12mo......... 1 25
BRIDGES on the Christian Ministry. 8vo.................... 1 50
—— On the Proverbs. 8vo.............................. 2 00
—— On the CXIX. Psalm. New edition. 8vo............... 1 00
—— Memoir of Mary Jane Graham. 8vo................... 1 00
—— Works. 3 vols. 8vo, containing the above.............. 5 00
BROWN'S Concordance. New and neat edition. 24mo....... 20
Do. Gilt edge.......................... 30
BUCHANAN'S Comfort in Affliction. 18mo................ 40
—— On the Holy Spirit. 18mo. Second edition.............. 50
BUNBURY'S Glory, Glory, Glory, and other Narratives........ 25
BUTLER'S (Bishop) Complete Works. 8vo.................. 1 50
—— Sermons, alone. 8vo................................ 1 00
—— Analogy, alone. 8vo................................ 75
—— and Wilson's Analogy. 8vo.......................... 1 25
BUNYAN'S Pilgrim's Progress, fine edition, large type. 12mo.. 1 00
Do. Gilt.......................... 1 50
Do. 18mo, close type.............. 50
—— Jerusalem Sinner Saved. 18mo....................... 50
—— Greatness of the Soul. 18mo.......................... 50
BURN'S (John) Christian Fragments. 18mo................ 40
BURNS' (Rev. Jabez) Parables and Miracles of Christ. 12mo.. 75
CALVIN—The Life and Times of John Calvin, the Great Reformer. By Paul Henry, D.D. 2 vols. 8vo, Portrait.......... 3 00
CAMERON'S (Mrs.) Farmer's Daughter. Illustrated......... 30

CATECHISMS—The Assembly's Catechism. Per hundred.... 1 25
—— with Proofs.... 3 00
—— Brown's Short Catechism. Per hundred.... 1 25
—— Brown on the Assembly's Catechism. 18mo.... 10
CECIL'S WORKS. 3 vols. 12mo, with Portrait.... 3 00
—— Sermons, separate.... 1 00
—— Miscellanies and Remains, separate.... 1 00
—— Original Thoughts, separate.... 1 00
—— (Catharine) Memoir of Mrs. Hawks, with Portrait.... 1 00
CHARNOCK'S Choice Works.... 60
CHALMERS' Sermons. 2 vols. 8vo. With a fine Portrait.... 3 00
—— Lectures on Romans. 8vo. " " 1 50
—— Miscellanies. 8vo. " " 1 50
—— Select Works; comprising the above. 4 vols. 8vo.... 6 00
—— Evidences of Christian Revelation. 2 vols.... 1 25
—— Natural Theology. 2 vols.... 1 25
—— Moral Philosophy.... 60
—— Commercial Discourses.... 60
—— Astronomical Discourses.... 60
CHEEVER'S Lectures on the Pilgrim's Progress. Illus. 12mo.. 1 00
CHRISTIAN RETIREMENT. 12mo.... 75
—— EXPERIENCE. By the same author. 12mo.... 75
CLARK'S (Rev. John A.,) Walk about Zion. 12mo.... 75
—— Pastor's Testimony.... 75
—— Awake, Thou Sleeper.... 75
—— Young Disciple.... 88
—— Gathered Fragments.... 1 00
CLARKE'S Daily Scripture Promises. 32mo, gilt.... 30
COLQUHOUN'S (Lady) World's Religion. New ed., 16mo.... 50
COMMANDMENT WITH PROMISE. By the Author of "The Week," &c. Illustrated by Howland. 16mo.... 75
COWPER—The Works of William Cowper; comprising his Life, Letters and Poems, now first collected by the introduction of Cowper's Private Correspondence. Edited by the Rev. T. S. Grimshaw. With numerous illustrations on steel, and a fine Portrait by Ritchie. 1 vol. royal 8vo.... 3 00
Do. do. cloth, extra gilt.... 4 00
Do. do. morocco extra.... 5 00
—— Poetical Works, complete, separate. 2 vols. 16mo. Illus. 1 50
CUMMING'S (Rev. John, D.D.) Message from God. 18mo.... 30
—— Christ Receiving Sinners.... 30
CUNNINGHAM'S World without Souls. 18mo.... 30
CUYLER'S (Rev. T. L.) Stray Arrows.... 30
DALE (Rev. Thomas)—The Golden Psalm. 16mo.... 60

DAVIES' Sermons. 3 vols. 12mo........................ 2 00
DAVIDSON'S (Dr.) Connexions. New edition. 8vo.......... 1 50
Do. do. 3 vols. 12mo.............. 1 50
DAVID'S PSALMS, in metre. Large type. 12mo, embossed.. 75
Do. do. gilt edge......... 1 00
Do. do. Turkey morocco...... 2 00
Do. 18mo, good type, plain sheep..................... 38
Do. 48mo, very neat pocket edition, sheep.............. 20
Do. " " " morocco............ 25
Do. " " " gilt edge.......... 31
Do. " " " tucks.............. 50
Do. with Brown's Notes. 18mo......................... 50
Do. " " morocco gilt.......... 1 00
D'AUBIGNE'S History of the Reformation. *Carefully Revised*, with various additions not hitherto published. 4 vols. in two. 12mo, cloth.. 1 50
Do. do. 8vo, complete in 1 vol......... 1 00
—— Life of Cromwell the Protector. 12mo.................. 50
—— Germany, England and Scotland. 12mo.................. 75
—— Luther and Calvin. 18mo.............................. 25
—— The Authority of God the true Barrier against Infidel and Romish Aggression.. 75
DICK'S (John, D.D.) Lectures on Theology. Fine edition, with Portrait. 2 vols. in one. Cloth............................ 2 50
Do. do sheep............................ 3 00
Do. do. in 2 vols. Cloth................... 3 00
—— Lectures on Acts. 8vo................................ 1 50
DICKINSON'S (Rev. R. W.) Scenes from Sacred History...... 1 00
—— Responses from the Sacred Oracles.................... 1 00
DODDRIDGE'S Rise and Progress. 18mo.................. 40
—— Life of Col. Gardiner. 18mo.......................... 30
DUNCAN'S Sacred Philosophy of the Seasons. 4 vols......... 3 00
—— Life. By his Son. With Portrait. 12mo............... 75
—— Tales of the Scottish Peasantry. 18mo. Illustrated....... 50
—— Cottage Fireside. 18mo. Illustrated................. 40
—— (Mrs.) Life of Mary Lundie Duncan. 16mo............. 75
—— —— Life of George A. Lundie. 18mo................... 50
—— —— Memoir of George B. Phillips. 18mo............... 25
—— —— Children of the Manse............................ 1 00
—— —— America as I saw it..............................
—— (Mary Lundie) Rhymes for my Children. Illustrated.... 25
EDGAR'S Variations of Popery. 8vo......................... 1 00
EDWARD'S (Jonathan, D.D.) Charity and its Fruits. Never before published. 16mo................................... 1 00

ERSKINE'S Gospel Sonnets. 18mo. Portrait........ 50
ENGLISH PULPIT. 8vo........ 1 50
EVIDENCES OF CHRISTIANITY. A Course of Lectures delivered before the University of Virginia. 8vo........ 2 50
Among the Lecturers are Drs. Alexander, Rice, Breckenridge, Plumer, Green, McGill, Sampson, &c.
FAR OFF; or, Asia and Australia Described. By the Author of the "Peep of Day," &c. Illustrated. 16mo........ 75
FAMILY WORSHIP. A Series of Prayers for every Morning and Evening throughout the year, adapted to Domestic Worship. By one hundred and eighty clergymen of Scotland. 8vo.. 3 00
Do. do. do. half morocco...... 4 00
Do. do. do. morocco........ 5 00
FERGUSON'S Roman Republic. 8vo........ 1 50
FISK'S Memorial of the Holy Land. With steel plates........ 1 00
FLEURY'S Life of David. 12mo........ 60
FOSTER'S Essays on Decision of Character, &c. Large type.. 75
Do. do. close type, 18mo.. 50
—— Essay on the Evils of Popular Ignorance. 12mo........ 75
FORD'S Decapolis. 18mo........ 25
FOX—Memoir of the Rev. Henry Watson Fox, Missionary to the Teloogoos. Illustrated. 12mo........ 1 00
FRANK NETHERTON; or, The Talisman. Illustrated. 16mo. 60
FRY (Caroline)—The Listener. Illustrated edition. 16mo...... 1 00
—— Christ on Law. 12mo........ 60
—— Sabbath Musings. 18mo........ 40
—— The Scripture Reader's Guide. 18mo........ 30
—— Christ our Example, and Autobiography. 16mo........
GEOLOGICAL COSMOGONY. By a Layman. 18mo...... 30
GOD IN THE STORM. 18mo........ 25
GOODE'S Better Covenant. 12mo........ 60
GRAHAM'S Test of Truth. 18mo........ 30
GREEN—The Life of the Rev. Ashbel Green, D.D. 8vo....... 2 00
GRIFFITH'S Live while you Live. 18mo........ 30
HALDANE'S Exposition of Romans. 8vo........ 2 50
HALL'S (Bishop) Select Works. 16mo........ 75
HAMILTON'S (Rev. James, D.D.) Life in Earnest. 18mo..... 30
—— Mount of Olives. 18mo........ 30
—— Harp on the Willows. 18mo........ 30
—— Thankfulness. 18mo........ 30
—— Life of Hall. 24mo, gilt........ 30
—— Happy Home. Illustrated. 18mo........ 50
—— Life of Lady Colquhoun. 16mo........ 75
—— The Royal Preacher. With Portrait. 16mo........ 85

HAWKER'S Poor Man's Morning Portion. 12mo............ 60
Do. do. Evening Portion. " 60
——— Zion's Pilgrim. 18mo............................... 30
HERVEY'S Meditations. 18mo............................... 40
HETHERINGTON'S History of the Church of Scotland..... 1 50
HENGSTENBERG on the Apocalypse. 2 vols. 8vo.........
HENRY'S (Matt.) Method for Prayer........................ 40
——— Communicant's Companion. 18mo...................... 40
——— Daily Communion with God. " 30
——— Pleasantness of a Religious Life. 24mo, gilt............ 30
——— Choice Works. 12mo................................. 60
HENRY, Philip, Life of. 18mo.............................. 50
HEWITSON—Memoir of the Rev. W. H. Hewitson, Free Church Minister at Dirleton, Scotland, with Portrait. 12mo............ 85
HILL'S (George) Lectures on Divinity. 8vo.................. 2 00
——— (Rowland) Life. By Sidney. 12mo...................... 75
HISTORY OF THE PURITANS IN ENGLAND, AND THE PILGRIM FATHERS. By Stowell and Wilson. 12mo. 1 00
HISTORY OF THE REFORMATION IN EUROPE...... 40
HOUSMAN'S Life and Remains. 12mo...................... 75
HORNE'S Introduction. 2 vols. royal 8vo, half cloth.......... 3 50
Do. do. 1 vol. sheep......................... 4 00
Do. do. 2 vols. cloth......................... 4 00
Do. do. 2 vols. library style 5 00
——— (Bishop,) Commentary on the Book of Psalms........... 1 50
HOWELL'S LIFE—Perfect Peace. 18mo.................... 30
HOWE'S Redeemer's Tears, and other Essays. 18mo.......... 50
HOWARD, (John,) or the Prison World of Europe. 12mo..... 1 00
HOOKER, (Rev. H.,) The Uses of Adversity. 18mo............ 30
——— Philosophy of Unbelief.............................. 75
HUSS, (John,) Life of. Translated from the German........... 25
INFANT'S PROGRESS. By the Author of " Little Henry and his Bearer." Illustrated. 16mo............................ 75
JACOBUS on Matthew. With a Harmony. Illustrated........ 75
——— Questions on do. 18mo.............................. 15
——— On Mark, Luke and John, (preparing,).................
JAMES' Anxious Inquirer. 18mo........................... 30
——— True Christian. 18mo................................ 30
——— Widow Directed. 18mo............................... 30
——— Young Man from Home................................ 30
——— Christian Professor. New edition. 12mo... 75
——— Christian Duty. 16mo................................ 75
JAMIE GORDON; or, The Orphan. Illustrated. 16mo..... 75
JANEWAY'S Heaven upon Earth. 18mo.................... 50

www.ingramcontent.com/pod-product-compliance
Lightning Source LLC
LaVergne TN
LVHW010200110826
845151LV00002B/566

* 9 7 8 1 4 2 5 5 3 6 4 7 3 *